WRITING POWER **4**

Writing Fluency • Language Use • Academic Writing • Social and Professional Writing

Sue Peterson

Dorothy Zemach

D0162103

Writing Power 4

Copyright © 2013 by Pearson Education, Inc.
All rights reserved.

Pearson Education, 10 Bank Street, White Plains, NY 10606

Staff credits: The people who made up the *Writing Power 4* team, representing editorial, production, design, and manufacturing, are Nan Clarke, Dave Dickey, Nancy Flaggman, Ann France, Shelley Gazes, Jaime Lieber, Amy McCormick, Liza Pleva, Massimo Rubini, and Jaimie Scanlon.

Cover images: (left) Lisa S./Shutterstock, (center left) Robnroll/Shutterstock, (center right) Blazej Lyjak/Shutterstock, (right) jocic/Shutterstock.
Text composition: TSI Graphics
Text font: 11.5/13 Adobe Caslon
Credits: See page viii

Library of Congress Cataloging-in-Publication Data
Blanchard, Karen Lourie
  Writing power. 1 : language use social and personal writing, academic writing, vocabulary building / Karen Blanchard.
    p. cm.
  ISBN 0-13-231484-3—ISBN 0-13-231485-1—ISBN 0-13-231486-X—ISBN 0-13-231487-8
  1. English language—Textbooks for foreign speakers.   2. English language—Rhetoric—Problems, exercises, etc.   3. Report writing—Problems, exercises, etc.   I. Title.
  PE1128.B5874   2012
  428.2'4—dc23
                                                                            2012006120

ISBN-10: 0-13-231487-8
ISBN-13: 978-0-13-231487-9

Printed in the United States of America
1 2 3 4 5 6 7 8 9 10—V011—17 16 15 14 13 12

Contents

Acknowledgments

The authors would like to acknowledge Beatrice S. Mikulecky and Linda Jeffries for their innovations in the *Reading Power* series, and the Pearson team for all of their efforts and contributions in making the *Writing Power* series a reality, especially Paula Van Ells, Amy McCormick, Massimo Rubini, Jaimie Scanlon, and series co-author Karen Blanchard. A special thanks goes to Development Editor Nan Clarke for her astuteness and steady hand throughout the writing of this text.

Sue Peterson would also like to dedicate this book to her parents—Paul and Carolyn. She is also deeply grateful to her friends, students, and colleagues including Mark, Greta, Martha, Marge, Roxa, and Patti. Finally, thank you to Sean, Jack, Carolyn, and Dan, for all your patience, support, and encouragement.

Writing Power 4 **Reviewers:**
The publisher would like to extend special thanks to the following individuals who reviewed *Writing Power* and whose comments were instrumental in developing this series.

Jeff Bette, Naugatuck Valley Community College; **Leslie Biaggi,** Miami-Dade Community College; **Linda Ciano,** American Language Institute, New York University; **Sally C. Gearhart,** Santa Rosa Community College; **Anthony Halderman,** Cuesta College, San Luis Obispo, CA; **Melissa L. Parisi,** Westchester Community College; **Jason Tannenbaum,** Pace University; **Joe Walther,** Korea

About the Authors

Sue Peterson has been in the TESOL field for twenty years and is currently the assistant director of the English Language Institute of St. John's University in New York City. She has taught reading, writing, listening, speaking, and grammar to college-level students and designed numerous courses. She has been a teacher trainer in the United States and Mexico and is a regular presenter at conferences. She holds a master's degree in TESOL from Hunter College, City University of New York, and her interests are in materials development, curriculum design, and technology.

Dorothy E. Zemach has taught ESL for over 18 years, in Asia, Africa, and the United States. She holds an MA in TESL from the School for International Training in Vermont, USA. Now she concentrates on writing and editing ELT materials and textbooks and conducting teacher training workshops. Her areas of specialty and interest are teaching writing, teaching reading, business English, academic English, testing, and humor. She is a frequent plenary speaker at international conferences, and a regular blogger for Teacher Talk at http://www.azargrammar.com.

Introduction to *Writing Power 4*

To the Teacher

Writing Power 4 is unlike most other writing textbooks. Rather than focusing on one area of writing, such as fluency, language use, academic writing, or professional writing, *Writing Power 4* includes all of them to give students practical skills for writing in many different situations. The book is also organized in a different way. It contains four separate Parts that concentrate on four important aspects of writing proficiency; therefore it is like four books in one. The book's structure is flexible, allowing you to assign work from different sections of the book concurrently and to target your students' greatest needs.

The four Parts of *Writing Power 4* are:
  - **Part 1: Writing Fluency**
  - **Part 2: Language Use**
  - **Part 3: Academic Writing**
  - **Part 4: Social and Professional Writing**

Writing Power 4 is designed to meet the needs of students in pre-college programs, college bridge programs, or college or university classes. As a result, it places an emphasis on the skills necessary for academic success. *Writing Power 4* is intended for students at the upper-intermediate level (CEFR C1).

The purpose of *Writing Power 4* is to develop students' writing skills for a variety of purposes. Exercises target both accuracy and fluency and give students the tools they need to express themselves in effective and interesting ways. Students learn appropriate vocabulary and structures for academic, professional, and social settings, as well as techniques for creative writing.

Students also work on writing fluency throughout the course, through journal and blog assignments. The Writing Power Blog can be found at http://pearsonELT.com/writingpowerblog. Log on to see instructions for how to set up a private class blog, where your students can post writing assignments and communicate with classmates in a fun online environment. The Further Practice boxes throughout the book give ideas for blog assignments, as well as journal topics and research projects.

A typical unit focuses on a central topic or theme and guides students through the full writing process. Students work individually, in pairs, and in groups to:
  - Brainstorm ideas
  - Select, organize, and develop ideas
  - Draft a text
  - Check and revise the text
  - "Publish" their work by sharing it with classmates and/or you

The final Writing Task at the end of the unit integrates all of the skills presented. To close the unit, students use the Check Your Writing checklist to review and revise their writing.

A separate Teacher's Guide contains the answer key, a rationale for the approach taken in *Writing Power 4*, specific suggestions for using it in the classroom, and a sample syllabus.

We hope you and your students will enjoy using *Writing Power 4*.

To the Student

Writing is an important part of academic, social, and professional life, both on paper and online. *Writing Power 4* teaches you skills to improve your writing in all of these areas. You will work on writing both fluently (quickly and easily) and accurately (correctly and appropriately).

This book is different from other writing textbooks. *Writing Power 4* is divided into four Parts. Instead of working on one part at a time, as in most books, you can and should work regularly on all four parts of the book.

Part 1: Writing Fluency To improve your writing fluency, it is important to write as often as you can about topics you are interested in. Units such as "Keeping a Journal" and "Blogging" will help you learn to write more quickly and easily and feel comfortable expressing yourself in writing. On the Writing Power Blog, located at http://pearsonELT.com/writingpowerblog, you and your classmates can post comments and have fun writing in English.

Part 2: Language Use This Part helps you work on writing more correctly. You will learn how to build your active vocabulary for writing, and to properly use pronouns, gerunds and infinitives, articles, and parallel structures. These skills will help you express your ideas clearly and effectively in writing.

Part 3: Academic Writing In this Part, you will learn strategies for researching, preparing to write, organizing ideas, and writing a full academic essay. The unit on Plagiarism, Quoting, and Paraphrasing focuses on how to incorporate source material and properly cite those sources to avoid plagiarism. The unit on Revision and Reference gives strategies for correcting and polishing your final work and formatting a reference page.

Part 4: Social and Professional Writing This Part covers the world of work and business. Units include Professional Networking, Opinion Writing, Business Correspondence, Résumés and Cover Letters, and Speech and Presentation Writing.

We hope you will enjoy studying with *Writing Power 4*! Begin by taking the Writing Questionnaire on the next page.

Questionnaire

What Does Writing Mean to You?

A.   Complete this questionnaire about writing in your life.

Writing Questionnaire

Name: _____   First Language: _____

1. What kinds of things do you write in your first language? In English? Check (✓) your answers. Add other ideas.

	In your language	In English
Blog posts		
Business letters		
Chat (online)		
Cover letters		
Diary or journal		
Emails		
Essays or compositions		
Memos		
Online reviews		
Personal letters		
Research papers		
Résumés		
Text messages		
Other (add your own):		

2. Do you enjoy writing in your first language? What is easy about it for you? What is challenging? _____

_____

3. Do you enjoy writing in English? What is easy about it for you? What is challenging?

_____

_____

4. What kinds of writing do you think you will do in English in the future? What skills might you need to do them? _____

_____

B.   Work in a group. Discuss and compare your answers to the questionnaire.

Credits

PART

1

Writing Fluency

Introduction

Learning to write in any language requires practice in **accuracy** and **fluency**. When you write accurately, you demonstrate that you know, understand, and can use various aspects of English such as grammar, vocabulary, spelling, and punctuation. In addition, accuracy can also mean following formatting rules, such as indenting and beginning a paragraph with a topic sentence. Accurate writing is essential in many different areas of life in addition to school. Whether you are writing for a teacher, an employer, or another reader, you need to communicate your ideas clearly.

Writing fluency is the ability to express your ideas smoothly and easily. Of course, the best way to become a fluent writer is to write! You can practice fluency by writing for a number of purposes and with different audiences in mind. Writing in a journal, for example, where you are your own audience, is a great way to practice fluency. You can freely express yourself without being concerned about how someone else may evaluate your writing. As your writing fluency develops, you may find that you are able to complete writing tasks more quickly and feel less stress when you write, even when accuracy is also important, such as for an exam or a class assignment.

A good writer is accurate and fluent. In most of the units in this book, the focus is on writing accurately. As you work through those units, you will need help answering questions and checking your work. You can practice writing fluently, however, on your own or by completing certain writing tasks in or outside of class—tasks that are designed to help increase your fluency.

In this part of *Writing Power 4*, you will learn about and practice three ways to work on your writing fluency:

- Keeping a Journal
- Writing a Blog
- Creative Writing

(See page v for information about the Writing Power Blog.)

You may not have time to both keep a journal *and* write a blog. Your teacher will let you know which one your class will do. However, you can practice creative writing anytime in your journal or blog or as in-class or homework assignments.

A. *Read these sentences. Are they related to accuracy or fluency? Write A (Accuracy) or F (Fluency). Write AF if you think it is related to both.*

_____ **1.** You begin writing without a specific topic in mind.

_____ **2.** You begin writing about one topic, but as new ideas come to you, you change topics one or more times.

_____ **3.** Before you begin writing, you make an outline to organize your thoughts.

_____ **4.** You brainstorm a list of ideas before you start to write.

_____ **5.** While you are writing, you stop to check information about the topic.

_____ **6.** You write a note to a family member or friend.

_____ **7.** As you write, you cross out or erase sentences because they don't seem just right.

_____ **8.** You guess at spelling words that you don't know.

_____ **9.** You use the spell check function on your computer or check spelling in a dictionary.

_____ **10.** When you don't know a word in English, you write it in your first language.

_____ **11.** You ask someone else to check what you've written and make suggestions for improvement.

_____ **12.** You write a report and put it aside. Then you reread and revise it.

B. *Work in a group. Compare your answers.*

A. *Write answers to these questions. Write about your first language and English.*

1. What are some types of writing you have done that focused on accuracy?

   First language _____

   English _____

2. What are some types of writing you have done that focused on fluency?

   First language _____

   English _____

3. What are some specific challenges for you in writing for accuracy?

   First language _____

   English _____

4. What are some specific challenges for you in writing for fluency?

   First language _____

   English _____

5. This year, what are some types of writing you will do where accuracy is more important?

   First language _____

   English _____

6. This year, what are some types of writing you will do where fluency is more important?

   First language _____

   English _____

B. *Work in a group. Discuss your answers. Then discuss them with the class.*

EXERCISE 3

Look back at your answers to questions 3 and 4 in Exercise 2. On a separate piece of paper, write one goal for writing fluency and one goal for writing accuracy for yourself in this course. List steps you will take to achieve your goal and how you will measure or recognize your results. Keep your writing to refer to at the end of this course.

UNIT 1

Keeping a Journal

A journal is a place to write thoughts, feelings, and impressions. Some writers use a particular notebook or create a computer journal. Some people write daily, and others write weekly or even less frequently. There is no right or wrong way to write a journal. It is a place to record experiences and ideas, and because it is unique to you, your journal is a reflection of who you are and how you view the world.

Keeping a journal is a useful way to get extensive writing practice and to build your writing fluency. You may already keep a journal on your own, but your teacher may also assign journal writing in your class. In this type of journal, you might write responses to questions or prompts from your teacher, or you might choose your own topics to write about. Most instructors don't grade grammar or spelling in a journal but instead check the length and frequency of your entries. The more you practice, the more your writing will improve.

In this unit, you will . . .

- learn about how keeping a journal can improve your writing.
- learn about different types of journals.
- give your teacher information about your journaling preferences.

Warm Up

Work in a group. Discuss these questions:

- Do you write differently when you know that your writing will not be corrected and you will not receive a grade? If so, explain how.

- Have you ever kept a journal in your first language, or do you keep one now?

- If yes, what kinds of things did/do you write about?

- If no, what kinds of things do you think you would enjoy writing about?

- If you decided to keep a journal, would you prefer writing by hand in a notebook or keeping a computer document? Why? How often do you think you'd like to write? Why?

Read the blog post from a professional writer. Then work with another student or group. Which of the reasons for journaling do you think are the most important? Why?

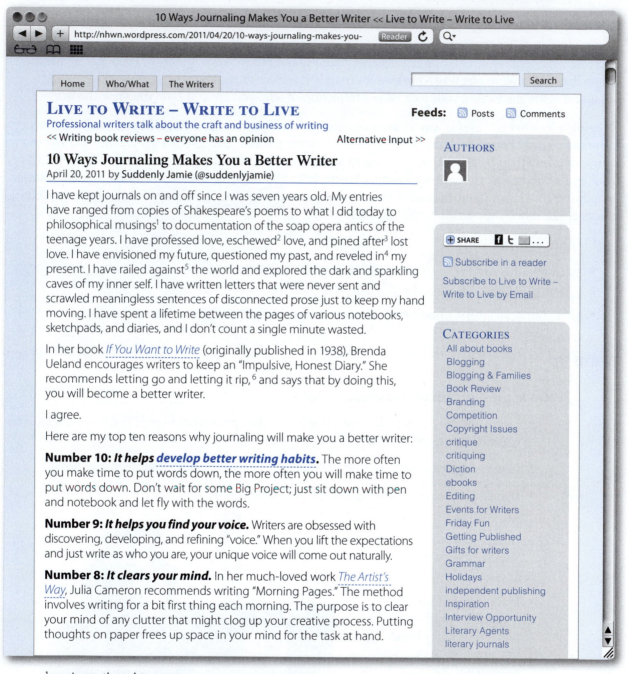

10 Ways Journaling Makes You a Better Writer << Live to Write – Write to Live

http://nhwn.wordpress.com/2011/04/20/10-ways-journaling-makes-you-   Reader

| Home | Who/What | The Writers |

Search

LIVE TO WRITE – WRITE TO LIVE
Professional writers talk about the craft and business of writing

<< Writing book reviews – everyone has an opinion   Alternative Input >>

Feeds: Posts Comments

10 Ways Journaling Makes You a Better Writer
April 20, 2011 by *Suddenly Jamie (@suddenlyjamie)*

I have kept journals on and off since I was seven years old. My entries have ranged from copies of Shakespeare's poems to what I did today to philosophical musings[1] to documentation of the soap opera antics of the teenage years. I have professed love, eschewed[2] love, and pined after[3] lost love. I have envisioned my future, questioned my past, and reveled in[4] my present. I have railed against[5] the world and explored the dark and sparkling caves of my inner self. I have written letters that were never sent and scrawled meaningless sentences of disconnected prose just to keep my hand moving. I have spent a lifetime between the pages of various notebooks, sketchpads, and diaries, and I don't count a single minute wasted.

In her book *If You Want to Write* (originally published in 1938), Brenda Ueland encourages writers to keep an "Impulsive, Honest Diary." She recommends letting go and letting it rip,[6] and says that by doing this, you will become a better writer.

I agree.

Here are my top ten reasons why journaling will make you a better writer:

Number 10: *It helps develop better writing habits*. The more often you make time to put words down, the more often you will make time to put words down. Don't wait for some Big Project; just sit down with pen and notebook and let fly with the words.

Number 9: *It helps you find your voice.* Writers are obsessed with discovering, developing, and refining "voice." When you lift the expectations and just write as who you are, your unique voice will come out naturally.

Number 8: *It clears your mind.* In her much-loved work *The Artist's Way*, Julia Cameron recommends writing "Morning Pages." The method involves writing for a bit first thing each morning. The purpose is to clear your mind of any clutter that might clog up your creative process. Putting thoughts on paper frees up space in your mind for the task at hand.

AUTHORS

SHARE

Subscribe in a reader

Subscribe to Live to Write – Write to Live by Email

CATEGORIES

All about books
Blogging
Blogging & Families
Book Review
Branding
Competition
Copyright Issues
critique
critiquing
Diction
ebooks
Editing
Events for Writers
Friday Fun
Getting Published
Gifts for writers
Grammar
Holidays
independent publishing
Inspiration
Interview Opportunity
Literary Agents
literary journals

[1] *musings*—thoughts
[2] *eschewed*—avoided
[3] *pined after*—longed for
[4] *reveled in*—had an enjoyable time
[5] *railed against*—protested
[6] *letting it rip*—doing something with energy and enthusiasm

Number 7: *It saves relationships.* A journal is an excellent place to blow off steam without the risk of saying something in haste that you won't be able to retract later. Angry at your friend? Write it down. Hating your job? Write it down. Have a problem with the neighbor next door? Well . . . you get the idea.

Number 6: *It brings you closer to perfect.* In his book *Outliers*, Malcolm Gladwell says that to be an expert at something, you must invest at least 10,000 hours in practice. The hours you spend journaling count. Start today!

Number 5: *It improves your health.* There have been a number of studies that demonstrate how people who write about their feelings (good and, especially, bad) have less stress and stronger immune systems. It's not surprising—keeping things bottled up inside is a recipe for disaster while learning about yourself is a good bet for increasing well-being and confidence.

Number 4: *It creates a vast personal archive.* Much of what I've written in my journals is unfit to be read, even by me. Still, there are also many ideas and snippets that could inspire stories or articles. I've even included writing exercises in my journals—practicing writing dialogue, description, action, etc. (Tip: If you think you'd like to go back into your journals and you're not using a searchable software, think about creating an index so you can locate passages later on.)

Number 3: *It delivers gems.* I can't tell you how many times I've gone back to reread a passage and thought, "Wow! Did I write that? It's pretty good!" When you free up your creative self and make the commitment to be completely honest and uncensored, good stuff is bound to come up. The diamonds will be buried amidst tons of rubble, but they will be there.

Number 2: *It flushes out the bad stuff.* We all write bad stuff. In another of my other favorite writing books—*Bird by Bird*—writer Anne Lamott talks about writing poor first drafts. We all do. It's part of the process. Journaling is the fastest, easiest way to get more of your bad stuff onto the page so you can get on with the business of writing your best stuff.

Number 1: *It alleviates the pressure to be "good."* Journaling frees you to write with joy, abandon, and creativity. Writers are often worried about living up to some standard. It paralyzes and stunts—sucking all the life out of our writing, leaving us with a diluted version that is limp and colorless and completely lacking in inspiration. A journal gives you permission to write without any fears, without editing, without any "shoulds." It lets you "just" write. What a gift.

And those are my top ten reasons. What are yours?

Jamie Lee Wallace *is a writer who, among other things, works as a marketing strategist and copywriter. She helps creative entrepreneurs (artists, writers, idea people, and creative consultants) discover their "natural" marketing groove so they can build their business with passion, story, and connection. She also blogs. A lot. She is a mom, a singer, and a dreamer who believes in small kindnesses, daily chocolate, and happy endings. Look her up on Facebook or follow her on Twitter. She doesn't bite . . . usually.*

RECENT COMMENTS

Work with another student. Write a list of five reasons a student learning English should keep a journal. Then share your list with another pair.

TYPES OF JOURNALS

There are several types of journals that teachers typically assign in writing classes. No matter what type of journal is assigned, the purpose of keeping one is to provide you with practice in expressing your ideas freely without having to think about the accuracy of your writing; it helps you develop your writing fluency. As was pointed out earlier, the ability to write fluently is helpful even in situations such as exams, where accuracy is also important. In this unit you will focus on these three types of journals:

1. **Freewriting Journals:** Students write freely on a topic (or topics) of their choice. The journal may be kept in a notebook or as a computer document. They are not edited for spelling or grammar, nor does anyone other than the writer read the journal.

2. **Guided Response Journals:** Students write answers to a specific question or write about an assigned topic. These might be assigned by the teacher or brainstormed by the class and may or may not be related to course content.

3. **Dialogue (Partner) Journals:** This type of journal resembles a conversation. Students write on a topic of their choice, and the teacher or another student writes a response to the journal entry. The response may include comments or questions. In the next entry, the student responds to comments and questions, and so on. This type of journal can be written via email with a partner in another classroom (or country!).

Your teacher may assign one of these types of journals or may give you various types of journal assignments at different times during the course.

Practice each type of journal on a separate piece of paper. Follow these instructions. You will share your writing with other students.

A. Freewrite for five minutes on a topic of your own choice.

B. Choose one of these topics. Write a guided response journal entry. Write for five minutes about the topic.

- A goal for the near future
- A time you felt sad
- A clothing style you like/dislike
- Something you learned in another class this week

C. *Practice a dialogue journal entry. Work with another student. Follow these steps:*

1. Write for two or three minutes about another topic from Exercise B.
2. Exchange papers.
3. Write a response to your partner's dialogue journal entry. Write for three minutes.
4. Return your partner's paper.
5. Write a response to your partner's comments or questions. Write for about one minute.

EXERCISE 4

A. *How should your class do journals? Complete the questionnaire about your journal preferences.*

	Agree	Not sure / It depends.	Disagree
1. I would like the teacher to read my journal.			
2. I would like my classmates to read my journal.			
3. I prefer to keep my journal in a notebook.			
4. I prefer using a computer to write my journal.			
5. I would like the teacher to choose the journal topics or questions.			
6. I prefer to choose my own topics to write about.			
7. I prefer to write freely, without a specific topic.			
8. I prefer writing in my journal only once a week.			
9. I prefer writing in my journal several times a week.			
10. I would like to receive a grade for my journal.			
11. Which types of journals interest you the most? (Circle one or more.)	Dialogue Freewriting Guided Response		

B. *Work in a group. Discuss your responses. Then share your ideas with the class.*

YOUR CLASS JOURNAL

Keep a journal throughout this course. Discuss these questions with your teacher and your whole class, and write the answers here:

1. Will the journal be done in a notebook or on the computer? _____

2. How often will you write in your journal? _____

3. About how long (time and length) should an entry be? _____

4. Will you write in your journal in class, at home, or both? _____

5. Will your teacher assign the topics, or will you choose them, or both? _____

6. Which type(s) of journal (diary, dialogue, etc.) will you do? _____

7. Will anyone read your journal? If so, who? _____

Journal Topic Ideas

Here are some journal topic ideas to help you and your class get started with keeping a journal:

- Write about a person who has influenced you and explain why.
- Write about a place you go when you need to relax.
- Describe a movie or book that had a surprising ending.
- How are you similar to most of your friends? How are you different?
- Write about a sport you enjoy playing or watching.
- Write about your most frightening experience.
- Describe the qualities of a good employer.
- What is a talent or skill you are proud of? Explain how you learned it.
- Write about an experience that changed your attitude about something or someone.
- Write your thoughts about one of these: a starry night sky, a full moon, space travel, the sound of the ocean, a thunderstorm, watching a sunset, watching a sunrise.

Work with another student or a group. Add at least five more ideas to the list.

Blogging

A **blog** is an online journal that is usually written by one person or a small group of people. In December 2011, there were over 175,000,000 blogs, and the number had been growing at the rate of nearly 3 million blogs per month. Bloggers write about political issues, social trends, hobbies, personal travel, academic topics . . . just about anything! Some people even set their blogs to private and use them as an online journal. However, most bloggers are hoping to share their interests and information with a wide variety of people, both in their home countries and around the world.

Your teacher can make a class blog at http://pearsonelt.com/writingpowerblog, where you and your classmates can practice posting on topics that interest you. You will be able to read each other's posts and make comments on them.

(See page v for more on how to set up your Writing Power 4 class blog.)

After practicing on your class blog, you can create a personal blog. There are several different popular blogging platforms (sitcs) that are free to use. Type the words *free blog* for a key word search on the Internet. You will find several URLs for free blogging platforms.

In this unit, you will . . .

- analyze a blog.
- decide what you want to write about for your own blog.
- plan features of your blog.

Warm Up

A. ***Work in a group. Discuss these questions:***

- Have you seen or visited any blogs? If yes, describe the content.

- How did you become interested in those blogs?

- Are there any particular blogs that you read regularly? If so, what topics do they discuss?

- Have you ever written a blog? If so, what is/was it about? What or who inspired you to write it?

- If you haven't previously visited or written a blog, explain why not. If you were to read or write a blog, what types of topics might interest you?

- How do you think blogging might help you improve your writing skills?

B. ***Work with another student. What types of features do blogs include (photos, video, and so on)? What are some things a blogger could do to attract more readers? Make a quick list, and then share your list with the whole class.***

THINKING ABOUT BLOGGERS

There is an abundance of different types of blogs. Sports, gardening, politics, the arts, interviews, advice—these are but a few of the topics people are blogging about. However for the most part, blogs that are the most widely read are about one topic, issue, or organization. Bloggers usually fall into one of five categories:

- **Hobby bloggers** are just posting for fun and aren't paid for writing. By some estimates, hobby bloggers make up more than half of all bloggers online.

- **Entrepreneurs** blog for a company, business, or organization that they own or manage.

- **Full-time professionals** are freelancers who make a living from blogging, either for one site or several.

- **Part-time professionals** are freelancers, often found in the technology industry, who treat blogging as a part-time job.

- **Corporate bloggers** work full-time on the blog of just one company. They might be employees of that company or freelancers.

A serious blog is a major commitment, even for hobby bloggers. Some bloggers host "guest bloggers" on their site from time to time to add a fresh perspective to the blog's topic. The blog should be updated regularly with new content—once a week at a minimum, or as often as once a day.

A. *Complete the survey about your blog interests. Check (✓) the appropriate columns.*

How interested would you be in reading a blog . . .	Very interested	Somewhat interested	Not interested
1. about events in your local community?	○	○	○
2. about national politics or events?	○	○	○
3. about international politics or events?	○	○	○
4. about books and literature? (If interested, what type of literature? _____)	○	○	○
5. about travel?	○	○	○
6. about music, dance, theater, or other art forms? (If interested, what type of art forms? _____)	○	○	○
7. a hobby or leisure activity? (If interested, what type? _____)	○	○	○
8. about a significant social issue?	○	○	○
9. about the latest in technology? (If interested, what type of technology? _____)	○	○	○
10. about a specific industry or professional field? (If interested what industry or field? _____)	○	○	○
11. about a sport? (If interested, what sport? _____)	○	○	○
12. about another topic? (What topic? _____)	○	○	○
13. that includes photos and/or videos?	○	○	○
14. that allows readers to post comments?	○	○	○
15. that has regular guest bloggers?	○	○	○

B. *Find three other students who share your interest in at least two topics. Discuss your choices.*

A. *Look at the blog homepage, the "about" link, and one post.*

Clouds in Your Coffee

http://cloudsinyourcoffee.wordpress.com/

Clouds in Your Coffee

Coffee Travels   How to Taste Coffee   Cafe Stay   About Clouds in Your Coffee

Costa Rica, Day 1
JANUARY 1, 2012
So this morning brought us to San Jose, Costa Rica's capital city. Finally! I'm a little tired, a little confused (my Spanish is good enough for "please" and "thank you" and of course "coffee" but that's about it), but mostly just very excited to be here. If you haven't traveled to Costa Rica before, [. . .]

Going to Costa Rica!
DECEMBER 25, 2011
Just found out that we'll be heading off to Costa Rica in early January to visit some coffee farms there and to meet some of the farmers. After drinking coffee for so long (granted, 'drinking coffee' is probably too simple of a word for the way that I feel about coffee, but you know what [. . .]

Cafe Stay: Bean Here, Done That
DECEMBER 15, 2011
Today's Cafe Stay was a trip to a little downtown place called Bean Here, Done That. From the outside, it's a pretty little building that was once a house. There are lots of lights in the windows and when you walk inside, there's a whole shelf full of books and games. The servers and baristas [. . .]

How to Taste Coffee, Part 1 (Flavor)
DECEMBER 10, 2011
If you're reading this blog, it means you probably enjoy coffee. At the very least, you've probably drank it over time. Maybe you've even had some experience making it. Coffee can be imbibed as part of a ritual, as an addiction or habit, as a way to connect with friends, and much more. And, yet, [. . .]

Welcome to Clouds in Your Coffee!
DECEMBER 1, 2011
Hello readers! Welcome to my blog, Clouds in Your Coffee. I love two things most of all in life: Great coffee and beautiful places. I started this blog to chronicle the two; sometimes separate, sometimes together. Thus Clouds in Your Coffee was created. I hope you'll come along with me on this journey toward amazing [. . .]

About Me

Hello readers! Welcome to my blog, Clouds in Your Coffee. I'm Stephen, and I love two things most of all in life: Great coffee and beautiful places. I started this blog to chronicle the two; sometimes separate, sometimes together. Thus Clouds in Your Coffee was created.
I hope you'll come along with me on this journey toward amazing cups of joe and incredible places to travel. Click on any of the links below to begin your travels in coffee.

Recent Posts
- Costa Rica, Day 1
- Going to Costa Rica!
- Cafe Stay: Bean Here, Done That
- How to Taste Coffee, Part 1 (Flavor)
- Welcome to Clouds in Your Coffee!

Recent Comments
- cloudsinyourcoffee on Cafe Stay: Bean Here, Done That
- Stephanie D. on How to Taste Coffee, Part 1 (Flavor)
- John S. Anders on Cafe Stay: Bean Here, Done That

Archives
- January 2012
- December 2011

Categories
- About Clouds in Your Coffee
- Cafe Stay
- Coffee Travels
- How to Taste Coffee

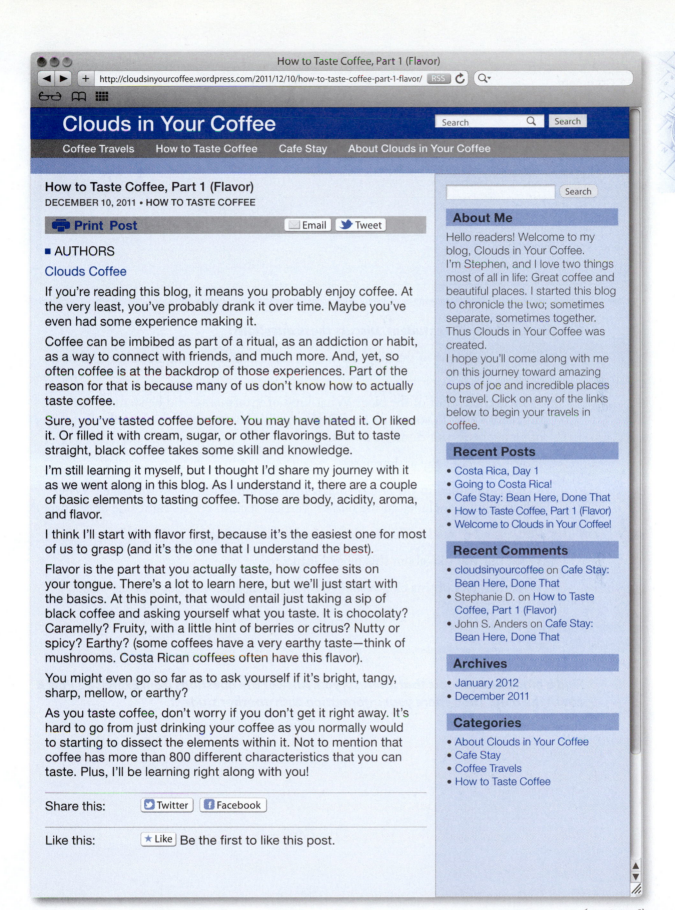

http://cloudsinyourcoffee.wordpress.com/2011/12/10/how-to-taste-coffee-part-1-flavor/

Clouds in Your Coffee

Search

Coffee Travels   How to Taste Coffee   Cafe Stay   About Clouds in Your Coffee

How to Taste Coffee, Part 1 (Flavor)
DECEMBER 10, 2011 • HOW TO TASTE COFFEE

🖶 **Print Post**   ✉ Email   🐦 Tweet

■ AUTHORS

Clouds Coffee

If you're reading this blog, it means you probably enjoy coffee. At the very least, you've probably drank it over time. Maybe you've even had some experience making it.

Coffee can be imbibed as part of a ritual, as an addiction or habit, as a way to connect with friends, and much more. And, yet, so often coffee is at the backdrop of those experiences. Part of the reason for that is because many of us don't know how to actually taste coffee.

Sure, you've tasted coffee before. You may have hated it. Or liked it. Or filled it with cream, sugar, or other flavorings. But to taste straight, black coffee takes some skill and knowledge.

I'm still learning it myself, but I thought I'd share my journey with it as we went along in this blog. As I understand it, there are a couple of basic elements to tasting coffee. Those are body, acidity, aroma, and flavor.

I think I'll start with flavor first, because it's the easiest one for most of us to grasp (and it's the one that I understand the best).

Flavor is the part that you actually taste, how coffee sits on your tongue. There's a lot to learn here, but we'll just start with the basics. At this point, that would entail just taking a sip of black coffee and asking yourself what you taste. It is chocolaty? Caramelly? Fruity, with a little hint of berries or citrus? Nutty or spicy? Earthy? (some coffees have a very earthy taste—think of mushrooms. Costa Rican coffees often have this flavor).

You might even go so far as to ask yourself if it's bright, tangy, sharp, mellow, or earthy?

As you taste coffee, don't worry if you don't get it right away. It's hard to go from just drinking your coffee as you normally would to starting to dissect the elements within it. Not to mention that coffee has more than 800 different characteristics that you can taste. Plus, I'll be learning right along with you!

Share this: 🐦 Twitter   f Facebook

Like this: ⭐ Like Be the first to like this post.

About Me

Hello readers! Welcome to my blog, Clouds in Your Coffee. I'm Stephen, and I love two things most of all in life: Great coffee and beautiful places. I started this blog to chronicle the two; sometimes separate, sometimes together. Thus Clouds in Your Coffee was created.
I hope you'll come along with me on this journey toward amazing cups of joe and incredible places to travel. Click on any of the links below to begin your travels in coffee.

Recent Posts
- Costa Rica, Day 1
- Going to Costa Rica!
- Cafe Stay: Bean Here, Done That
- How to Taste Coffee, Part 1 (Flavor)
- Welcome to Clouds in Your Coffee!

Recent Comments
- cloudsinyourcoffee on Cafe Stay: Bean Here, Done That
- Stephanie D. on How to Taste Coffee, Part 1 (Flavor)
- John S. Anders on Cafe Stay: Bean Here, Done That

Archives
- January 2012
- December 2011

Categories
- About Clouds in Your Coffee
- Cafe Stay
- Coffee Travels
- How to Taste Coffee

(continued)

1 Comment   Comments RSS

Stephanie D.   *January 6, 2012*

Thank you for this. I just moved to Seattle and there are good coffee shops everywhere. I am trying to learn more about how to taste coffee, so I look forward to reading the rest of your posts.

Reply

Leave a Reply

Enter your comment here . . .

B. *Work with another student. Discuss these questions:*

- What is the topic of the blog? How long did it take you to figure it out, and how did you know?

- Who is the author of the blog? What kind of information did he share about himself? Why do you think he did not post his last name? Which of the five types of bloggers do you think he is? Why?

- How often does the author post?

- What is included in the *header* (horizontal section at the top of the page)? What information is included in the *sidebar* (vertical section on the right side of the page)?

- What kind of readers do you think would visit this blog?

- What did you like about this blog? Dislike?

- What features of this blog would you want to include in a blog of your own?

EXERCISE 3

Find a blog about a topic that interests you. Answer the questions from Exercise 2 Part B about the blog. Then share your information with another student.

A BLOG OF YOUR OWN

Keep a blog throughout this course or for a time period set by your teacher. Choose a topic of interest to you that you will be able to write about during this course. Your blog can include information about you and why you're blogging.

A. **Use this idea web to plan your own blog. Add as many ideas as you can.**

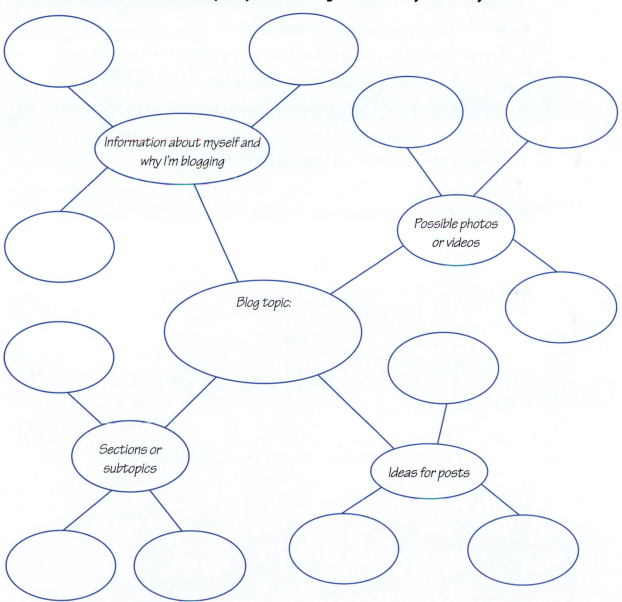

B. **Work with another student. Share your idea webs. Make suggestions for what to include on each other's blogs.**

C. *Discuss these questions with your teacher and your class. Write the answers here:*

1. By when should you have your blog set up? _____

2. What are one or two topics that you want to blog about? _____

    _____

3. How often do you have to post on your blog? _____

4. What should the length (how many words) of each post be? _____

5. Are you required to read classmates' blogs? If so, how many and how often?

    _____

6. Are you also required to leave comments? _____

7. Are you required to, or allowed to, have guest posters? If so, how often?

    _____

8. Are any other features such as photos or videos required? If so, which ones?

    _____

9. What additional rules or guidelines are there for the blog? _____

    _____

10. What will be the content of your first post? _____

    _____

Creative Writing

Some writers hear the words *creative writing* and wonder, "Do I have to be an artist?" However, creative writing can be enjoyable and achievable. Writing a fictional story, for example, can be simple once you understand its key elements.

In this unit, you will . . .

- learn about character, plot, and setting—the three key elements of a short story.
- learn about some common plot patterns found in short stories.
- work with a partner to write a short story together.

Warm Up

Work in a group. Discuss these questions:

- What kinds of stories do you enjoy reading?
- What is the last story you read? Was it assigned for school, or did you choose it? Briefly describe it.
- What kinds of stories do you not enjoy? Why?
- Have you ever written a story? Why? What was it about?

CHARACTER

A **character** in a story is usually a person (though it could also be a robot, an alien, or even an animal) who experiences the events. Many stories have more than one character. If there is a conflict between characters, there is usually a **protagonist** (the leading character; the hero/heroine) and an **antagonist** (the person or force who acts against the protagonist).

Characters can be described from the perspective of a narrator, who is perhaps another character or even the author. They may also be described by other characters, or their personalities may become apparent through what they say to each other—their dialogue—or their actions.

EXERCISE 1

A. **Work with another student. Think about different characteristics of people (or story characters). For five minutes, brainstorm vocabulary to complete the chart. Follow the examples in the chart.**

Physical Characteristics	Personality	
	Positive	**Negative**
tall	cheerful	cruel
thin	patient	lazy
brown hair	kind	stingy
weak	intelligent	

B. **Work with another pair. Share your charts. Add any words from the other pair's chart that you particularly like.**

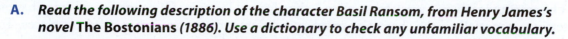

A. *Read the following description of the character Basil Ransom, from Henry James's novel* **The Bostonians** *(1886). Use a dictionary to check any unfamiliar vocabulary.*

And, indeed, he was very long, Basil Ransom, and he even looked a little hard and discouraging, like a column of figures, in spite of the friendly face which he bent upon his hostess's deputy, and which, in its thinness, had a deep dry line, a sort of premature wrinkle, on either side of the mouth. He was tall and lean, and dressed throughout in black; his shirt-collar was low and wide, and the triangle of linen, a little crumpled, exhibited by the opening of his waistcoat, was adorned by a pin containing a small red stone. In spite of this decoration the young man looked poor— as poor as a young man could look who had such a fine head and such magnificent eyes. Those of Basil Ransom were dark, deep, and glowing; his head had a character of elevation which fairly added to his stature; it was a head to be seen above the level of a crowd, on some judicial bench or political platform, or even on a bronze medal. His forehead was high and broad, and his thick black hair, perfectly straight and glossy, and without any division, rolled back from it in a leonine manner. These things, the eyes especially, with their smouldering fire, might have indicated that he was to be a great American statesman; or, on the other hand, they might simply have proved that he came from Carolina or Alabama. He came, in fact, from Mississippi, and he spoke very perceptibly with the accent of that country.

B. *Work with another student. Discuss these questions:*

• Without looking back at the passage, describe Basil Ransom's appearance.

• The description of Mr. Ransom was mostly of his physical appearance. What do you imagine his personality was like?

A. *Write for five minutes. Describe a character in a familiar story, book, movie, poem, or television show.*

B. *Write for five minutes. Describe a person you know from your own life, or invent an imaginary character.*

C. *Work with another student or in a group. Share your character descriptions from Exercises A and B. Were the characteristics you described positive or negative? How do you know? Did you concentrate more on physical characteristics or personality?*

SETTING

The **setting** is where a story takes place—the physical location. Of course, novels may have several settings, especially if the characters travel or if different characters live in different places. To describe a setting, writers often give sensory details—information about the sights, sounds, and even smells of a location. Use a dictionary to check any unfamiliar vocabulary.

EXERCISE 4

A.   Read this excerpt from Tickets, Please! (1919) by D. H. Lawrence.

Old-fashioned tramcar

There is in the North a single-line system of tramcars which boldly leaves the county town and plunges off into the black, industrial countryside, up hill and down dale, through the long, ugly villages of workmen's houses, over canals and railways, past churches perched high and nobly over the smoke and shadows, through dark, grimy, cold little market-places, tilting away in a rush past cinemas and shops down to the hollow where the collieries[1] are, then up again, past a little rural church under the ash-trees, on in a bolt to the terminus, the last little ugly place of industry, the cold little town that shivers on the edge of the wild, gloomy country beyond. There the blue and creamy coloured tramcar seems to pause and purr with curious satisfaction.

B.   Work with another student. Discuss these questions:

• What kind of impression do you have from the setting—is it a nice place? Poor or wealthy? Rural or urban?

• This is the opening paragraph of a short story. What do you imagine the story will be like? What might it be about?

[1]*colliery—a* coal mine and its related buildings and equipment

A. *Think of a place that is familiar to your classmates. Write a brief description of it, but don't give the name.*

B. *Exchange descriptions with another student. Guess what setting your partner described. Explain your answer.*

PLOT

The **plot** is what happens in a story—the sequence of events or the storyline. As a result of these events, something happens to the character or characters; there is some kind of a change. Plots vary somewhat in different cultures and in different time periods, but a plot structure generally involves some kind of conflict and then a resolution. That is, there is a problem or a question and then a solution or an answer. Note that the resolution to a conflict is not always positive or happy. Sometimes the plot has an unexpected development, or twist.

Work with a partner. Take turns describing one or two plots from books or movies you know. How brief can you make the description? (As in the classic example—Boy meets girl; boy loses girl; boy wins girl back.)

A. *Read the story by O. Henry, an American writer known for having twists in his plots. Use a dictionary to check any unfamiliar vocabulary.*

After Twenty Years

The policeman on the beat moved up the avenue impressively. The impressiveness was habitual and not for show, for spectators were few. The time was barely 10 o'clock at night, but chilly gusts of wind with a taste of rain in them had well nigh de-peopled the streets.

Trying doors as he went, twirling his club with many intricate and artful movements, turning now and then to cast his watchful eye adown the pacific thoroughfare, the officer, with his stalwart form and slight swagger, made a fine picture of a guardian of the peace. The vicinity was one that kept early hours. Now and then you might see the lights of a cigar store or of an all-night lunch counter; but the majority of the doors belonged to business places that had long since been closed.

(continued)

When about midway of a certain block the policeman suddenly slowed his walk. In the doorway of a darkened hardware store a man leaned, with an unlighted cigar in his mouth. As the policeman walked up to him the man spoke up quickly.

"It's all right, officer," he said, reassuringly. "I'm just waiting for a friend. It's an appointment made twenty years ago. Sounds a little funny to you, doesn't it? Well, I'll explain if you'd like to make certain it's all straight. About that long ago there used to be a restaurant where this store stands—'Big Joe' Brady's restaurant."

"Until five years ago," said the policeman. "It was torn down then."

The man in the doorway struck a match and lit his cigar. The light showed a pale, square-jawed face with keen eyes, and a little white scar near his right eyebrow. His scarfpin was a large diamond, oddly set.

"Twenty years ago to-night," said the man, "I dined here at 'Big Joe' Brady's with Jimmy Wells, my best chum, and the finest chap in the world. He and I were raised here in New York, just like two brothers, together. I was eighteen and Jimmy was twenty. The next morning I was to start for the West to make my fortune. You couldn't have dragged Jimmy out of New York; he thought it was the only place on earth. Well, we agreed that night that we would meet here again exactly twenty years from that date and time, no matter what our conditions might be or from what distance we might have to come. We figured that in twenty years each of us ought to have our destiny worked out and our fortunes made, whatever they were going to be."

"It sounds pretty interesting," said the policeman. "Rather a long time between meets, though, it seems to me. Haven't you heard from your friend since you left?"

"Well, yes, for a time we corresponded," said the other. "But after a year or two we lost track of each other. You see, the West is a pretty big proposition, and I kept hustling around over it pretty lively. But I know Jimmy will meet me here if he's alive, for he always was the truest, stanchest old chap in the world. He'll never forget. I came a thousand miles to stand in this door to-night, and it's worth it if my old partner turns up."

The waiting man pulled out a handsome watch, the lids of it set with small diamonds.

"Three minutes to ten," he announced. "It was exactly ten o'clock when we parted here at the restaurant door."

"Did pretty well out West, didn't you?" asked the policeman.

"You bet! I hope Jimmy has done half as well. He was a kind of plodder, though, good fellow as he was. I've had to compete with some of the sharpest wits going to get my pile. A man gets in a groove in New York. It takes the West to put a razor-edge on him."

The policeman twirled his club and took a step or two.

"I'll be on my way. Hope your friend comes around all right. Going to call time on him sharp?"

"I should say not!" said the other. "I'll give him half an hour at least. If Jimmy is alive on earth he'll be here by that time. So long, officer."

"Good-night, sir," said the policeman, passing on along his beat, trying doors as he went.

There was now a fine, cold drizzle falling, and the wind had risen from its uncertain puffs into a steady blow. The few foot passengers astir in that quarter hurried dismally and silently along with coat collars turned high and pocketed hands. And in the door of the hardware store the man who had come a thousand miles to fill an appointment, uncertain almost to absurdity, with the friend of his youth, smoked his cigar and waited.

About twenty minutes he waited, and then a tall man in a long overcoat, with collar turned up to his ears, hurried across from the opposite side of the street. He went directly to the waiting man.

"Is that you, Bob?" he asked, doubtfully.

"Is that you, Jimmy Wells?" cried the man in the door.

"Bless my heart!" exclaimed the new arrival, grasping both the other's hands with his own. "It's Bob, sure as fate. I was certain I'd find you here if you were still in existence. Well, well, well!—twenty years is a long time. The old restaurant's gone, Bob; I wish it had lasted, so we could have had another dinner there. How has the West treated you, old man?"

"Bully; it has given me everything I asked it for. You've changed lots, Jimmy. I never thought you were so tall by two or three inches."

"Oh, I grew a bit after I was twenty."

"Doing well in New York, Jimmy?"

"Moderately. I have a position in one of the city departments. Come on, Bob; we'll go around to a place I know of, and have a good long talk about old times."

The two men started up the street, arm in arm. The man from the West, his egotism enlarged by success, was beginning to outline the history of his career. The other, submerged in his overcoat, listened with interest.

At the corner stood a drug store, brilliant with electric lights. When they came into this glare each of them turned simultaneously to gaze upon the other's face.

The man from the West stopped suddenly and released his arm.

"You're not Jimmy Wells," he snapped. "Twenty years is a long time, but not long enough to change a man's nose from a Roman to a pug."

"It sometimes changes a good man into a bad one," said the tall man. "You've been under arrest for ten minutes, 'Silky' Bob. Chicago thinks you may have dropped over our way and wires us she wants to have a chat with you. Going quietly, are you? That's sensible. Now, before we go on to the station here's a note I was asked to hand you. You may read it here at the window. It's from Patrolman Wells."

The man from the West unfolded the little piece of paper handed him. His hand was steady when he began to read, but it trembled a little by the time he had finished. The note was rather short.

Bob: I was at the appointed place on time. When you struck the match to light your cigar I saw it was the face of the man wanted in Chicago. Somehow I couldn't do it myself, so I went around and got a plain clothes man to do the job.

JIMMY.

B. Work in a group. Discuss these questions:

- Describe the characters. Is there a protagonist and/or antagonist? If so, which character is the protagonist? Which is the antagonist?

- Describe the setting.

- Briefly summarize the plot. What was the twist?

WRITING TASK

Write a short story.

A. Work with another student to write a short story. First, complete the chart.

Setting:	Words and phrases to describe the setting:
Character 1 (Protagonist):	Words and phrases to describe Character 1: Physical characteristics: Personality characteristics
Character 2 (Antagonist):	Words and phrases to describe Character 2: Physical characteristics: Personality characteristics:
Other characters:	Words and phrases to describe other characters: Physical characteristics: Personality characteristics:
Brief plot outline: **Problem:** **Solution:**	

B. Together, write a two-to-three page story.

Check Your Writing

A. *Use this form to check your story, or exchange stories with another pair and check each other's writing.*

Story Checklist

1. What is the setting? _____

2. Was the setting described so that you could easily imagine it? _____

3. How many main characters are there? _____

4. Is there a protagonist? _____ Is there an antagonist? _____

5. Describe one of the characters. _____

_____

_____

6. Briefly summarize the plot. _____

_____

_____

_____

7. Underline one or two favorite sentences from the story.

8. Do you have any other comments or suggestions for the writers? If so, write them here:

_____

_____

_____

_____

_____

B. *Make changes to improve your story. Remember to check your writing for grammar, spelling, and punctuation errors.*

Language Use

Introduction

In this part of *Writing Power 4*, you will work on developing language skills for writing in many different situations—how to build a rich vocabulary that you can draw upon for your writing, and how to write sentences and paragraphs in English that are correct and that effectively communicate the ideas, information, and feelings you want to express. These units will help you understand and practice some of the more complex skills that are often difficult for students of English.

Skills introduced in Part 2 include:

- Building Vocabulary
- Pronouns
- Gerunds and Infinitives
- Articles
- Parallel Structure

Vocabulary Building

Building a rich vocabulary will help you write clearly and in a way that expresses exactly what you want to convey. A broad vocabulary gives your writing variety and makes it sound more natural. You have already learned many words as you have worked toward becoming a more accomplished writer in English.

In this unit, you will . . .

- learn about yourself as a vocabulary learner.
- learn and practice strategies for finding and selecting relevant words.
- learn about ways you can collect and review vocabulary to improve your writing.
- learn how to select the most appropriate strategies for yourself.

Strategies for building vocabulary include . . .

- selecting useful words.
- keeping a notebook for new vocabulary.
- using visuals and graphic organizers.
- planning your vocabulary learning.

Using these strategies will help you better understand information and decide which new words will be useful for your writing.

You can also focus on specific areas for vocabulary study, such as . . .

- word families.
- synonyms and antonyms.
- collocations and phrases.

Note: For this unit and the rest of this course, you will need a Vocabulary Notebook. You will use this notebook especially for keeping words that will be useful in your writing.

Warm Up

A. *What kind of learner are you? Take this vocabulary learning survey. Check (✓) a maximum of three styles which describe you very well. Then check your learning style(s) at the bottom of the page.*

I learn vocabulary best by . . .

☐ **1.** listening and repeating new words and writing them down.

☐ **2.** connecting words to a song or a rhythm; focusing on pronunciation and word stress.

☐ **3.** acting out words and relating them to movement.

☐ **4.** visualizing the words and connecting them to images or colors.

☐ **5.** connecting words to ideas or topics; creating logical patterns.

☐ **6.** practicing with other people, doing exercises, or testing each other.

☐ **7.** studying on my own; relating words to my own personal experiences.

B. *Read the description(s) of your style(s) below. If you checked more than one, which one describes you the best? If you checked only one, does the description match your style? Why or why not?*

C. *Compare your learning style with your classmates. How are your learning styles similar or different? Then discuss these questions:*

- Do you have a vocabulary notebook? How is it organized? What does it include? Does it contain just lists of words and definitions, or does it also contain graphic organizers, pictures, and diagrams?

- Where and how do you usually practice learning vocabulary? Do you listen to music at the same time? Do you practice alone or with others?

- Look at the descriptions of your preferred learning styles again. What steps could you take to ensure that the way you learn vocabulary fits your learning style?

You are probably a _____ learner:

1. verbal-linguistic This person enjoys reading and writing; is expressive in speaking and writing; likes playing with words sounds; makes an effort to learn and use new words.

2. musical-rhythmical This person likes to work with sound and music; has a good sense of rhythm and pitch; usually can sing, play an instrument, or identify the sounds of instruments; associates music with emotions; notices background music; often hums a song; songs often pop into thoughts.

3. kinesthetic This type of learner uses body and sense of touch to learn; likes sports and exercise; likes to think through issues while exercising; notices and appreciates textures; likes making things or working on puzzles.

4. visual This person prefers using images, colors, and maps to organize information; easily visualizes objects, plans, and outcomes; has a good sense of space and direction; uses maps easily and rarely gets lost.

5. logical-mathematical This type of learner likes to use logical and mathematical reasoning; recognizes patterns and connections easily; prefers to classify and group information; works well with numbers.

6. interpersonal This person communicates well verbally and nonverbally; is sensitive to others' motivations, feelings, or moods; is a good listener; prefers learning in groups.

7. intrapersonal This type of learner is private, introspective, and independent; can concentrate well; is aware of own thinking; analyzes own ways of thinking and feeling; likes to be alone; often keeps a journal or diary.

NOTE: Most people have 2–3 preferred learning styles.

SELECTING USEFUL WORDS

Reading in English is an extremely practical way to build your English vocabulary. You will often find new words when you read a textbook, article, or novel. Knowing how to choose which words are important and useful for you to learn is an important skill.

As you know, understanding new words and expressions is often necessary for comprehending information when you read. Sometimes you can guess the meaning of new words from **context**—the other words and sentences around it. Other times this may not be possible. Using your dictionary to look up new words is part of learning vocabulary. However, if you stop your reading to check the dictionary too often, it is difficult to follow the general meaning of the text.

When you find a new word in your reading, underline or highlight it. At the end of one or two pages, look back at the words and decide which ones will be useful for you to learn.

How do you decide which words will be useful for your writing? Which words do you want to add to your vocabulary notebook? Words and expressions that are important are often **repeated in the text**, or they may describe or explain **a key aspect** of the topic. A word is also useful for you if it is related to your studies, work, or interests.

Not all words are equally important, so before you spend time learning a word, check first to find out if a word is common or useful. You could check to see if it is included on **word lists** such as the Pearson International Corpus of Academic English (PICAE) or the Academic Writing List (AWL).

The **Pearson International Corpus of Academic English** lists 3,000 of the most frequently used words in English. Knowing these words is necessary for general comprehension. *(See Appendix, page 00.)*

The **Academic Word List** (available online) contains 570 of the most frequently used words found in academic texts, articles, and journals. Learning these words will help you to understand your academic readings as well as to write using a proper academic tone.

Guidelines for Selecting Useful Words

To decide whether a word will be useful for your writing, ask yourself these questions:

- Is the word repeated in the text?

- Does the word relate to or explain a key aspect of the topic?

- Do I need to look up the word to understand the text better?

- Is it on a word list such as the Pearson International Corpus of Academic English or Academic Word List?

- Is the word related to my school, work, or personal interests?

If you answer *yes* to two or more of the questions, the word is probably useful for your writing. Look it up in the dictionary and write it in your vocabulary notebook.

Read the following passages. Follow these instructions for each passage:

1. Write the topic of the passage on the line below it.

2. Circle any words you know that relate to the topic.

3. As you read, underline or highlight any words or phrases that are new to you. Do not stop to look them up in a dictionary!

4. Choose three words you underlined or highlighted and try to guess their meaning from the context. Then check the meanings in the dictionary. Were your guesses correct? Write the words that you guessed incorrectly on the line below the passage.

5. Check for each word on the PICAE (*See the Appendix*) or the AWL. Write the ones you find on the line under each passage. Then ask yourself the Guidelines questions to decide which words and phrases are useful to learn. Write the words on the line below the passage and in your vocabulary notebook.

Passage 1

Last weekend I watched an outstanding CNN program called "Bullying: It stops here!" Bullying is a real problem in schools today, in part because schoolchildren receive threatening emails and other forms of cyberattacks. In my day, there were plenty of mean and intimidating bullies around, but at least when we left the school building, we could go home and get out from under their noses. On the other hand, it was worse in my schooldays because bullies were protected by teachers and even hero-worshipped by some teachers. Anyway, good for CNN for raising awareness of this important topic!

Topic: _____

Words I guessed incorrectly from context: _____

Words on word lists: _____

Useful words for my writing: _____

Passage 2

As a Human Resources Manager, you will find that dealing with problems in the workplace is not as easy as it might appear. Not everyone should be managed in the same way—and furthermore, not everyone will respond to the same treatment. Take the "Fire Hose," for example. This is a person who dampens enthusiasm and assumes that everything will fail. You might find that you can change the Fire Hose's negative attitude subtly by encouraging him to look for solutions, not problems. This takes time, but can be successfully managed. The "Sniper," on the other hand, needs a very different kind of management technique. Snipers have a habit of attacking people in such a subtle way that people rarely notice. Snipers also withhold key information and exclude key people from important situations. The best response to this kind of person is to bring it out in the open: Find out what the resistance is about. You may even need to confirm with the other staff what is happening behind the scenes. If you consider the situation unmanageable, you may have to ask the Sniper to see a counselor.

Page 7

Topic: _____

Words I guessed incorrectly from context: _____

Words on word lists: _____

Useful words for my writing: _____

(continued)

CAVE FORMATIONS

Snottites

Unlike rigid stalactites, found hanging from the ceilings of caves, viscous **snottites** can cover the walls as well. These bacterial single-celled microbes grow in colonies, and obtain their energy from chemosynthesis—a process fuelled by chemical rather than solar energy. Chemosynthesis of volcanic sulfur compounds produces snottites, so named because they have the consistency of the mucus found in the nasal passages of vertebrates. These highly acidic biofilms have chemical properties similar to the acid in a typical battery.

Topic: _____

Words I guessed incorrectly from context: _____

Words on word lists: _____

Useful words for my writing: _____

VOCABULARY NOTEBOOKS

Many students keep a special notebook for vocabulary study. It helps them organize and keep track of new words. You can start a vocabulary notebook to write down useful new words and phrases you encounter in *Writing Power 4* and from other sources.

Vocabulary notebook entries can include information about a word, such as . . .

- the part of speech of the word—noun, verb, adjective, adverb, and so on.
- the definition.
- a visual, such as a simple drawing or diagram, to help you remember the meaning.
- the sentence in which the word was found.
- new sentences with the new word; you can write them yourself or copy an example sentence from the dictionary.

Your vocabulary notebook can be organized in a number of different ways:

- alphabetically
- in word categories, such as "sports words," "science words," or "AWL words"
- by date
- by part of speech
- by specific topics

Your notebook can also include information that will help you understand and remember the words and use them accurately.

EXERCISE 2

A. **Start a vocabulary notebook using the vocabulary you marked "useful words" in Exercise 1. Choose a way to organize your notebook from the list above. Then follow these instructions for each word:**

1. On the left side of the page, write the word or phrase.

2. Under the word, write the sentence where you found it.

3. Look up the word in the dictionary.

4. To the right of the word, write the part of speech, the definition, and/or provide a visual to help you remember the meaning.

5. Write or find a new sentence using the word.
   Example:

bullying–n., the act of intimidating another person; using persistent and aggressive behavior against a weaker person "Bullying is a real problem in schools today, in part because schoolchildren receive threatening emails and other forms of cyberattacks."

Bullying was common among the boys in my school; however, the girls didn't bully each other much.

B. **Compare notebooks with another student. Did you choose any of the same useful words?**

C. **Think back to the Warm Up. According to your own learning style, what kinds of activities will help you remember these new words? Share your ideas with the class.**

COGNITIVE STRATEGIES: VISUALS AND GRAPHIC ORGANIZERS

A **cognitive strategy** is the process by which information is obtained, stored, retrieved, and used.

Research studies show that learning or remembering a new word takes repeated exposure to that word—at least seven or eight times—over time. Everyone has his or her own way of memorizing information, and the strategies you use depend on the kind of learner you are (linguistic, visual, musical-rhythmical, logical-mathematical, and so on).

Learners who are visual, musical, logical, and kinesthetic may find that strategies such as making word lists or copying out sentences do not help them very much. Instead, they need to see some kind of visual representation of the word, such as a picture or a graphic organizer.

One visual way to memorize your new vocabulary is to make **flashcards**. Also, drawing or labeling photos and pictures can help you remember new words. In Exercise 1, the phrases *Get out from under their noses* and *fire hose* are ideal examples of phrases for which it might be helpful to draw a picture in your vocabulary notebook.

fire hose

A logical-mathematical learner may find it more helpful to create charts and tables. For example, flowcharts help some learners to memorize the language used in a process. Finally, don't forget word maps—these can help you organize and therefore *remember* the language.

Study these visual graphic organizers.

Flow Chart

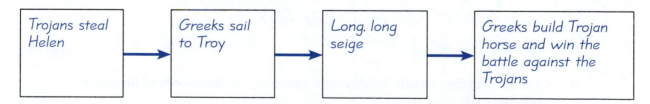

| Trojans steal Helen | Greeks sail to Troy | Long, long seige | Greeks build Trojan horse and win the battle against the Trojans |

Cycle

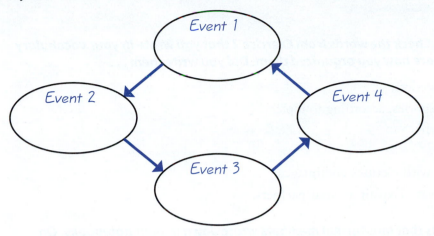

Collocation Chart

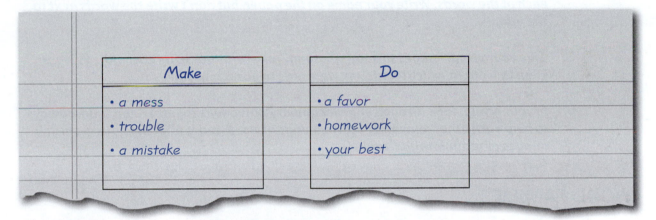

Make	Do
• a mess	• a favor
• trouble	• homework
• a mistake	• your best

Word Map

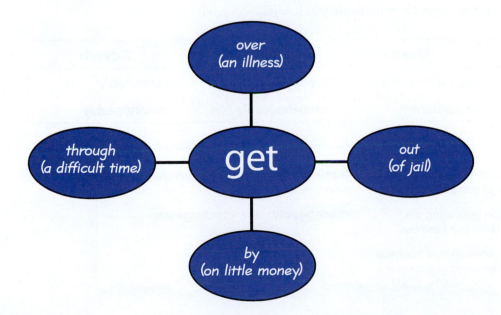

A. *Work in a group. Check the words from Exercise 2 that you wrote in your vocabulary notebook. Compare how you organized them. Did you write them . . .*

- in alphabetical order?
- in different categories, according to topic?
- by part of speech?
- by date?
- as word lists or with pictures and images?
- in some other way? Explain to your partners.

B. *Choose five words that most group members wrote down in their notebooks. On a separate piece of paper, each member draws a graphic organizer or visual for each of the words. Write your name on the paper, but don't write the words next to the visual!*

C. *Give your visual images to another group. Take turns guessing each other's words. Then talk about which words you were able to guess and why.*

D. *In your group, look through your vocabulary notebooks together and think of ways to help each other remember the meanings of words more effectively, using visual images or graphic organizers.*

WORD FAMILIES

Every word belongs to a **word family**—words that share the same root. For example, look at the different forms of the word *manage*. How many do you know?

Verb	Noun	Adjective	Adverb
manage	manager	manageable	manageably
mismanage	management	unmanageable	unmanageably

manage *v.* to take charge of, take control of, regulate, be manager of someone else

manager *n.* the person controlling the activities of a person or team in a business

management *n.* administration of business concerns, or the people engaged in a company

manageable *adj.* easily controlled (antonym: **unmanageable**)

manageably *adv.* of manageable

Although words may share the same root and have related meanings, each meaning is distinct. Look again at the forms for the word *manage*. Notice how the word changes meaning.

> **Note:** When you write a word in your vocabulary notebook, you can write other words that you know or find in the same family.

Dictionary Listings

If a word has several meanings, the dictionary numbers each definition and lists the one most frequently used first.

A. *Work with another student. Complete the chart with as many word forms as you can for each word from this unit. An X means no form exists.*

Verb	Noun	Adjective	Adverb
consider			
	definition		
energize	energy		
enthuse	enthusiasm		
extend			extensively
X		important	
inform			X

B. *Check your word forms with the class. Write any new words in your vocabulary notebook.*

C. *Make visuals or a graphic organizer for some of the new words. Compare your idea with another student. If possible, one of you should have a **visual** or **logical** learning style, based on the quiz at the beginning of the unit. For each word, say the definition and at least one other word in the same word family.*

Synonyms and Antonyms

Learning **synonyms** (words with similar meanings) or **antonyms** (words with opposite meanings) will increase your writing fluency and also give your writing variety.

A word may have many synonyms and antonyms. Each synonym expresses a slightly different aspect or tone of the word. Knowing which one to use will give your writing precision. Antonyms are also important, especially if you are comparing or contrasting something or need to show the opposite meaning.

Dictionaries often mark synonyms and antonyms along with the definitions.

quite /kwaɪt/ *adv., quantifier* **1** very, but not extremely SYNONYM: pretty: *He's quite fat.* | *It became quite clear that we needed help.*

sen•si•tive /ˈsɛnsətɪv/ *adj.* **1** a sensitive person is able to understand the feelings, problems, etc. of other people ANTONYM: insensitive

Some dictionaries and word processing software also often include a **thesaurus**. A thesaurus is a dictionary that lists synonyms and antonyms.

For example, maybe you are writing about the reason something happens. The word *reason* may be needed repeatedly throughout your essay. Look at the thesaurus entry from the Longman Dictionary of American English for the word *reason* and you will find a number of synonyms.

rea•son¹ /ˈrizən/ *n.* **1** [C] the cause or fact that explains why something happens or exists: *Did he **give** any **reason for** quitting?* | *There are many **reasons why** people develop heart disease.* | *One of the **reasons (that)** she came to Boston is her family.*

THESAURUS: reason

explanation a reason that you give for why something happened or why you did something: *Is there any explanation for his behavior?*

excuse a reason that you give for why you did something bad: *I hope she has a good excuse for being late again.*

motive a reason that makes someone do something, expecially something bad: *The police have found no motive for the attack.*

rationale (formal) the reasons and principles on which a decision, plan, etc. is based: *What is the Pope's rationale for not allowing women to be priests?*

grounds a good reason for doing, believing, or saying something: *Abusive behavior is grounds for divorce.*

A. *Work in a group. Write synonyms and antonyms for the words in the chart. Not all words have antonyms.*

Word	Synonyms	Antonyms
difficult		
normal		
interesting		
similar		
most		
thin		
amusing		

B. *Compare these two passages. Underline the words that are different.*

Passage 1

Sometimes it's hard to believe that my two brothers and I are from the same family. Although we look similar, we have completely different personality types. My older brother Seth is serious, introverted, and resembles a "fire hose" at times, always saying that everything we do as a family is boring. In contrast, my younger brother Lewis is enthusiastic, fun, and amusing. He can be an attention seeker, but psychologists say that's quite normal behavior for the youngest child in the majority of families. You wouldn't believe that we get along, but we do.

Passage 2

At times it's difficult to believe that my two brothers and I come from the same family. We look alike, but our personality types differ completely. My older brother Seth is serious, introspective, and is like a "fire hose" at times, always saying that everything we do as a family doesn't interest him. In contrast, my younger brother Lewis is excited about things, he's fun, and he makes us laugh. He often looks for attention. However, psychologists state that's quite typical behavior for the youngest child in most families. You'd find it hard to believe that we get along with each other, but we do.

C. *Write a paragraph of four or five sentences about some different personalities in your family, using as many synonyms and antonyms as you can. Then share your sentences with the class.*

Collocations and Phrases

Collocations are words that are usually used together in a phrase. Learning to use collocations will make your writing sound more natural. The best way to learn collocations is to notice words you often see or hear used together. If you hear or see a phrase several times in different places, it is probably a collocation. In addition, your dictionary will list collocations for some nouns, verbs, and adjectives. Make it a point to always check for collocations when you look up a new word.

Collocation Patterns

Here are some of the most common ways collocations occur:

Adjective + noun
> *Examples:*
>> a **low price**
>> a **common feature**
>> **careful attention** (x careless attention)
>> in **alphabetical order**

Verb + noun
> *Examples:*
>> *When reading, don't **interrupt the flow** of the text by stopping to look up every word in a dictionary.*
>> *I like programs that **raise awareness** of topics like modern-day bullying in schools.*

Verb + adverb
> *Example:*
>> *My brothers and I **get along well** despite our different personalities.*

Adverb + adjective
> *Examples:*
>> *My brothers and I are **completely different**.*
>> *Working late into the night is **totally unacceptable**.*
>> *You are **absolutely right**.*

A. *Work in a group. Complete the chart with these common verb + noun collocations from the box. Add more if you can. Use your dictionary to help you.*

> ~~a goal~~   every opportunity   a deadline   attention   a target
> ~~a risk~~   (yourself) a compliment   a break   off

set + noun	*take* + noun	*pay* + noun / preposition
set a goal	take a risk	

B. *Add any new collocations to your vocabulary notebook.*

A. *Read the text about learning vocabulary. Complete the sentences with phrases from the box in Exercise 6. Change the form where necessary.*

Vocabulary Learning Strategies

There is an old saying: "No one can *teach* you vocabulary; you have to learn it." In other words, it is essential to plan, monitor, and evaluate how you are going to study vocabulary. Here are some tips to help you in your planning:

1. _____ a weekly goal. Know how many words you want to learn each week. At the start, just _____ a low target. Then, gradually increase the quantity.

(continued)

2. Don't study for hours and hours! It's more effective to study for 2 hours a day than all day once a week. If you study for hours, make sure you _____ regular breaks.

3. Don't continue studying into the night. Plan what time you are going to stop and _____ a deadline! When you finish your day's work, _____ yourself a compliment, because you deserve it.

4. When you study vocabulary, _____ careful attention to your learning style. If writing lists doesn't work for you, try another method.

All of this _____ off. You will learn a lot. But the work doesn't stop there. Your next task is to _____ every opportunity to USE the language. Even if you are not sure it is correct, _____ a risk, because we learn from our mistakes!

B. ***Compare your answers with another student. Then discuss how you can make your vocabulary learning more effective using advice from the text. For example:***

"I need to set a deadline of two hours a day. I can't study for longer because . . ."

Common Phrases in Academic Writing

Certain phrases are especially useful for the kinds of writing you may do in school. You will find these types of phrases in textbooks and academic articles.

Examples:

__In other words__, it is essential for every student to plan, monitor, and evaluate.

Many people, __such as__ schoolmates and even teachers, actually support bullying.

__In contrast__, my younger brother Lewis is enthusiastic, fun, and amusing.

__In fact__, psychologists state that this is quite typical behavior for the youngest child in most families.

Bullying is a real problem in schools today, __in part because__ schoolchildren receive threatening emails.

Take the "Fire Hose," __for example__.

The "Sniper," __on the other hand__, needs a very different kind of management technique.

Note: You will learn more about these phrases in Part 3, Academic Writing.

Complete the sentences with phrases from the box. There may be more than one correct answer for some sentences. Not all phrases will be used.

because	in contrast	in other words	on the other hand
for example	in fact	in part	such as

People learn in a variety of different ways. **1.** _____, it is thought that there are seven common learning styles. A verbal-linguistic learner makes an effort to learn new words **2.** _____ that type of learner enjoys reading and writing. The kinesthetic learner uses the body and sense of touch.
3. _____, he or she will often think through issues while exercising.
4. _____, a logical-mathematical learner uses logic and reasoning.
A visual learner can easily visualize things **5.** _____ objects, plans, and outcomes. The interpersonal learner prefers learning in groups.
6. _____, this type of learner likes to work with others.
7. _____, an intrapersonal learner is private and introspective and likes to learn alone.

Pronouns

Writers use pronouns to make their writing sound more fluent and natural. However, you must take care to use the correct form of pronouns, which can be tricky even for native speakers, and to ensure that your pronouns are just as clear to your readers as they are to you.

In this unit, you will study some common problem areas of pronouns:

- subject vs. object pronouns
- pronoun-antecedent agreement
- impersonal pronouns

Warm Up

A. **Work in a group. Discuss these questions:**

- What sports do you like to watch? What sports do you like to play?

- What are some reasons that people play sports? What are some reasons people watch sports?

- Is there a sports team associated with your home town or area? If so, describe it.

- Do you prefer to play to win a game or just for fun?

B. **Work alone. Write for at least five minutes about one of the questions in Exercise A. Keep your writing to work on throughout this unit.**

SUBJECT AND OBJECT PRONOUNS

As you know, a noun is a word that names a person, place, thing, or idea. **Pronouns** replace nouns. There are different types of pronouns that can take the place of nouns or even long noun phrases.

Examples:

Subject   Replaced by   Subject pronoun
The car is new. → *It is new.*

Subject   Replaced by   Subject pronoun
The notion that it is not particularly difficult to communicate with someone on the other side of the world is new. → *It is new.*

Direct object   Replaced by   Object pronoun
Mr. and Mrs. Bonilla bought a new car last week. → *Mr. and Mrs. Bonilla bought it last week.*

Indirect object   Replaced by   Object pronoun
Mr. and Mrs. Bonilla gave Joaquin the car. → *Mr. and Mrs. Bonilla gave him the car.*

EXERCISE 1

A. **Work with another student. Read these sentences. Discuss whether the underlined words are subject or object pronouns and explain why.**

1. They lost the game.
2. The Tigers beat us again last week.
3. Salim passed the ball to me. / Salim passed me the ball.

B. **Work with another student. Complete the chart of subject and object pronouns.**

Subject pronouns	Object pronouns
I	me
	you
he	
	her
it	
	us
you	
	them
who	

C. Complete the rules by writing SP for subject pronoun or OP for object pronoun in the blanks.

1. A/an _____ is used to name who or what is performing the action in a sentence or a clause. Most commonly, it comes before the verb.

2. A/an _____ is always used after a preposition.

3. A/an _____ receives the action of the verb.

4. A/an _____ can be either direct or indirect.

Common Problems with Subject and Object Pronouns

Plural Subjects and Objects

Which is correct, "You and I" or "You and me"? You have probably heard both, and for a good reason—both are correct, but in different positions in a sentence. As you can see from the chart you completed in Exercise 1B, *I* is a subject pronoun and *me* is an object pronoun. Therefore, both of these sentences are correct:

Examples:

You and I are going to the beach this weekend.

My friend will give driving directions to you and me.

As you can see from the chart, the pronoun *you* is the same as both a subject pronoun and an object pronoun. Your ear becomes used to hearing subject pronouns together (*he and I*) and object pronouns together (*them and us*), but hearing (or seeing) the pronoun *you* doesn't alert your ear as to whether *I* or *me* should follow. You have to think more carefully about whether the sentence structure requires a subject or an object pronoun.

Comparatives

Be careful with comparative sentences. Words such as *than* and *as* in sentences can present special problems. Look at these examples. Would you use the subject or object pronouns to complete these sentences?

Jack is taller than . . .

I am not as tall as . . .

In casual English, speakers often use object pronouns. Many people, including native speakers, might say *Jack is taller than me* and *I am not as tall as her*. However the more formal, correct form, especially in written English, is the subject pronoun. For example:

Jack is taller than I.

I am not as tall as she.

Nobody would say, *Jack is taller than me am* or *I am not as tall as her is*. When you are unsure about sentences with *than* or *as*, complete the sentence by adding the verb. Then it will be easier for you to hear or see what is correct. For example:

Jack is taller than I (am).

I am not as tall as she (is).

Read the paragraph from a student's composition. Complete it by circling the subject or object pronoun. Then compare answers with another student.

My friends and (**1.** I / me) enjoy playing sports, but I am not as competitive as (**2.** they / them). For example, (**3.** I / me) like to play without even keeping score, but whenever I suggest that to (**4.** they / them), (**5.** they / them) disagree. I would rather play with (**6.** they / them) than argue about it, so I participate, although at times my teammates get impatient with (**7.** I / me) because I feel bad about beating the other team. If my team is far ahead of the others, I would rather let (**8.** they / them) score a few more points so the score is more even. (**9.** Who / Whom) is right? I think that my friends and (**10.** I / me) have an equal love of the game, but my friends are just more interested in the outcome than (**11.** I / me). However, I don't mind playing with competitive people as long as they don't expect (**12.** I / me) to change.

Note: Constructions such as "taller than me," while technically incorrect, are common in spoken English. In fact, they are so common that the correct construction can sound overly formal in casual written English, such as in an email to a friend. To solve this problem, use the more complete sentence form "taller than I am," and it will sound natural in both formal and informal situations.

A. *Look at the freewriting you did for the Warm Up on page 48. Underline the pronouns you used. Label subject pronouns S and object pronouns O. Remember that there are other types of pronouns, too, so you will not label every one.*

B. *Work with a partner. Discuss these questions:*
   - How many times did you use the correct forms?
   - In which sentences was it challenging to decide which form was correct? Why?

C. *Make any necessary corrections. You may also add some content if you wish.*

Pronouns and Agreement

The noun that a pronoun replaces is called its **antecedent**—literally meaning something that "comes before." Usually, the noun—the antecedent—comes before the pronoun in a prior clause or sentence. The pronoun and its antecedent must agree in **gender**, **person**, and **number**.

Gender refers to whether a person is male or female. In the example sentences below, Jill is a woman's name; therefore, the correct pronouns for *Jill* are *she* and *her*.

> **Examples:**
>
> **Incorrect:** *Roberta was upset with Jill because he forgot to bring a tennis racket.*
> **Correct:** *Roberta was upset with Jill because she forgot to bring a tennis racket.*
>
> **Incorrect:** *Because Jill forgot to bring a tennis racket, Roberta was upset with him.*
> **Correct:** *Because Jill forgot to bring a tennis racket, Roberta was upset with her.*

Most mistakes that students make with pronouns and gender are the result of carelessness or simply not knowing whether a certain name is male or female.

Person and *number* can be trickier. **Person** refers to whom the sentence is about—first person (*I*), second person (*you*), or third person (a singular noun or *he*, *she*, or *it*).

> **Example:**
>
> **Incorrect:** *If a person wants to improve at sports, you have to practice for a long time.*
> **Correct:** *If a person wants to improve at sports, he or she has to practice for a long time.*

Number refers to whether the antecedent is singular or plural. Problems with number can also be related to person.

> **Example:**
>
> **Incorrect:** *I play on three different soccer teams, so I have a different uniform for each of it.*
> **Correct:** *I play on three different soccer teams, so I have a different uniform for each of them.*

(See Part 3, Unit 7 for more on pronouns and antecedents.)

> **Note:** Some collective nouns are singular in American English but plural in British English. These include family, staff, team, company (meaning "business"), as well as the names of individual companies. However, when these nouns are antecedents for pronouns, the pronoun is often plural because it refers to the individual members of a family, staff, or team.

EXERCISE 4

Complete the sentences with the appropriate pronoun.

1. When I tell people that I don't participate in sports, _____ usually think that means I don't get any exercise, which isn't true.

2. My family is very active, and I do a lot of activities with _____.

3. For example, we go hiking and canoeing in the summer, and in the winter

   _____ go skiing or snowboarding.

4. Are these sports? I'm not really sure. I don't play _____ competitively, so it's not the same as playing a game of basketball.

5. On the other hand, my brother is a ski racer, so when _____ skis, it's definitely competitive.

6. His wife was a ski racer when _____ was a child, and

   _____ taught _____ to ski when _____ got married.

7. My sister-in-law doesn't ski competitively any more because _____

   is busy with children and her job, but my brother trained more

   and more until _____ was able to compete—and win.

8. Now _____ goes skiing with his wife and _____

   sometimes, but _____ and I just ski for fun, and we let

   _____ race on ahead.

Possessive Pronouns and Possessive Adjectives

Some pronouns function as possessives. They express to whom something belongs. When they are used alone, they are called **possessive pronouns**. When they are used with nouns, they are called **possessive adjectives**. In both cases, they express ownership.

Examples:

Possessive Pronoun: *This uniform is **hers**.*
Possessive Adjective: *This is **her** uniform.*

Possessive Pronoun: *The tennis rackets on the bench are **theirs**.*
Possessive Adjective: ***Their** tennis rackets are on the bench.*

Possessive pronouns and possessive adjectives must also agree with their antecedents in gender, person, and number.

Examples:

*The coach was upset with the <u>player</u> because he forgot **his** uniform.*
*The uniform over there is **his**.*
*The coach was upset with the <u>players</u> because they forgot **their** uniforms.*
*The uniforms over there are **theirs**.*

Work with another student. Complete the chart of possessive pronouns and possessive pronoun adjectives.

Possessive adjectives	Possessive pronouns
my	*mine*
	yours
his	
	hers
its	
	ours
your	
	theirs
whose	

Indefinite Pronouns

It is easy to tell with many nouns whether they are singular or plural—*the player* is singular, *the players* is plural. However, English has a few pronouns that can seem plural in idea, but are singular in grammar. These are **indefinite pronouns**. Some common indefinite pronouns are:

- *everybody/everyone*
- *anybody/anyone*
- *nobody/no one*
- *somebody/someone*

Example:

Incorrect: *Everyone who wants to play on the team next spring has to pay their registration fee by Friday.*

Correct: *Everyone who wants to play on the team next spring has to pay his or her registration fee by Friday.*

Some writers think using "his or her" is awkward. The sentence could also be written this way:

All players who want to be on the team next spring have to pay their registration fee by Friday.

A. *Read the paragraph. There are five mistakes with pronouns. Circle the pronouns that are not correct.*

My parents were worried about my joining a baseball team when I was in elementary school. They said that too much competition wasn't good for children because it made me feel too much pressure to win. I think it's because my dad remembered that when they were kids, he was on a soccer team, and he didn't really like the competitive aspect. If someone made a mistake, the other players got upset with them. However, my baseball team was different. Everyone did their best to help the team, and nobody got angry if someone made a mistake. Their mistake was just that—a mistake. It was a very supportive group. In fact, I'm still friends with people from that team, and I think it'll be friends for life.

B. *Rewrite the five sentences from the paragraph in Exercise A so that they are correct. You may have to change other words in the sentences. Then compare your sentences with another student. Did you rewrite the sentences in the same way?*

Exchange the freewriting you revised in Exercise 3 with another student. Check your partner's pronouns, and draw an arrow from each pronoun to its antecedent. Not all pronouns will have an antecedent. Check to see if they agree in gender, person, and number. If you are not sure, write a question mark above the sentence.

Further Practice

Journal or Blog Topic *(See Part 1, Units 1 and 2.)*
- Write a paragraph about whether you feel you are a competitive person. In what ways does competition help you? In what ways does it harm or impede you?

Research and Write
- Survey at least ten people in your class about what sports they like to play and what sports they like to watch. Take notes on their answers. Then write a paragraph about the results, OR choose one person and write a profile about that person and his or her preferences.

Impersonal Pronouns

English has a few different ways to refer to people in general. Common pronouns for this are, in order of formality: *one*, *they*, and *you*. These pronouns mean "any person" or "all people."

> **Examples:**
>
> *What causes <u>one</u> to be a loyal sports fan, even when one's team loses for several years in a row?*
>
> <u>*They*</u> *say loyal sports fans follow their teams no matter what.*
>
> *How can <u>you</u> be a loyal sports fan, even when your team loses for several years in a row?*

It is also possible to use indefinite pronouns such as **someone** or **somebody**, but because they are singular, you will need to use *his* or *her* to refer to them, which can become awkward in longer sentences and paragraphs.

> *What causes someone to be a loyal sports fan, even when his or her sports team loses for several years in a row?*

EXERCISE 8

Change the formal paragraph using "one" to an informal paragraph using "they" or "you." Rewrite the paragraph on a separate piece of paper. Then compare your paragraph with a partner. How were your paragraphs similar? How were they different?

The word *fan* comes from *fanatic*, meaning "a person filled with excessive and single-minded enthusiasm." Sports fans are an excellent example of this. One chooses to support a certain team just because one lives in the same town as that team (whose players, of course, probably come from different areas). When one's team does well, one is filled with pride. When one's team loses, one strengthens one's resolve and supports them all the more. Even when one moves far away, one still cheers for one's home team.

WRITING TASK

Write a short composition.

Choose one of the following topics. Brainstorm ideas, and then write a three to five paragraph composition.

- Do you think sports or physical education classes should be required for high school or university students? Why or why not?

- Do you think team sports provide any benefits that individual sports do not? Why or why not? Are there any disadvantages to playing team sports?

- Do you think individual sports provide any benefits that team sports do not? Why or why not? Are there any disadvantages to playing individual sports?

- Top athletes in some countries receive very high salaries. Do you think this practice is justified? Why or why not? Supplement your composition with some Internet research.

Check Your Writing

A. *Use this form to check your writing, or exchange compositions with another student and check each other's writing.*

Composition Checklist

1. How many paragraphs does the composition have? _____

2. What is the main idea of the composition? _____

3. Were any object pronouns used? _____

4. Did you find any pronouns that you thought did not agree in gender, person, or number? If so, circle them.

5. Were any indefinite or impersonal pronouns used? If so, do you think they were used appropriately? If not, explain here:

_____

_____

_____

_____

6. Underline one or two sentences that you particularly liked.

7. What ideas or suggestions do you have to improve the composition? Write your suggested changes here:

_____

_____

_____

_____

_____

B. *Make changes to improve your composition. Remember to check your writing for grammar, spelling, and punctuation errors.*

Gerunds and Infinitives

Gerunds and **infinitives** are noun forms of verbs. Like other nouns, they are used as subjects and objects in a sentence. Gerunds end in *-ing*, while infinitives are usually preceded by the word *to*. Gerunds and infinitives can be tricky because—like irregular past participles—you need to learn which one to use in each situation. In some cases there are no rules governing their use.

In this unit you will study some common problem areas of gerunds and infinitives:

- specific verbs used with gerunds and infinitives
- how to use gerunds with prepositions
- changes in meaning with gerunds and infinitives

Warm Up

A. Work in a group. Discuss these questions:

- Which parts of your own country—or which other countries—have you traveled to on vacation? What was one of your best experiences? One of your worst experiences?

- Which parts of your own country—or which other countries—would you love to visit? Why?

- Do you know any movies, books, or TV programs about travel? Describe one.

- What are some reasons people choose to travel abroad?

- Some people say that if you want to travel, it is better to watch a good travel documentary on TV in the comfort of your own home than to go there yourself. What are the advantages of staying at home? How is traveling better? Which would you prefer to do? Why?

Note: *Trip* and *travel* are both nouns. However, *trip* is a count noun; *travel* is noncount.

Example:

Incorrect: *We took a travel to Australia.*

Correct: *We took a trip to Australia.*

B. On your own, make a list of five advantages and disadvantages of traveling. Keep your notes for later writing assignments in this unit.

Advantages	Disadvantages
It's exciting.	

GERUNDS

Gerunds are nouns that always end in *-ing*. For example, *traveling/going/seeing/taking* can all be gerunds. Some verbs are always followed by a gerund rather than an infinitive, such as the verbs *avoid*, *resent*, and *enjoy*.

Examples:

Incorrect: *My dad **avoids** to fly.*

Correct: *My dad **avoids** flying.*

Incorrect: *The manager **resents** to spend money on first class tickets.*

Correct: *The manager **resents** spending money on first class tickets.*

Incorrect: *Most people **enjoy** to watch adventure movies which are set in foreign countries.*

Correct: *Most people **enjoy** watching adventure movies which are set in foreign countries.*

However, as you know, many verbs, such as *arrange*, are followed by the infinitive instead.

Examples:

Incorrect: *We **arranged** traveling through China on a tour.*

Correct: *We **arranged** to travel through China on a tour.*

Verb + Gerund: Common Verbs

How do we know which verbs use the gerund and which ones use the infinitive? Unfortunately, there are few rules. Much like irregular past participles, these must be studied and learned as individual vocabulary items. Study the chart. Make sure that you know the meaning of all the verbs.

Verbs followed by gerund	Example sentence
admit	The thief admitted stealing the tourists' money.
appreciate	We appreciated receiving a refund.
consider	The airline considered canceling the flight due to bad weather.
delay	We delayed going to the airport until we were certain about the flight.
discuss	We discussed traveling to Guatemala, but we didn't make a decision.
enjoy	Some travelers really enjoy staying at hostels, but I prefer hotels.
entail/involve	This tour entails/involves going camping. What do you think?
justify	How can the hotel justify charging so much money for a room?
recommend	The author highly recommends getting inoculations before the trip.
resent	I resent paying high prices for airline tickets when service is so poor.
resist	I couldn't resist giving the guide a tip. He was so helpful.
risk	Why did you risk getting sick? You know you shouldn't eat shellfish.
suggest	My parents suggested not* taking a vacation this year.
tolerate	I can't tolerate waiting in long lines.

*Note that the negative *not* is placed directly before the gerund.

Verb + Particle + Gerund

Two-part verbs consist of a verb plus a **particle**—a preposition such as *about, of, for,* or *in*. These verbs are easier for learners since they must be followed by either a regular noun or a gerund. The verb may be followed by one or more particles.

Examples:

With a gerund	**With a regular noun**
*I **apologized for** responding irritably.*	*I **apologized for** my irritable response.*
*I **look forward to** seeing you.*	*I **look forward to** the occasion.*

Other common two-part verbs that are followed by a gerund include:

complain about   *We didn't **complain about** sleeping under the stars. It was a fantastic experience!*

look after   *The tour company **looked after** getting visas for us.*

insist on   *I **insist on** traveling on my own this year. It's so much easier than traveling in a group.*

object to   *The manager **objects to** taking long journeys, so her assistant usually goes instead.*

plan on *Do you **plan on** taking a first-aid kit?*

take care of *The guide will **take care of** transporting you to the airport.*

win by *The judges were almost certain that the man **won by** cheating, but they didn't say anything.*

Verb + Noun/Pronoun + Particle + Gerund

Certain gerunds must be used with a noun or pronoun.

accuse (someone) of *The police **accused** the three travelers **of** smuggling contraband.*

blame (someone) for *You can't **blame** anyone **for** having bad weather. That's life!*

fine (someone) for *The police officer **fined** the couple **for** jaywalking although they didn't know it was a criminal offence.*

prevent (someone) from *The guide **prevented** us **from** walking on the path that the turtles take.*

stop (someone) from *Your parents can't **stop** you **from** living abroad. You're an adult now.*

thank (someone) for *It's only polite to **thank** someone **for** helping you out when you get lost.*

Be + Adjective + Preposition + Gerund

There are many *be* + adjective structures that are followed by a preposition + a gerund.

be capable of *Are you **capable of** climbing mountains, hiking, and doing strenuous activities?*

be excited about *I'm so **excited about** traveling to Asia. This will be my first time there.*

be interested in *We're **interested in** learning about the local culture when we go on trips abroad.*

be responsible for *Who is **responsible for** organizing our rooms?*

be tired of *I'm **tired of** going to the beach every year. How about trying an adventure trip this year?*

be used to *An experienced traveler **is used to** waiting in lines, waiting for buses, and so on.*

EXERCISE 1

A. Match the sentences to form four short conversations.

_____ **1.** If she resents waiting in line at airports so much, why does she fly?

_____ **2.** The author said that a true traveler is not interested in arriving. I don't understand!

_____ **3.** I wish someone would stop tourists from throwing trash on the ground.

_____ **4.** Airlines often apologize for canceling flights, but that's not good enough, in my opinion.

a. I agree. But you can't really blame people for doing it if there aren't any trashcans.

b. Totally. When they canceled our flight last year, we insisted on being put on another airline.

c. It means that the true traveler is more excited about experiencing what happens along the way.

d. I don't think she needs to avoid flying. She just needs to learn to be more tolerant.

B. *Identify the different gerund structures in each conversation in Exercise A. Write the number of the dialogue that matches the description of the gerund structure.*

_____ verb + gerund

_____ verb + particle + gerund

_____ verb + noun/pronoun + particle + gerund

_____ *to be* + adjective + preposition + gerund

EXERCISE 2

A. *Complete the paragraph by adding the correct particle. If none is needed, leave the space blank. Then compare answers with another student.*

Although many people don't enjoy (**1.**) _____ reading these days, Bill Bryson still remains one of the most popular travel writers in the world. Why? When you read one of his travel books, you can sense that he's really excited (**2.**) _____ exploring the country. Of course, he complains (**3.**) _____ people who treat him rudely and he objects (**4.**) _____ paying a lot of money for things, but he is capable (**5.**) _____ describing these events with tremendous humor. Sometimes I think he's guilty (**6.**) _____ judging people too harshly, and he tends to blame them (**7.**) _____ acting in a way that is typical of their culture, but on the whole, I'm really interested (**8.**) _____ reading about the things he says. No one can accuse him (**9.**) _____ being boring! I'm really looking forward (**10.**) _____ buying his next book.

B. *Work with another student. Answer the questions. Then freewrite about one of the questions for five minutes.*

- What (or whom) do you often complain about on vacations?

- What do you get excited about before you set off on your vacation?

- What do you object to when you travel on airlines and other forms of transportation?

- What are you most interested in doing when you reach your destination?

- Have you ever considered writing about your travel experiences?

A. Look at the notes you made for the Warm Up on pages 58–59. For each advantage and disadvantage, write a sentence with a gerund that means the same as or something similar to the original. If possible, add a personal example too.

Advantages	Disadvantages
It's exciting.	It's expensive.

Example:

It's exciting. = I get very excited about traveling. There's so much to see and do.

It's expensive. = They overcharge tourists in many places. I object to paying so much money.

B. Work with another student. Discuss these questions:

- How many times did you use a gerund form?
- In which sentences was it challenging to find an example using a gerund? Why?

C. Help each other make any necessary changes or improvements. You may also add some more content if you wish.

INFINITIVES

Infinitives are used after many common verbs, such as *hope*, *need*, and *want*.

Examples:

We **need** to buy some food for this afternoon.

The manager **hopes** to send me to a conference in Indonesia soon. I really **want** to go.

As with gerunds, there are many examples of verb + infinitive structures which simply have to be learned. There are a few rules. One rule is that we <u>do not</u> use the infinitive after prepositions.

Example:

Incorrect: *Let's go. I'm tired of to wait around.*

Correct: *Let's go. I'm tired of waiting around.*

There are a number of typical structures with infinitives. Study these groups of structures and examples. Use a dictionary if necessary to help you understand the meaning of the verbs.

Verb + Infinitive: Common Verbs

There are many other common verbs which are followed by the infinitive.

appear   *There **appears** to be a mistake in the price list here.*

arrange   *Let's **arrange** to meet by the square at noon.*

fail   *Despite all the good things we heard about the place, it **failed** to live up to our expectations.*

hesitate   *If you have any problems, don't **hesitate** to call and ask for help.*

intend   *I **intended** to study the language before going, but I didn't have time. That was a mistake.*

promise   *You **promised** to find us a hotel. Now we don't have anywhere to stay!*

manage   *We got lost, but **managed** to find our way back to the hotel. Actually, it was fun.*

offer   *We **offered** to take the stranded passengers with us in our car.*

volunteer   *The best time I ever spent abroad was when I **volunteered** to teach in Tanzania.*

wait   *The kids can't **wait** to go down to the beach. They're so excited.*

Verb + Noun/Pronoun + Infinitive

Certain verbs must be used with a noun or pronoun if they are followed by an infinitive.

advise (someone)   *I'd **advise** you not* to say anything about this. We could get into trouble.*

allow (someone)   *Excuse me. Will you **allow** me to use your phone?*

ask (someone)   *Let's **ask** that guy to take a photo of us.*

cause (someone)   *Bad weather **caused** us to delay our day out.*

convince (someone)   *They **convinced** us to go on vacation with them.*

encourage (someone)   *I'm so glad he **encouraged** me to visit Vietnam. It's a great country!*

force (someone)   *The police **forced** the tourists to take a different route.*

hire (someone)   *The hike to the ruins was exhausting. Fortunately we **hired** porters to carry our stuff.*

invite (someone)   *The Middle East is famous for its hospitality. People **invite** you to visit their homes.*

persuade (someone)   *Can't you **persuade** your sister not* to travel by herself?*

remind (someone)   *The receptionist **reminded** me to take an umbrella. That was really thoughtful.*

warn (someone)   *I wish someone had **warned** me not* to take buses in this place!*

*Note that the negative *not* is placed directly before the infinitive.

Infinitives and Gerunds as the Subject or Object of a Sentence

Infinitives with the word *to* can function as the subject or the object of a sentence. For example:

Infinitive as Subject

***To travel** in a new country is exciting.*

***To learn** a new language and culture broadens your mind.*

Infinitive as Direct Object

*When I fly, I like **to listen** to music.*

*I've always wanted **to volunteer** in another country.*

Gerunds can also function as subjects or objects of a sentence. For example:

Gerund as Subject

Traveling in a new country is exciting.
Learning a new language and culture broadens your mind.

Gerund as Object

When I fly, I like **listening** *to music.*
I really would love **volunteering** *in another country.*

EXERCISE 4

A. **Complete the paragraphs by circling the correct verb form.**

There's no doubt that travel can be a challenge. Day 1: Bad weather forced you
(**1.** changing / to change) your plans. Day 2: You planned on (**2.** going / to go) to the
beach together but now all the kids have had an argument. Day 3: The place you read
about in the guidebook failed (**3.** living / to live) up to your expectations. Day 4: You
got lost because your husband managed (**4.** reading / to read) the map wrong. Oh,
and that's not to mention the sunburn you suffered on Day 6 because you risked
(**5.** sitting / to sit) in the sun for too long on Day 5, and the rental car that broke down
in the mountains on Day 7 because someone intended (**6.** checking / to check) the
engine but forgot. No wonder you and the kids can't wait (**7.** getting / to get) home!

But hold on! Remember the generous people who invited you (**8.** eating / to eat)
in their home while you were waiting for the car to be fixed? And the hotel manager
who suggested (**9.** taking / to take) you to the clinic when you got sunburned? Or
the woman who didn't hesitate (**10.** driving / to drive) you back to your hotel when
you were lost? Half the fun of travel is enjoying what happens when it doesn't go
as planned!

B. **Work with another student. Describe something that went wrong on a trip you once
took and something good that happened as a result. Use verb + infinitive and verb +
gerund structures.**

C. **Revise the advantages and disadvantages list you made in Exercise 3. Add any
new ideas you have. Then choose a maximum of three advantages and three
disadvantages that you would like to include in your final writing exercise. Cross out
the other ideas.**

D. **Rewrite the advantages so that they form a short coherent paragraph. Then do the
same for the disadvantages.**

A. *Read the quotes. Decide if the infinitive or gerund is used as the S (subject) or O (object) in each quote.*

_____ **1.** "*To travel* is to discover that everyone is wrong about other countries."—Aldous Huxley

_____ **2.** "*Traveling* . . . forces you to trust strangers and to lose sight of all that familiar comfort of home and friends. . . . Nothing is yours except the essential things—air, sleep, dreams, the sea, the sky . . . "—Cesare Pavese

_____ **3.** "When a person spends all his time in foreign travel, he ends by *having* many acquaintances, but no friends."—Seneca

_____ **4.** "*To awaken* quite alone in a strange town is one of the pleasantest* sensations in the world."—Freya Stark.

_____ **5.** "All travel has its advantages. If the passenger visits better countries, he may learn *to improve* his own. And if fortune carries him to worse, he may learn *to enjoy* it."—Samuel Johnson

pleasantest is a less common superlative form of *pleasant*

B. *Work with another student. Discuss what you think each author means. Then discuss which quotes you agree with or like best and explain why.*

EXERCISE 6

Read the quotes in Exercise 5 again. Paraphrase (restate in your own words) one of the quotes or invent one of your own. Include a gerund or infinitive in your paraphrase. Then use it to write an introductory comment for a short composition. Do the same in order to create a short conclusion.

Note: Do not use the quotes in their original form. *(See Part 3, Unit 3 for more on paraphrasing.)*

EXERCISE 7

Look at the two paragraphs you wrote for Exercise 4C. Then write a short composition about the advantages and disadvantages of travel. Be sure to include . . .

- a short introductory comment about travel.
- a paragraph discussing three advantages.
- a paragraph discussing three disadvantages.
- a short conclusion.

Gerunds and Infinitives: Change of Meaning

Some verbs can be followed by either an infinitive or a gerund, such as the verb *like*:

> I like **traveling** *with a well-informed guide.*
> I like **to travel** *with a well-informed guide.*

In this case, you can use the infinitive or gerund and there is no difference in meaning.

Other verbs that can be followed by a gerund or infinitive without a change in meaning are: *begin, start, continue, love, prefer,* and *hate.*

Some verbs can be followed by either the infinitive or gerund, but their meanings are not the same. Compare the sentences in each set of examples.

Forget

> *I won't* **forget** *to meet the man. (= I don't know him yet, but I will be sure to go and meet him.)*
> *I won't* **forget** *meeting the man. (= I will not lose the memory. It was very special to meet him.)*

Note: *Remember* is similar to *forget. Remember* + infinitive = a future event that I need to remember; *remember* + gerund = something in the past that I do not intend to forget.

Go on

> *The woman* **went on** *to say that it was a national holiday. (= She finished saying something, and after that, she told us it was a national holiday.)*
> *The woman* **went on** *saying that it was a national holiday. (= We understood her the first time, but she repeated herself many times.)*

Regret

> *He* **regrets** *to say he can't help us. (= He's saying he can't help us right now. He's apologizing for this.)*
> *He* **regrets** *saying he couldn't help us. (= He said that he couldn't help in the past and now he is sorry that he said it.)*

Stop

> *We* **stopped** *to take photos. (= We interrupted our activity and took photos.)*
> *We* **stopped** *taking photos. (= We didn't take photos anymore.)*

A. Read the pairs of sentences. Check (✓) the sentence that has the correct meaning.

1. ☐ **a.** Colombia was treated by the media for years as a no-go area. But they've stopped writing such negative reports, and now it's a popular tourist destination.

   ☐ **b.** Colombia was treated by the media for years as a no-go area. But they've stopped to write such negative reports and now it's a popular tourist destination.

2. ☐ **a.** I regret going to Thailand for the New Year. It was too crowded.

   ☐ **b.** I regret to go to Thailand for the New Year. It was too crowded.

3. ☐ **a.** When Dave arrived in North Korea, the woman told him she regretted saying that the country's leader had died and that everything would be closed.

   ☐ **b.** When Dave arrived in North Korea, the woman told him she regretted to say that the country's leader had died and that everything would be closed.

4. ☐ **a.** You don't have to suffer from jet lag. Remember drinking plenty of water on the flight and remember not drinking alcohol on board.

   ☐ **b.** You don't have to suffer from jet lag. Remember to drink plenty of water on the flight and remember not to drink alcohol on board.

5. ☐ **a.** Remember that the objective of travel is not just to get to your destination quickly. So, stop looking at things on the way.

   ☐ **b.** Remember that the objective of travel is not just to get to your destination quickly. So, stop to look at things on the way.

B. Work with another student. Discuss these questions. Use the correct form and meaning of the verbs.

- Think of a trip you really enjoyed. What will you never forget doing? Is there anyone you'll never forget meeting?

- Imagine you are going on vacation in twenty-four hours. What last-minute things should you remember to do? Is there something you always forget to do when you go on vacation?

- Did you ever have the opportunity to travel somewhere interesting, but you didn't take the chance while you had it? What happened? Do you regret missing that chance?

- Since the digital camera and other developments, have you stopped printing out your vacation photos and putting them in a photo album? What do you do with the photos now?

WRITING TASK

Write a short composition.

Write a final draft of the three to five paragraph composition you drafted in Exercise 7. Focus specifically on one of these types of travel:

- Traveling abroad
- Traveling in your home country
- Traveling with your family or friends
- Traveling on your own
- Organized travel

Check Your Writing

A. *Use this form to check your writing, or exchange compositions with another student and check each other's writing.*

Composition Checklist

1. How many paragraphs does the composition have? _____

2. What is the main focus of the composition? _____

3. Do the paragraphs have a clear order (introduction, advantages, disadvantages, conclusion)? _____

4. Were any infinitives or gerunds used? _____

5. Did you find any places where a verb with infinitive or gerund could be included? If so, circle them and suggest the verb in the column (e.g., *managed* + infinitive, *avoided* + gerund).

6. Did you find any places where an infinitive or gerund was used incorrectly? If so, underline them and write a question mark (?) there.

7. Underline one or two sentences that you particularly liked.

8. Do you have any other comments or suggestions for the writer? If so, write them here:

_____

_____

_____

_____

B. *Make changes to improve your composition. Remember to check your writing for grammar, spelling, and punctuation errors.*

Gerunds and Infinitives **69**

Articles

Articles—*a, an*, and *the*—are as tricky for advanced learners of English as they are for beginners. Although there are rules for their usage, as is the case for any grammar rules, there are plenty of exceptions. However, improper use of articles is one of the first things that will catch the eye of a native English-speaking reader, so it's important to continue to study article usage and to learn how to proofread your writing for mistakes in this area.

In this unit, you will learn about . . .

- articles with count versus noncount nouns.
- articles general versus specific nouns.
- other common noun markers.

Warm Up

A. *The national symbol of the United States is the bald eagle. However, Benjamin Franklin (1706–1790), an early American politician, once had a different idea. Read an excerpt from a letter Benjamin Franklin wrote to his sister in 1784. Underline the articles. Then compare your results with a partner.*

For my own part I wish the Bald Eagle had not been chosen the Representative of our Country. He is a Bird of bad moral Character. He does not get his Living honestly. You may have seen him perched on some dead Tree near the River, where, too lazy to fish for himself, he watches the Labour of the Fishing Hawk; and when that diligent Bird has at length taken a Fish, and is bearing it to his Nest for the Support of his Mate and young Ones, the Bald Eagle pursues him and takes it from him.

With all this Injustice, he is never in good Case but like those among Men who live by Sharping & Robbing he is generally poor and often very lousy. Besides he is a rank Coward: The little *King Bird* not bigger than a Sparrow attacks him boldly and drives him out of the District. He is therefore by no means a proper Emblem for the brave and honest Cincinnati of America who have driven all the *King birds* from our Country . . .

I am on this account not displeased that the Figure is not known as a Bald Eagle, but looks more like a Turkey. For the Truth the Turkey is in Comparison a much more respectable Bird, and withal a true original Native of America . . . He is besides, though a little vain & silly, a Bird of Courage, and would not hesitate to attack a Grenadier of the British Guards who should presume to invade his Farm Yard with a red Coat on.

B. *Work in a group. Discuss these questions:*

- Is there an animal that represents your country? If so, what is it? Why do you think it was chosen?

- If you could choose any animal to represent your hometown, what would you choose? Why?

- Why do many sports teams choose animals as mascots? Which animals do you know about that are associated with sports teams? What qualities do those animals have?

C. *On your own, write for at least five minutes about one of the questions in Exercise B. Keep your writing to work on throughout this unit.*

COUNT VERSUS NONCOUNT NOUNS

There are two main types of nouns in English: **count nouns** and **noncount nouns**. **Count nouns** are separate items that can be counted, for example, *eggs, birds, trees*. To some extent, you can use logic to determine this.

- Objects that can be picked up separately can be counted: *apples, books, pillows*.
- Objects that are one distinct item can be counted: *cars, children, houses*.

Noncount nouns can be . . .

- masses or substances that cannot be counted, for example: *water, air, milk*.
- concepts, feelings, or ideas that cannot be counted, for example: *love, honesty, courage*.

Nouns that have a plural form are count nouns. Note that while many plurals end in *-s—eagles, turkeys, guards—*not all do, for example, *children* or *teeth*. Furthermore, some nouns that end in *-s* are not plural—*physics, economics, news*.

Noncount nouns are often used with quantifiers: *a piece of bread, a cup of tea, a can of corn*.

Some nouns can be either count or noncount, but with a difference in meaning.

I read the paper this morning. = **a newspaper**
The printer is out of paper. = **something to write, type, or print on**

Look at all those chickens! = **birds**
I don't eat much chicken. = **meat from a chicken**

Logic does not always work, however. In English, we count *suitcases*, but not *luggage*. We count *peas*, but not *corn*. When you learn a new noun in English, make sure you know whether it is used as a count noun or a noncount noun. If you aren't sure, check a dictionary.

EXERCISE 1

Read the paragraph. Look at the underlined nouns. Above each one, write C for count or NC for non-count.

This semester I had to do some research on an animal that is not common in this country. I chose the water buffalo because they are common in Southeast Asia, but not here. These animals are quite large and are well-known for their strength. In many countries, they are highly valued for both their meat and their milk. They have dark gray fur and long curved horns, and their average weight is 600 pounds (270 kg). An individual water buffalo can live for about 25 years in captivity. During the day, they spend much of their time under water. They usually live in herds of about 30 animals. In the wild, they typically eat grass, although domesticated water buffalo will also eat grain. It seems strange to me that an animal known for its meat would be a vegetarian.

Work with another student. Take turns looking at the freewriting you did for Exercise C of the Warm Up. Identify all the nouns. Circle the count nouns and underline the noncount nouns. Don't make any changes with articles.

General vs. Specific

Count and noncount nouns can be **specific** or **general**. A noun is *specific* when the writer wants to talk about a particular thing or things. When the writer wants to make a generalization about something, a noun is *general*.

Articles are used before nouns in some situations. Look at the summary chart:

	count		noncount
	singular	**plural**	
general	*a/an*	Ø **(no article)**	Ø
	I have never seen **an eagle**.	Bald **eagles** used to be an endangered species in the U.S.	The turkey is a bird of **courage**.
specific	*the*	*the*	*the*
	The eagle I saw must have been injured.	Not many people have seen **the eagles** that live in the forest near my house.	**The courage** of the turkey inspired Benjamin Franklin.

A general noun is preceded by either *a/an* if it is a count noun or no article if it is a noncount noun. However, a specific noun of either type is preceded by *the*. Clearly it is important to know whether a noun is general or specific. This, more than any other area, causes difficulty for people whose native language is not English.

Match the sentence with the description of the underlined noun or noun phrase.

_____ **1.** <u>Mosquitoes</u> are responsible for spreading malaria among humans.

_____ **2.** Worldwide, <u>malaria</u> caused more than 650,000 deaths in 2010.

_____ **3.** You shouldn't scratch <u>a mosquito bite</u>.

_____ **4.** <u>The water</u> in which mosquitoes breed can be treated to kill the insects.

_____ **5.** <u>The malaria vaccines</u> developed in recent years have saved many lives.

_____ **6.** I didn't see <u>the mosquito</u> that bit me.

   a. general singular count noun
   b. general plural count noun
   c. specific singular count noun
   d. specific plural count noun
   e. general noncount noun
   f. specific noncount noun

A noun can be specific in four ways:

1. When the object itself is unique. If there is only one of something, then it is specific. Thus, we speak about *the sun, the moon,* or *the beginning* of a story. Nouns modified by a superlative are unique—*the tallest tree, the most expensive restaurant.*

2. When both the reader and the writer (or the speaker and the listener) understand from context which specific item is meant. Look at the example:

    He walked into <u>the living room</u> and closed <u>the door</u>.

    We understand that *the living room* is the one in his house, and *the door* is the door through which he just walked.

3. When the noun is made specific by explicit information in the sentence—usually a prepositional phrase or a relative clause. For example:

    She signed her name at the bottom of the contract.

    Give your ticket to the man behind the counter.

    The bottom is specific because it is the bottom of the page. *Behind the counter* specifies which man is being discussed.

4. When the noun has been previously mentioned in a sentence that comes before.

    The first time I saw a tiger was in a zoo. <u>The tiger</u> was asleep.

    Since *the tiger* in the second sentence refers to *a tiger* in the first sentence, it is specific.

There are, of course, more rules (and more exceptions) to using articles; but if you can understand the difference between count and noncount nouns and between general and specific nouns, you will be able to catch many of the errors in your writing.

Checking for correct article usage in something you have written takes time. As you check your writing, identify each noun and first ask yourself, "Is it a count or a noncount noun?" Then ask yourself, "Is it general or specific?"

Remember that other words such as possessive adjectives can take the place of articles:

There's the cat he lost!

There's his cat!

EXERCISE 4

Work with another student. Explain why the underlined nouns are specific.

Ever since I was a child, I've wanted to own a horse. I read all of the <u>books</u> about horses that I could find, and I took lessons at the local <u>riding school</u>. I didn't get a horse until I was 26, though, and the <u>horse</u> I bought wasn't a beautiful black race horse like the <u>ones</u> in the <u>books</u> I read. Instead, he was old and not very attractive, but to me, he was still the most beautiful <u>horse</u> I had ever seen—because he was mine. I never thought I'd have the <u>money</u> to be able to keep a horse of my own, but fortunately, I do. I couldn't afford a saddle at first, so I just used an old blanket. The <u>saddle</u> I have now was given to me by a friend. I keep him in a pasture at my friend's farm in the <u>summer</u>, and in the <u>winter</u>, she lets me keep him in the <u>barn</u>.

EXERCISE 5

A. **Complete the passage with "a," "an," "the," or Ø (no article).**

_____ piranhas are _____ type of _____ fish that live in South America. They live in _____ rivers and _____ lakes. _____ Piranhas are _____ carnivores; that is, they eat _____ meat and _____ other fish. In fact, one of _____ most famous attributes of _____ these fish is _____ their very sharp teeth. _____ piranhas have _____ row of teeth on both _____ upper and _____ lower jaw. If _____ tooth is broken or falls out, _____ new tooth will grow to replace it. There is _____ some disagreement over whether _____ piranhas are aggressive. _____ some scientists say they travel in _____ groups (called "_____ schools") because that makes it easier to attack _____ fish; however, _____ most biologists feel that this behavior is typical of _____ fish, and that _____ piranha is not different from other fish except for having _____ very sharp teeth.

(continued)

Do ____ piranhas really eat ____ people? That is certainly ____ popular belief. Occasionally, ____ swimmer in ____ river or lake with piranhas will get bitten. It is very unusual, though, for such ____ encounter to lead to ____ injury or ____ death. It is far more common, actually, for ____ humans to eat ____ piranhas than ____ other way around.

B. *Compare answers with another student. Explain your choices.*

EXERCISE 6

Look again at the freewriting you did in the Warm Up. Determine whether the nouns you used are general or specific. Then check to make sure you used articles correctly. Correct any mistake in your usage of articles.

Further Practice

Journal or Blog Topic *(See Part 1, Units 1 and 2.)*

• Have you ever been to a zoo? What are some reasons that people visit zoos? What are some positive aspects of zoos? What are some negative aspects?

Research and Write

• Choose one of these types of animals to research online, and write a paragraph about it. Check at least two different Internet sites to get information.
  - a dangerous animal
  - a beautiful animal
  - a useful animal
  - an endangered animal

OTHER COMMON NOUN MARKERS

In addition to possessive adjectives, here are some other words and expressions that commonly signal nouns and that can be used in place of articles. Note that many of them also depend on whether a noun is count or noncount:

used with count nouns		used with noncount nouns	used with both
singular	**plural**	much	no
every	many	little	(hardly) any
each	few	a little	some
	a few	a great deal of	plenty of
	a couple (of)	a large amount of	a lot of
	a (large/small) number of		most
	several		all

EXERCISE 7

Circle all of the words that are possible in each sentence.

(**1.** Many / Little / Some / Plenty of) parents believe that taking care of pets will help children learn responsibility. I have known (**2.** a little / a few / a lot of / several) children who kept pets, and I'm not sure this is always true. (**3.** A couple of / A few / A great deal of) kids I knew when I was young had pets they didn't take care of, and this caused (**4.** some / a lot of / much / many) problems for their parents. A child might be interested in a new pet at first, but then lose interest after (**5.** much / little / several) months or even (**6.** a few / most / a couple of) weeks. I live in a college town—that is, there are (**7.** a few / a large amount of / a number of) colleges and universities nearby. Every year, (**8.** some / each / a little) students get a puppy or a kitten—and then realize they don't have (**9.** many / a lot of / any / a great deal of) time to take care of it. Furthermore, when they graduate, they might need to move into an apartment that doesn't allow (**10.** no / any / several) pets. Before taking on the responsibility of taking care of an animal, (**11.** a few / few / every / all) person needs to think carefully about whether he or she will be able to meet that responsibility for as long as the animal lives.

WRITING TASK

> Write a short composition about an animal or pet.

Choose one of these topics. Brainstorm ideas, and then write a composition of three to five paragraphs.

- What animal best represents you, and why?

- Research an interesting animal online and then describe it.

- What kinds of animals are typically used for work? Choose one or two, and discuss the kind of work they do.

- Why do people keep pets? What are some benefits to keeping pets?

- Write about a dangerous or harmful animal and explain why it is dangerous or harmful.

Check Your Writing

A. *Use this form to check your writing, or exchange compositions with another student and check each other's writing.*

Composition Checklist

1. How many paragraphs does the composition have? _____

2. What is the main idea of the composition? _____

3. Check each noun in the composition. Decide if it is count or noncount, singular or plural, or general or specific. Then determine whether articles were used correctly. If you find something that might be a mistake or if you have any questions, circle the phrase.

4. Double underline noun markers from the chart on page 77 and the nouns they were used with. Circle any noun markers you think were used incorrectly.

5. Underline your one or two favorite sentences from the composition.

6. What ideas or suggestions do you have to improve the composition? Write your suggested changes here:

   _____

   _____

   _____

   _____

B. *Make changes to improve your composition. Remember to check your writing for grammar, spelling, and punctuation errors.*

Parallel Structure

The word "parallel" can be used to mean *having the same qualities*. In writing, parallel structure (also called parallelism) involves choosing the same grammatical pattern for words, phrases, clauses, and sometimes in more than one sentence.

Using parallel structure can help you write more clearly and concisely and give your writing a smooth rhythm and flow. It can also help you highlight important ideas and create interest or suspense in your writing. Parallel structure is an effective technique for clear, powerful, memorable writing.

In this unit, you will . . .

- learn to recognize different types of parallel structures.
- create and use parallel structures in your own writing.

Warm Up

A. *On your own, write your answers to these questions.*

- What types of group leisure activities do you do (or have you done), such as playing a team sport, singing in a chorus, or playing in a band? What do you enjoy about these activities?

- What kinds of individual activities do you do in your free time, such as playing video games, reading, or gardening? Why do you enjoy them?

- What are some leisure activities you have done in the past, but no longer do? Why did you stop?

- What is an activity you would like to try but haven't yet? Why does it interest you?

B. *Discuss your answers in a group. Save your writing to use later in this unit.*

PARALLEL SERIES

A common use of parallel structure is for series (lists) of similar items or ideas.

An important rule of parallelism is this: *Similar ideas should use similar structures.* This means that when you list related ideas, examples, or details in the same sentence, you should list them in the same way (e.g., with the same verb, word order, or in the same form).

Nouns

It is important to keep the form the same when listing nouns as subjects, objects, or complements.
Examples:
Not parallel: *The game of chess requires skill, patience, and to be able to concentrate.*
Parallel: *The game of chess requires skill, patience, and concentration.*
OR
The game of chess requires skill, patience, and the ability to concentrate.

Not parallel: *A surfboard, a wetsuit, and loving the ocean are all you need to start surfing.*
Parallel: *A surfboard, a wetsuit, and a love of the ocean are all you need to start surfing.*

Verbs

When listing actions or activities, be careful not to mix verb forms.
Examples:
Not parallel: *Almost every evening when I was in high school, I ate dinner, finished my homework, and was playing computer games until after midnight.*
Parallel: *Almost every evening when I was in high school, I ate dinner, finished my homework, and played computer games until after midnight.*

Adjectives and Adverbs

It is important to keep the form the same when listing multiple adjectives and adverbs in a description.
Examples:
Not parallel: *A good musician is dedicated, persistent, and has a lot of patience.*
Parallel: *A good musician is dedicated, persistent, and patient.*

Not parallel: *Grace sings beautifully and with confidence.*
Parallel: *Grace sings beautifully and confidently.*

> **Work with another student. On a separate piece of paper, rewrite these sentences using parallel structure.**
>
> 1. A good soccer player is strong, agile, and moves quickly.
>
> 2. My sister is an amazing painter, musician, and loves photography.
>
> 3. As we watched the ballet performance, we were amazed at how skillfully and with grace the dancers moved.
>
> 4. Last week, Carlos played three tennis matches, went mountain biking, and had attended yoga class twice.
>
> 5. The members of the book club agreed that the novel was slow-moving, uninspiring, and it bored us.
>
> 6. Energy, enthusiasm, and to be patient are just some of the qualities of a good coach.
>
> 7. Sometimes I wish I had listened to my parents when I was young and didn't quit my violin lessons.
>
> 8. Paola is quite a skillful downhill skier and skates gracefully.

PARALLEL GERUNDS AND INFINITIVES

Gerunds (verb + *ing*) and **infinitives** (*to* + verb) are noun forms of verbs. Like other nouns, they can be subjects, objects, or subject complements. *(See Part 2, Unit 3 for more on Gerunds and Infinitives.)* When using these forms to list actions and activities, do not mix gerunds and infinitives. Choose one form and stick with it.

Examples:

Not parallel: *I think I'd like sculpting or to make pottery because I enjoy working with my hands.*

Parallel: *I think I'd like sculpting or making pottery because I enjoy working with my hands.*

Not parallel: *Participating in team sports is a great way to make new friends, get in shape, and building confidence.*

Parallel: *Participating in team sports is a great way to make new friends, get in shape, and build confidence.*

Note: When you begin a list or activities with an infinitive form, you do not need to repeat the subject, or add a new verb. You can use either the infinitive or the base form to continue the list.

Example:

Not parallel: *This summer, I plan to take a drawing class, and I will grow a vegetable garden, and build a birdhouse.*

Parallel: *This summer, I plan to take a drawing class, (to) grow a vegetable garden and (to) build a birdhouse.*

Look back at your answers to the questions from the Warm Up. Complete these sentences using parallel structure.

Example:

Playing chess is important to me because it allows me to challenge my mind, learn from my opponents, and develop new strategies.

1. Three activities I enjoy doing are . . .

2. I enjoy / don't enjoy taking part in team sports or group activities because (three reasons) . . .

3. I enjoy / don't enjoy individual activities because (three reasons) . . .

4. My favorite thing to do in my free time is . . . . In order to do it, you need . . . (three things)

5. Playing / Doing / Practicing [your favorite activity] is important to me because (three reasons) . . .

6. Someday I'd like to try . . . because (three reasons) . . .

A. Work in a group. Brainstorm at least three ideas for each list.

Reasons for exercising regularly	Steps to become a successful artist	Things all good actors do
Activities that are more enjoyable with a group	**Reasons people should travel abroad**	**Suggestions for overcoming stage fright**

B. *With your group, use the information in Exercise A to complete these sentences on a separate piece of paper. Use parallel structure.*

1. Three reasons for exercising regularly are . . .
2. . . . are the key steps to become a successful artist.
3. All good actors need . . .
4. . . . are much more fun in a group than alone.
5. International travel gives people a chance to . . .
6. . . . are just a few suggestions for overcoming stage fright.

PARALLEL PHRASES

In addition to lists of words and phrases in shorter sentences, parallel structure is important in longer sentences, for example, when phrases or clauses are joined by coordinating conjunctions (*for, and, nor, but, or, yet, so*) or by correlative conjunctions (*neither . . . nor, either . . . or, not only . . . but also*).

Checking for Parallelism in Longer Sentences

There are two steps to check for parallel structure:

1. Find the list in the sentence.
2. Make sure the parts of the list have the same structure.

Example:

The Museum of Fine Arts is an amazing place to see famous European paintings and sculptures, you can learn about Japanese pottery, or explore ancient Middle Eastern artifacts.

The Museum of Fine Arts is an amazing place . . .
1. *to see famous European paintings and sculptures,*
2. *you can learn about Japanese pottery,* OR   } **not parallel**
3. *explore ancient Middle Eastern artifacts.*

The Museum of Fine Arts is an amazing place . . .
1. *to see famous European paintings and sculptures,*
2. *to learn about Japanese pottery,* OR   } **parallel**
3. *to explore ancient Middle Eastern artifacts.*

Coordinating Conjunctions

Two similar parts of a sentence—or two whole sentences—can be joined by **coordinating conjunctions** (*for, and, nor, but, or, yet, so*). In each case, the conjunction balances a pair of equal ideas using parallel structures.

> ### *Examples:*
>
> **Not parallel:** *According to my guitar instructor, I <u>can wait</u> until next spring to join the advanced class, or <u>start</u> as early as this fall.*
>
> **Parallel:** *According to my guitar instructor, I <u>can wait</u> until next spring to join the advanced class, or <u>I can start</u> as early as this fall.*
>
> **Not parallel:** *The captain of the Northside soccer team says her greatest positive influences have been <u>the advice</u> of her high school coach, <u>attending professional matches</u> when she was younger, and <u>her family supported her.</u>*
>
> **Parallel:** *The captain of the Northside soccer team says her greatest positive influences have been <u>the advice</u> of her high school coach, <u>the professional matches</u> she attended when she was younger, and <u>the support</u> of her family.*

Correlative Conjunctions

Certain joining words always work together as a pair, such as *neither . . . nor; either . . . or; not only . . . but also.* These pairs are called **correlative conjunctions**. Correlative conjunctions also balance a pair of equal ideas using parallel structures.

> ### *Examples:*
>
> *He is <u>neither</u> the best runner in our school <u>nor</u> the worst.* **(parallel items: the best runner, the worst [runner])**
>
> *You can try out for <u>either</u> the marching band <u>or</u> the jazz band, but you can't do both.* **(parallel items: the marching band, the jazz band)**
>
> *David Robinson was <u>not only</u> an outstanding athlete, <u>but also</u> a prominent member of the community.* **(parallel items: an outstanding athlete, a prominent member)**

> **Note:** When you use parallel structure, be aware of introductory words such as articles (*a, an, the*) and prepositions. You can either use the introductory word once, at the beginning of the series (if it fits for each item) or use the introductory word (or that type of word) before every item in the series.
>
> ### *Examples:*
>
> **Articles:**
>
> **Not parallel:** *We competed against <u>the</u> French, Spanish, and <u>the</u> Chinese volleyball teams.*
>
> **Parallel:** *We competed against <u>the</u> French, Spanish, and Chinese volleyball teams.*
>
> **Parallel:** *We competed against <u>the</u> French, <u>the</u> Spanish, and <u>the</u> Chinese volleyball teams.*
>
> **Prepositions:**
>
> **Not parallel:** *My sister's rock band performed <u>in</u> schools, <u>parks</u>, and <u>at</u> local events.*
>
> **Parallel:** *My sister's rock band performed <u>in</u> schools, <u>in</u> parks, and <u>at</u> local events.*

Read the paragraph. Underline the examples of incorrect parallel structure and correct them.

My brother Morris is surprising, amazing, and inspires me. He's both a talented artist and accomplished musician. He can do just about anything you can imagine: paint watercolor pictures, excellent photography, or play classical violin. Whether he's drawing in his sketchbook, playing a musical piece, or takes photos of his flower garden, he does it effortlessly, with passion, and is creative. He's not only a great artist, but can cook well. Whenever I visit his house, he invites me to sit back and relaxing while he cooks a fantastic gourmet meal for us. While we eat, we often listen to music by one of his favorite classical composers, usually either Bach, or by Mozart. Once I asked him how he got to be so good at everything. He told me there were three reasons: practice, more practicing, and to practice again.

PARALLEL CLAUSES

As with series and phrases, it is important to use parallelism to balance the structures in clauses. Check that the format and wording of the first clause is the same in the later clause(s). Be sure to check the nouns, the verb tenses, the adjectives, the adverbs.

Example:

Not parallel: *The students rehearsed for many hours before the holiday concert, but there was still a lot of anxiety about the event.*

Parallel: *The students rehearsed for many hours before the holiday concert, but they still felt very nervous about the event.*

With relative clauses (clauses that start with a relative pronoun: *who*, *which*, or *that*), the relative pronoun may be repeated to create parallel structure.

Example:

Chess is a game that can be challenging to learn at first, but that can provide many hours of enjoyment.

In longer sentences with multiple clauses, it is better to avoid repeating the relative pronoun and the subject.

Example:

Not parallel: *Before every big game, the coach sends the team a text message to remind us that we should get a good night's sleep, we need to eat a good breakfast, and to be on time for warm ups.*

Parallel: *Before every big game, the coach sends the team a text message to remind us that we should get a good night's sleep, eat a good breakfast, and be on time for warm ups.*

On a separate piece of paper, rewrite these sentences using parallel structure.

1. Raul explained that he enjoys snowboarding, but skiing wasn't as enjoyable for him.

2. Fishing is a sport which requires familiarity with different types of fish, and you need to know about what they like to eat.

3. Mr. Davis is the piano teacher who gave me an understanding of the importance of hard work, and I learned from him to appreciate the learning process.

4. When I started my first vegetable garden, the seeds didn't grow well, there were insects that ate most of my plants, and it was taken over by weeds.

5. Emiko made the difficult decision to drop out of the marathon, not because she was unable to continue, but there was a fear of injuring her knee.

PARALLEL COMPARATIVES

Another place to pay attention to parallel structure in your writing is when making comparisons. These phrases are used in comparative sentences:

X is *similar to* Y
X is *the same as* Y
X is *as [big] as* Y

X is *[bigger] than* Y
X is *more [interesting] than* Y
X is *less [interesting] than* Y

X is *different from* Y

Without parallel structure, the meaning of comparative sentences can be confusing. The grammatical structure of both items being compared needs to be the same.

Examples:

Not parallel: *Jakob's musical tastes are similar to his sister.* **(Compares musical tastes to a person)**

Parallel: *Jakob's musical tastes are similar to his sister's.* **(Compares two people's musical tastes)**

Not parallel: *The basketball team at Franklin School is bigger than Simon School.* **(Compares a team to a school)**

Parallel: *The basketball team at Franklin School is bigger than the basketball team at Simon School.* **(Compares two teams)**

Choose one of the pairs of items below. On a separate piece of paper, write a paragraph comparing the two items. Use the expressions in the box to discuss both similarities and differences. Use parallel structure.

> as . . . as   more . . . than
> different from   similar to
> . . . -er than   the same as
> less . . . than

- your interests / your best friend's interests
- learning to ride a bicycle / learning to speak English
- classical music / hip-hop music
- playing a computer game / playing a board game
- the game of baseball / the game of chess
- Van Gogh's paintings / Picasso's paintings
- traveling in your own country / traveling overseas

A. Complete the paragraph by circling the best choices. Keep the structures parallel.

To watch a karate match in person is (**1.** experiencing / to experience) the thrill of a great traditional sport. Before my friend Toshi invited me to a match, I was familiar with the rules of boxing, but not (**2.** karate's / of karate). I sometimes play a karate game on my computer, but I soon found out that a video game is very different from (**3.** doing the real thing / the real thing.) I've always been interested in trying martial arts myself, so I looked forward to (**4.** sit / sitting) in the front row and (**5.** watch / watching) the action up close. To begin the match, the two fighters approached the center of the ring and (**6.** bowing / bowed) politely to each other. Then the referee signaled the start of the match, and the fighters (**7.** moved / had moved) toward each other, at first slowly and (**8.** with caution / cautiously). Then suddenly, one fighter lunged forward and let loose with a series of rapid kicks and (**9.** punch / punches). The people in the audience began to applaud and (**10.** cheering / cheer) loudly. The (**11.** thing / things) that amazed me the most (**12.** was / were) the speed,

(continued)

(**13.** accuracy / the accuracy), and the height of both fighters' kicks. They were not only incredibly strong and fast, but also (**14.** had amazing flexibility / amazingly flexible). The match was over in just a few minutes, which felt too quick, and (**15.** that left / which left) me wanting more. But in those few minutes, several things became clear to me: that I would try karate myself someday, that (**16.** I would need / that I needed) to work extremely hard, and that, hopefully, I (**17.** will / would) never have to be in the ring with one of those same fighters.

B. **Compare answers with another student. Take turns reading the sentences aloud.**

COMBINING SENTENCES WITH PARALLEL STRUCTURE

In many cases, parallel structure can be used to combine sentences in order to avoid repeating words and phrases. This helps to make your writing sound smoother, clearer, and more concise.

Example:

Separate sentences: *My family enjoys spending time together outdoors. We often go on long camping trips. In addition, we have a small boat, which we sail on the lake.*

Combined: *My family enjoys spending time together outdoors, going on long camping trips, or sailing our small boat on the lake.*

EXERCISE 8

A. **Read the paragraph. Notice the repetition in the underlined sentences. How does it affect the smoothness and flow of the paragraph?**

A good coach can make a big difference in your life. A coach can do this by making you feel welcome on a team. He or she can build up your confidence. A coach can gradually introduce you to new skills and greater challenges. In first and second grade, our only coach was our teacher, Miss Woodward. She was tiny. She had gray hair. She wore glasses. Yet she knew all there was to know about choosing teams. She also knew all there was to know about playing kickball. If you remember kickball, you know that you can get the runners out by throwing the relatively large rubber ball at them. One day I threw the ball at Maria, the smallest girl in our class. It hit her pretty hard. It knocked her down. I felt guilty. I felt embarrassed. It was because I threw the ball too hard. Maria got up. She had scraped her knees. She had scraped her palms. She even had a scrape on her chin. I went over to her. I told her I had thrown the ball.

I apologized. Later, Miss Woodward called me aside to speak to me. "A real athlete like you should look out for other players," she said. "I bet you could have thrown that ball a lot easier." I felt foolish. But I also felt proud. I also felt strong. No one had ever called me an "athlete" before. I wanted to be worthy of it. All these years later, I remember Miss Woodward as a great coach. You know why? A good coach encourages all her players. A good coach develops all her players. In addition, she challenges all her players. But great coaches do one more thing: they teach you about something bigger than sports.

B. *Combine each group of underlined sentences into a single sentence with a parallel structure. Write your new sentences on a separate piece of paper.*

C. *Work with another student. Take turns reading aloud the paragraph with your combined sentences.*

WRITING TASK

Write a short composition about a game, a sport, or a leisure activity.

A. *Think of a game, a sport, or another type of leisure activity that you have experience with. It can be something that you currently enjoy doing (or watching), or one that you have done in the past. Choose one of these topics for your composition.*

- A funny story about when you were first learning to do the activity

- An emotional experience you had (exciting, embarrassing, moving, inspiring) while watching, or doing the sport/activity

- An athlete, a coach, or another person who has inspired or encouraged you

- A person you know who has many different talents

- An activity that you quit, but that you wish you hadn't quit

B. *Write a three- to five- paragraph composition about your chosen topic. Use at least five examples of different types of parallel structure introduced in this unit.*

Check Your Writing

A. *Use this form to check your writing, or exchange compositions with another student and check each other's writing.*

Composition Checklist

1. How many paragraphs does the composition have? _____

2. What is the main topic of the composition? _____

3. Does the composition use at least five examples of parallel structure? _____

4. Are all items in a series (list) parallel, including nouns, verb forms, adjectives, and adverbs? _____ . If no, circle the items that are not.

5. Do all gerunds and infinitive forms have parallel structure? _____

6. Are there any sentences that can be combined with parallel structure? Underline them.

7. Do you have any other comments or suggestions for the writer? If so, write them here:

   _____

   _____

   _____

   _____

B. *Make changes to improve your composition. Remember to check your writing for grammar, spelling, and punctuation errors.*

Academic Writing

Introduction

In this part of *Writing Power 4*, you will work on developing skills for academic writing. You will study and practice all of the skills needed to write an academic essay—the kind of writing you need to do for high school or university classes.

Academic writing requires special skills. As you progress through the units in Part 3, you will learn and practice these skills individually, and then you will put them together to write a persuasive essay. Skills introduced in Part 3 include:

- Using Formal Register
- Working with Source Materials
- Plagiarism, Quoting, and Paraphrasing
- Summary Writing
- Prewriting Techniques
- Thesis Statements, Introductions, and Conclusions
- Essay Support
- Organizing and Drafting
- Revision and Reference

What Is Academic Writing?

Academic writing is writing you do for school. You may be required to write a report about a book you have read, an essay that responds to a particular topic or question, or a research paper about an issue. For this type of writing, you are usually required to analyze and explain a topic, form and clearly state an opinion, and give information to support it. Therefore, academic writing has a specific purpose. Often that purpose is to persuade the reader to agree with and/or take action on a point of view or opinion about an issue. Then, to clarify and support that opinion, the writer may make comparisons or contrasts, show causes and effects, explain a problem and present a solution, or discuss the advantages or disadvantages of a particular action related to the issue.

Academic writing requires special skills and knowledge. There are certain rules for format and language use that you need to follow; these are most often not necessary for other types of writing.

In this unit you will learn about what makes academic writing different from other types of writing and practice the specific skills you need to be successful.

Warm Up

Look at the reasons why people write. Add as many more reasons as you can. Work with the whole class. Discuss which reasons may apply to the writing you do for school.

People write to . . .

- report about a story or an event.
- express emotions, attitudes, and opinions.
- communicate with one person or many.
- be remembered.
- complete an assignment.
- record memories.
- _____
- _____
- _____
- _____
- _____
- _____

WRITING FOR AN AUDIENCE

Whenever and whatever you write, you are writing for a particular reader or audience. In writing you do outside of school, your audience may be a friend or family member, a future employer, or even you, yourself. When you write for academic purposes, your audience is your teacher or sometimes your classmates.

In addition to the topic, the audience is what determines the type of language, tone, and style of a piece of writing.

EXERCISE 1

A. *Write the correct topic and audience from the box on the line under each passage.*

Topic	Audience
a comparison about two languages in a book	the writer himself
a response to an advertisement	an old friend
a plan	a future employer
a response to an unexpected email	a professor

1.

> To Whom It May Concern:
>
> I am very interested in your job posting for the full-time sales representative with your company. I have been a sales representative for the past five years and . . .

Topic: _____   Audience: _____

2.

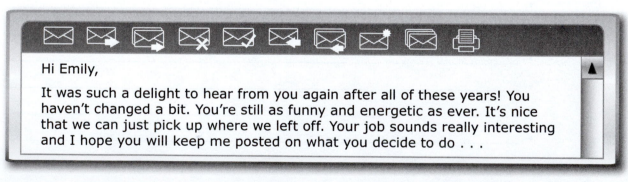

Hi Emily,

It was such a delight to hear from you again after all of these years! You haven't changed a bit. You're still as funny and energetic as ever. It's nice that we can just pick up where we left off. Your job sounds really interesting and I hope you will keep me posted on what you decide to do . . .

Topic: _____   Audience: _____

3.

> In *The Number Sense*, French neurologist and mathematician, Stanislas Dehaene (1997) explains that the Chinese have a greater ability for memorizing numbers in a two-second time span because their words for numbers are short. Other languages like English have longer words for numbers, so English speakers need more time to remember the longer words. For example, it takes longer to speak or hear the number seven than the shorter Chinese word *qi* for the number seven. He points out that Chinese who speak the Cantonese dialect can memorize up to ten numbers in a two-second time span . . .

Topic: _____   Audience: _____

4.

To do: Friday
class
laundry
~~call dentist~~
vacuum bedroom
groceries: milk, bread, eggs, cheese, bananas, carrots
homework chapter 1, exs. 5-8
library return books
~~email Tina, Joey~~

Topic: _____   Audience: _____

B. **Compare answers with another student. What differences do you notice about the language each writer uses?**

Tone and Register

Every piece of writing expresses the attitude or mood of the writer. This is referred to as the **tone**. The tone may be humorous, serious, sarcastic, sad, friendly, and so on. For academic writing you need to use the words and phrases that express a more serious tone. **Register** refers to the kinds of language (words, phrases, and expressions) you choose to express your ideas.

There are two main types of register: **formal** and **informal**. We speak and write differently, depending on the formality of the situation or status of a person. Think about the way you speak to your friends, parents, boss, or teacher. How do you change the way you speak to each of them?

Academic classes are considered a formal setting. Depending on your class, you, your classmates, and your teacher may use more informal or casual language when you speak. However, no matter how informally you may speak to one another, when you write academic assignments, you will need to use formal language.

Learning the difference between formal and informal register may be a challenge. However, with time and practice, you can achieve your end goal—a well-written academic essay.

Guidelines for Using Formal Register

- Using formal language means choosing the kind of vocabulary found in textbooks or formal documents.
  Examples: *Perhaps, . . . However, . . . In addition, . . .*

- Avoid slang (overly casual language) and incorrect spelling.
  Examples:

    ~~Kids~~ → *children*   ~~See ya~~ → *Goodbye*   ~~Gonna~~ → *going to*

- Avoid certain casual-sounding phrasal verbs; try to use single verbs that express the same meaning.
  Examples:

    The researchers conducted a study to ~~check out~~ whether multivitamins can be a substitute for an unhealthy diet. → *The researchers conducted a study to **investigate** whether multivitamins can be a substitute for an unhealthy diet.*

    The scientists were trying to ~~figure out~~ how climate change might cause severe weather systems. → *The scientists were trying to **understand** how climate change might cause severe weather systems.*

- Avoid contractions, such as *I'm* or *Where's*. Write out the full word: *I am . . . , Where is . . .*

- Avoid abbreviations, such as *i.e., e.g.,* or *Oct*. Write out the full word or phrase instead: *in other words, . . . for example, . . . October . . .*

Examples:

What're you doing? → *What are you doing?*

Agave nectar ~~doesn't~~ have as many antioxidants that other natural sweeteners contain; ~~i.e.,~~ ~~it's~~ no better for you than processed sugar. → *Agave nectar does not have the amount of antioxidants that other natural sweeteners contain;* **in other words**, *it is no better for you than processed sugar.*

Overuse of CT scans may be causing cancer; ~~e.g.,~~ one CT scan is equal to about 450 chest X-rays. → *Overuse of CT scans may be causing cancer;* **for example**, *one CT scan is equal to about 450 chest X-rays.*

CT scans have saved thousands of lives because they can find hard-to-detect cancers such as lung, pancreatic, kidney, ~~etc.~~ → *CT scans have saved thousands of lives because they can find hard-to-detect cancers such as lung, pancreatic, kidney,* **and so on**.

- Use a variety of sentence types and structures, including simple, compound, and complex sentences.

- Avoid personal pronouns, where possible. Instead, use impersonal words like *There is/are, It is,* and passive verb forms.

- Use passive verb forms to avoid use of the personal pronoun or when the subject is unknown or the person who performs the action is unimportant.

Examples:

Personal pronoun: *~~I have read about several ways to increase an online profile.~~*
Impersonal words: *There are several ways to increase an online profile.*

Personal pronoun: *~~I surveyed some people about how they used the Internet.~~*
Passive: *Various people were surveyed about their Internet usage.*

Individual subjects are unknown: *~~People speak Arabic in Saudi Arabia.~~*
Passive: *Arabic is spoken in Saudi Arabia.*

People performing action are unimportant: *~~Some students wrote good essays.~~*
Passive: *The essays were well-written.*

- Avoid use of the exclamation point. Exclamation points are not considered appropriate in formal writing.

Example:

On social media sites people should not upload photos that their grandmother would consider inappropriate!!! → *On social media sites people should not upload photos that their grandmother would consider inappropriate.*

Circle the word or phrase that is more appropriate for academic writing.

but / however	cause / because
and / in addition	In other words, / I mean
have to / hafta	you should / it is recommended
I think / In my opinion	maybe / perhaps
there is / there's	frequently / all the time
wrong / incorrect	wanna / want to
lots of / many	kind of / somewhat
guy / man	hot topic / controversial topic
things / stuff	unacceptable / horrible
wonderful / awesome	gonna / going to
also / furthermore	kid / child

EXERCISE 3

A. *Read the descriptions of formal and informal language.*

Formal	Informal
• Uses formal (textbook-like) vocabulary and phrases (*Perhaps, . . . However, . . . In addition, . . .*) • Includes longer, varied sentence types (simple, compound, complex) • Uses correct grammar, spelling, and punctuation • Uses a mix of active and passive verb forms • Uses proper formatting to acknowledge source materials (the author, title, publisher, URL)	• Starts sentences with coordinating conjunctions such as *and, so,* and *but* • Uses slang or casual expressions • Uses contractions and abbreviations • Uses exclamation points

B. *Read the sentences. Write **F** for formal. Write **I** for informal.*

_____ **1.** In his book, *Dialogue Concerning the Two Chief Systems of the World* (1632), physicist, mathematician, astronomer, and philosopher Galileo Galilei argued for the theory of Copernicanism, which supports the view that the earth revolves around the sun.

     2. I think free, public mail service should be available to every citizen in the world cause not everyone has a home computer with access to email.

     3. I can get lots of helpful information online about jobs, e.g., I can check out new products, pricing, and reader reviews about items.

     4. Uffe Ravnskov, MD and researcher, refutes long-held beliefs that high cholesterol decreases life spans. Dr. Ravnskov contradicts many health and nutrition experts by stating that saturated fat is good for you.

     5. Colleges and universities may view an applicant's social media site to get another view of the student's "hidden" personality and compare it to what the student presents on his/her application.

  C. ***On a separate piece of paper, rewrite the sentences you marked with an I. Make them appropriate for academic writing. Then compare your work with another student.***

ACADEMIC ESSAYS

Most academic essays consist of four or more paragraphs and are about 500–800 words long. Academic essays present a **thesis**—the controlling idea of the essay and the writer's opinion about the topic. Then the essay logically presents evidence to support the writer's thesis. Although a personal experience may be used as an example to support the thesis, academic topics are not usually personal and require additional research. Sources must be properly referenced, or cited, in an academic essay. **Citations** give detailed information about the sources such as the author, title, publisher, and so on.

Essay Structure and Format

As you have already learned in this unit, audience and register are important considerations. In addition, all academic writing has certain features and follows the same general structure or form.

An academic essay . . .

- uses formal language.
- is about one topic.
- has a controlling idea—thesis statement—which presents the writer's point of view or opinion.
- begins with an introductory paragraph and ends with a concluding paragraph.
- has body paragraphs that develop the controlling idea expressed in the thesis statement.
- restates the thesis in the concluding paragraph.
- uses standard essay format.
- cites sources properly.

A. *Read the sample essay.*

Carolina Gonzales
October 16, 2012
Writing 104
Professor Lee

<u>Free Workers to Surf</u>

According to Internet World Statistics (2011), over 3 billion people use the Internet every day. They connect to the Internet on their home computers, portable devices like smartphones or tablets, or at work. At work, companies worry that employees' productivity might be affected by their spending time on the Internet. However, according to a study by Dr. Brent Coker (2009) from the University of Melbourne, the opposite may be true. Companies need to realize that workers will be more productive, more creative, and happier if allowed to freely use the Internet in the workplace.

In their study, Lee, McCann, and Messenger (2007) found that workers around the world are working 22 percent longer hours than the standard forty-hour week. With longer work days, employees need the freedom to do what they feel is best for themselves during their break times, in order to return to work re-energized. One break-time activity workers find relaxing is using the Internet. It offers them an easy way to escape their work environment without leaving the office. For example, they can shop, go on their social media sites, read a book, or even do a yoga routine with an online video program. This type of online usage may cause some companies to worry about computer viruses. However, all computers are vulnerable to viruses, so it is a company's responsibility to have good security systems that protect its computers from invaders. In addition, companies should have Internet usage policies that state which sites are not appropriate on workplace computers. As the Coker (2009) study found, employees who spent a small part of their work day surfing the Internet for pleasure were more productive than employees who did not. With safe systems and firm policies, workers should be able to use the Internet responsibly so they can return to their duties refreshed and ready to concentrate more fully.

Giving workers access to the Internet during break times not only will make workers more productive (Coker, 2009) but also may promote creative thinking. For example, while casually surfing the Net, a worker in the marketing department may find something that sparks a new idea or way to promote new products. With instant information on the Net, a company has to be ahead of the competition, not a step behind. Letting workers control where they want to travel on the Net may help a company keep its competitive edge. The images, creative websites, videos, or music a worker clicks on may be the inspiration for a company's next product, ad campaign, or marketing strategy. These are just some of the benefits a company may gain if employees are allowed a few minutes of relief time from their normal work duties to surf the Net.

Last but not least, letting workers relax via the Internet may help build a feeling of connection among workers. Many companies do not have the land or money to create beautiful, outdoor spaces so their employees can relax together. Furthermore, they do not have the indoor office space or funds for a basketball hoop or ping-pong table so that employees can participate in team-building activities. Companies that are lucky enough to have resources like these give their workers a way to enjoy time together and create a happier workplace. For companies without these resources, the Internet is a cost-effective way for employees to share time together enjoying the entertainment it offers. Instead of feeling isolated in an office space, workers can connect online and have some fun whether they share the same office space or not. What company would ever want to discourage employees from enjoying being at work and building relationships with coworkers?

In conclusion, the Internet is everywhere. At work, employees who are allowed to access it during breaks will be more effective, innovative, and content. With advanced Internet safety software and Internet usage guidelines, companies can no longer deny workers a tool that has the potential for increased job satisfaction.

References

Internet users in the world distribution by world regions. (2011). Retrieved September 15, 2012 from http://www.internetworldstats.com/stats.htm

Lee, S., McCann, D., & Messenger, J. C. (2007). *Working time around the world: Trends in working hours, laws, and policies in a global comparative perspective.* USA/Canada: Routledge.

The Melbourne Newsroom. (2009). *Freedom to surf: Workers more productive if allowed to use the internet for leisure.* Retrieved September 15, 2012 from the University of Melbourne website: http://newsroom.melbourne.edu/news/n-19

- How many topics are there in the sample essay?

- In which paragraph does the writer introduce the topic of the essay?

- Which sentence in the introduction expresses the writer's opinion about the topic? Underline it.

- Based on the writer's opinion statement, what main points do you expect to be developed in the body paragraphs?

- What are some of the examples the writer uses to support the main idea of each of the body paragraphs?

- What kind of detailed information does the writer give about her sources?

- How does the writer restate her opinion in the concluding paragraph? Double underline the sentence(s).

- What are some examples of formal register used in the essay?

WRITING TASK

> Write a short essay that expresses and supports your opinion about a topic.

A. **Choose one of these topics.**

- Physical education class should not be required.

- Internet newspapers and magazines are as accurate as print newspapers and magazines.

- The main goal of education is to prepare students for jobs.

- Drivers should not be allowed to use cell phones while driving.

B. **Use this outline to organize your ideas.**

Topic: _____

Introduction:

What is some general information you know about the topic?

_____

_____

What is your opinion about the topic? Do you agree or disagree with the statement?

_____

Write a sentence that clearly states your opinion about the topic.

_____

Body:

What are some reasons for your opinion? Why are they important?

_____

_____

_____

What are some specific examples that support your opinion?

_____

_____

_____

_____

_____

Conclusion:

Restate the sentence from your introduction in which you stated your opinion. Use different words. What kind of final comment, if any, do you want to add?

_____

_____

_____

_____

C. *Write a four- to five-paragraph essay on a separate piece of paper. Follow these instructions for format and structure:*

1. Write the following single-spaced in the upper left corner:
   - your name
   - the date
   - the course title
   - your teacher's name

2. Write a title for your essay. Center it above the introductory paragraph.

3. Write four or five paragraphs:
   - introduction—1 paragraph
   - body—2–3 paragraphs
   - conclusion—1 paragraph

4. Use double spacing for the main text.

5. Indent each paragraph.

Check Your Writing

A. *Use this form to check your writing, or exchange essays with another student and check each other's writing.*

Essay Checklist

The essay . . .

1. is the right length. ☐

2. is formatted correctly. ☐

3. follows the guidelines for formal register. ☐

4. focuses on one topic. ☐

5. includes an introduction with some general information about the topic. ☐

6. clearly expresses the writer's opinion in a sentence in the introduction. ☐

7. includes examples that support the writer's opinion. ☐

8. has a conclusion. ☐

9. Were there any sentences you didn't understand? If so, write a question mark (?) in front of them on the essay.

10. Underline one or two sentences in the essay that you particularly liked.

11. What changes do you suggest to improve the essay?

   _____

   _____

B. *Make changes to improve your essay. Remember to check your writing for grammar, spelling, and punctuation errors.*

2

Working with Source Materials

In colleges and universities, writing assignments require students to give information about, analyze, or argue a topic. Since academic topics usually focus on social, cultural, or scientific issues, students spend time gathering and studying information from source materials such as books, interview transcripts, and various types of web, magazine, newspaper, or academic journal articles. Later, they use this information from source materials to develop and support their writing with details, examples, facts, statistics, and explanations.

Sometimes source materials are provided by the teacher, but often students are responsible for finding them on their own. Knowing how to judge the **reliability** (trustworthiness) of a source and its usefulness to your assignment are essential for good academic writing.

In this unit you will study and practice . . .

- judging the reliability of source materials.
- determining usefulness of sources.
- taking notes and keeping track of sources.

Warm Up

Look at the sources in the chart. Work in a group. Discuss these questions:

- Which types of sources have you used the most? Why?
- What are some of the advantages and disadvantages of these sources?
- How do you check whether the information is accurate or not?

a large metropolitan newspaper	a tabloid (a newspaper that has small pages, many photographs, short stories, and not much serious news)	an online encyclopedia (such as wikipedia.com)	an interview with an expert in a particular field
a business website	a government website	a television news broadcast	an encyclopedia
an interview with a friend	a library database	an academic journal (a publication with articles about topics that have been researched and studied seriously by experts)	a textbook
an online video	a website recommended by your friend	a website recommended by your teacher	

TYPES OF SOURCES

A wide variety of publications is available to use as sources for research. Some of these are:

- **Academic journals** are publications written by scholars about academic subjects and research. The articles are reviewed and judged by other academics to make sure proper research methods were followed.

- **Major newspapers and magazines** publish articles about the news, current events, and items of general interest. These publications are connected to a large metropolitan area or have a large national or global readership. Articles are checked carefully by writers and editors to confirm that the information is accurate and true. The writers may be journalists, scholars, or experts in their fields.

- **Popular magazines** publish articles of special interest such as sports, technology, or entertainment. These publications usually follow the same verification process that major publications do.

- **Online and print encyclopedias** publish information written about a general topic. Print versions often take years to publish, so online versions often provide more up-to-date information. However, many online encyclopedias can be written or edited by anyone and therefore can be less reliable.

- **Websites** publish materials about a wide variety of topics. It is important to be aware of the different types of Internet sources. The last part of the URL (web address) will provide you with important information:

.com commercial or business	.edu college or university	.net network or Internet service provider	.org non-profit	.gov federal government	~ personal page

Reliable Sources

As you use various sources to explore your writing topic, you will not only learn about the topic but also begin to shape and build the ideas you will express in your writing.

To ensure that your ideas and opinions are based on accurate information, you will need to use reliable and credible sources. Because so much information is available, especially online, it can be difficult to know which sources are reliable. Depending on the quality of a source, the information may be accurate or seriously flawed. Sources may also contain information that is biased (based on the opinion of the author, rather than on facts). Being able to distinguish these qualities is important if you want your writing to be taken seriously.

To determine if a source is reliable, look at these guidelines.

Guidelines for Determining Reliable Sources

The author . . .

- is an authority or expert.
- has a distinguished title before his or her name such as Doctor, Professor, or Director.
- holds an advanced degree indicated by letters after the name—M.D., Ph.D., M.A., M.S., LLD.
- is affiliated with a reputable institution or organization, but not connected to a special interest group or political organization with biased[1] views or opinions.
- uses quotations or **cites**—refers to—reliable sources.

The content . . .

- is factual.
- presents a well-informed viewpoint that considers more than one perspective about an issue.
- cites sources and lists references.
- uses facts, quotations, and/or statistics from other reputable sources.
- is not trying to sell something.
- is verifiable—can be found in other places.
- is up-to-date.

The website . . .

- includes contact information such as the name of the author or owner of the site.
- does not promote a product.
- has a domain name connected to established, well-known institutions such as *.edu*, *.gov*, or *.org*.
- includes the current date.
- includes active links.

The online encyclopedia . . .

- may contain information that can be written or edited by anyone.
- has collaborative and evolving content; it may be more up-to-date than printed version.
- may be a good source to begin research, but content should be verified from other sources.
- should not be used as the only source.

[1]*biased*—unfairly preferring one person or group over another

Work with another student. Read the information from various sources. Circle Yes for reliable or No for not reliable. Use the Guidelines for Determining Reliable Sources to help you. Write the reason(s) for your answer on the line.

1. Uffe Ravnskov, M.D., a world-renowned researcher, refutes long-held beliefs that high cholesterol decreases life spans. He reviews a number of research studies with results that support his findings. Dr. Ravnskov contradicts many health and nutrition experts by stating that saturated fat is good for you . . .
From: Wikipedia.com

   Reliable: Yes / No

   Reason: _____

2. In his book *The Number Sense*, French neurologist and mathematician Stanislas Dehaene (1997) explains that the Chinese have a greater ability for memorizing numbers in a two-second time span because their words for numbers are short. Other languages like English have longer words for numbers, so English speakers need more time to remember the longer words. For example, it takes longer to speak or hear the number seven than the shorter Chinese word *qi* for the number seven. He points out that Chinese who speak the Cantonese dialect can memorize up to ten numbers in a two-second time span.

   Reliable: Yes / No

   Reason: _____

3. "Since your risk of heart disease and heart attacks is associated with high cholesterol, you may want to think about medication to lower your cholesterol. You can also make changes in your lifestyle to reduce cholesterol levels. Lifestyle changes can help improve the cholesterol-lowering effect of medication as well."
By Allain Clinic Staff

   Our senior medical editors are Allain Clinic educators and practitioners who have extensive knowledge in a wide variety of medical specialties. They work closely with Web content specialists and editors to guarantee that information is accurate, comprehensible, and relevant. Our medical editors are leaders in their specialized areas.
   From: www.theallainclinic.org

   Reliable: Yes / No

   Reason: _____

4. *Americans and Text Messaging*
Aaron Smith
September 19, 2011

"Some 83% of American adults own cell phones, and three-quarters of them (73%) send and receive text messages. The Pew Research Center's Internet & American Life Project asked those texters in a survey how they prefer to be contacted on their cell phone, and 31% said they preferred texts to talking on the phone, while 53% said they preferred a voice call to a text message."
From: http://pewinternet.org/Reports/2011/Cell-Phone-Texting-2011/Summary-of-Findings.aspx

Reliable: Yes / No

Reason: _____

5. Amy was filled with cancer and her doctors said there was nothing they could do for her. She was despondent and had lost all hope until she found out about the New Ways Cancer Clinic. At New Ways, Amy started the clinic's exclusive detoxifying treatments and specially formulated natural foods nutrition plan. In three weeks, she went home cancer-free.
From: New Ways Cancer Clinic brochure

Reliable: Yes / No

Reason: _____

6. In *Cosmographia (1524)*, mathematician Petrus Apianus reviews the Ptolemaic system in which the sun revolves around the earth.

Reliable: Yes / No

Reason: _____

7. In his book, *Dialogue Concerning the Two Chief Systems of the World* (1632), physicist, mathematician, astronomer, and philosopher, Galileo Galilei argued for the theory of Copernicanism, which supports the view that the earth revolves around the sun.

Reliable: Yes / No

Reason: _____

EXERCISE 2

A. ***Work with another student. Compare these pages from two websites about vitamins and dietary supplements. Discuss any similarities or differences you notice.***

Website 1

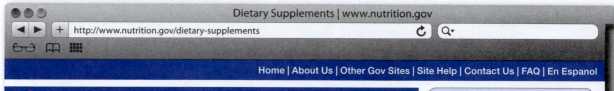

Dietary Supplements | www.nutrition.gov

http://www.nutrition.gov/dietary-supplements

Home | About Us | Other Gov Sites | Site Help | Contact Us | FAQ | En Espanol

Dietary Supplements

Questions to Ask Before Taking Vitamin and Mineral Supplements

United States Department of Agriculture, National Agricultural Library, Food and Nutrition Information Center.

Are you considering vitamin or mineral supplements? Do you think you need them? Or that they "can't hurt"? Here are some questions to ask before you decide to take them.

MedlinePlus: Dietary Supplements

DHHS. NIH. National Library of Medicine.

A wealth of information on supplements from government and health-related agencies.

Dietary Supplement Fact Sheets

Department of Health and Human Services, National Institutes of Health, Office of Dietary Supplements.

Fact sheets on the functions, food sources, intake recommendations and more for many dietary supplements.

About Us

Expert Nutrition Information at Your Fingertips

Nutrition.gov provides easy access to food and nutrition information. It serves as a gateway to reliable information on nutrition, healthy eating, physical activity, and food safety for consumers.

Providing science-based dietary guidance is critical to enhance the public's ability to make healthy choices. Since dietary needs change throughout the lifespan, specialized nutrition information is provided about infants, children, teens, adult women and men, and seniors. The site is kept fresh with the latest news and features links to interesting sites.

Food and Nutrition Experts Working for You

Nutrition.gov was revitalized by the staff at the Food and Nutrition Information Center (FNIC) and the National Agricultural Library (NAL) in cooperation with a panel of food and nutrition expert advisors from agencies within United States Department of Agriculture (USDA) and Department of Health and Human Services (DHHS). FNIC's staff of trained nutrition professionals, most of whom are Registered Dietitians (R.D.), provide information on food and human nutrition.

Thank you for visiting Nutrition.gov!

Dietary Supplements

- Questions To Ask Before Taking Vitamin and Mineral Supplements
- Herbal Supplements
- Safety and Health Claims
- Dietary Supplements for Athletes
- Commonly Asked Questions (FAQs)

See Also

- FDA Basics: Dietary Supplements

I Want To

- Print the Nutrition.gov Brochure

About Us

- Site Credits

Website 2

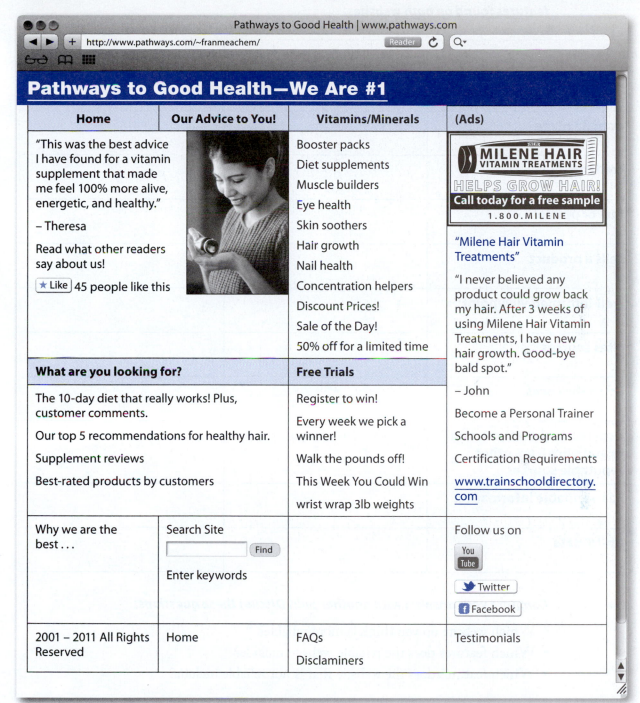

Pathways to Good Health—We Are #1

Home	Our Advice to You!	Vitamins/Minerals	(Ads)
"This was the best advice I have found for a vitamin supplement that made me feel 100% more alive, energetic, and healthy." – Theresa Read what other readers say about us! ★ Like 45 people like this		Booster packs Diet supplements Muscle builders Eye health Skin soothers Hair growth Nail health Concentration helpers Discount Prices! Sale of the Day! 50% off for a limited time	
What are you looking for?		**Free Trials**	"Milene Hair Vitamin Treatments" "I never believed any product could grow back my hair. After 3 weeks of using Milene Hair Vitamin Treatments, I have new hair growth. Good-bye bald spot." – John
The 10-day diet that really works! Plus, customer comments. Our top 5 recommendations for healthy hair. Supplement reviews Best-rated products by customers		Register to win! Every week we pick a winner! Walk the pounds off! This Week You Could Win wrist wrap 3lb weights	Become a Personal Trainer Schools and Programs Certification Requirements www.trainschooldirectory.com
Why we are the best . . .	Search Site [ ] Find Enter keywords		Follow us on You Tube 🐦 Twitter f Facebook
2001 – 2011 All Rights Reserved	Home	FAQs Disclaminers	Testimonials

B. *Use the Guidelines for Determining Reliable Sources and fill in the chart with features found on both websites.*

	Website 1	Website 2
author credentials		
domain name		
content:		
fact or opinion		
sells a product		
well-informed viewpoint		
cites sources		
lists references		
uses facts, quotations, and/or statistics from other reputable sources		
has verifiable information		
up-to-date		

C. *Compare your answers with another pair. Discuss these questions:*

- Which website do you think is more reliable?
- Which features does the reliable website include?
- Which features does the website that is not reliable include?

Further Practice

Research and Write

On your own, go online to a website you have visited for information in the past. Decide if the website is reliable or not. Use the Guidelines for Determining Reliable Sources and the chart in Exercise 2B to help you. Take notes on the features that make it a reliable or unreliable source. Present your findings to the class.

Usefulness of Source Materials

In addition to deciding if a source is reliable, you will need to determine if the information will be useful or relevant to the topic you are researching. Ask yourself these questions.

- Will the source provide background knowledge about the topic?
- Will it provide examples and explanations?
- Will it explain special terms or concepts?
- Will it include expert opinions or information?
- What type of publication is it?

EXERCISE 3

Work with another student. Imagine you need to do research for the sample topics given. Check (✓) the source(s) you think will be useful for each topic. Next, decide how the source(s) will be useful. Then use the questions above to decide what kind of information the source(s) will provide. Write your answer in the box. Add more sources if you can.

Topic 1. Explain the process of photosynthesis.

☐ "Accretion of Rocky Planets by Hot Jupiters" by Jacob A. Ketchum, Fred C. Adams, and Anthony M. Bloch From: *The Astrophysical Journal Letters*, Volume 741, Number 1 October 2011	☐ National Science Foundation Press Release, "Scientists Offer New View of Photosynthesis" May 7, 2007 www.nsf.gov
☐ a librarian or library	☐ an online encyclopedia
Other sources you know that might be useful:	Types of information the source might include:

Topic 2. Rate cars for their fuel efficiency and choose the best one.

☐ "Emission Facts: Average Annual Emissions and Fuel Consumption for Cars and Light Trucks" April 2000 http://www.epa.gov/oms/consumer/f00013.htm	☐ "Best and Worst Fuel Economy" www.consumerreports.org
☐ "Why I Like These 5 Cars" Jdanvers/autoreviews.blog.com	☐ "Our 10 Best Cars" Dolvian Car Company's Annual Report
Other sources you know that might be useful:	Types of information the source might include:

Topic 3. Is the universe expanding?

☐ October 4, 2011 2011 Nobel Prize in Physics: Discovery of Expanding Universe by Observing Distant Supernovae Science Daily.com http://www.sciencedaily.com/releases/2011/10/111004091704.htm	☐ a physics textbook
☐ an academic journal	☐ a television show
Other sources you know that might be useful:	Types of information the source might include:

Topic 4. Should employers limit the amount of time employees can use the Internet at work?

☐ *Business Week* (magazine) over 300,000 subscribers	☐ "Freedom to surf: Workers More Productive If Allowed to Use the Internet for Leisure" http://newsroom.melbourne.edu/news/n-19
☐ a dictionary	☐ people you know
Other sources you know that might be useful:	Types of information the source might include:

STUDYING SOURCE MATERIALS

Underlining, Highlighting, and Taking Notes

Once you have determined that a source is reliable and useful for your writing assignment, it is time to study the materials. **Underlining or highlighting texts** is one way to help you study the information and remember important ideas. It can be done in different ways. Usually, students develop their own style. These are some suggestions.

When you underline or highlight . . .

- look for the main ideas and important points.
- identify key words and phrases.
- identify details that give an example or explanation.
- identify quotes and figures you may need to refer to later.
- choose entire sentences or sections of text if it helps you connect and remember ideas.

Taking notes is another way to help you remember important ideas and key terms in source materials.

When you take notes . . .

- use the margins or empty spaces on the page for your notes *or* write them in a separate place such as on note cards or a notebook.
- write only important words and phrases (complete sentences are not necessary).
- write the main ideas in your own words.
- add your own ideas, reactions, or questions.

EXERCISE 4

A. **Read the text. Use the suggestions for underlining and highlighting above to identify the important ideas.**

In their study, Lee, McCann, and Messenger (2007) found that workers around the world are working 22 percent longer hours than the standard forty-hour week. With longer work days, employees need the freedom to do what they feel is best for themselves during their break times in order to return to work re-energized and ready to concentrate. One break-time activity that workers find relaxing is using the Internet. It offers them an easy way to escape their work environment without leaving the office. For example, they can shop, go on their social media sites, read a book, or even do a yoga routine with an online video program. This type of online usage may cause companies to worry about computer viruses. However, all computers are vulnerable to viruses, so it is a company's responsibility to have good security systems that protect its computers from invaders. In addition, companies should have Internet usage policies that state which sites are not appropriate on workplace computers. As

(continued)

the Coker (2009) study found, employees who spent a part of their work day surfing the Internet for pleasure were more productive than employees who did not.

Companies should seriously consider rethinking their move to ban or limit Internet usage because of fears of viruses and wasted time. With safe systems and firm policies, workers should be able to use the Internet responsibly so they can return to their duties refreshed and ready to concentrate more fully.

B. *Read the text and take notes. Use the suggestions for taking notes above to help you.*

Last but not least, letting workers relax via the Internet may help build a feeling of connection among workers. Many companies do not have the real estate or money to create beautiful, outdoor spaces so their employees can relax together. Furthermore, they do not have the indoor office space or funds for a basketball hoop or ping-pong table so that employees can participate in team-building activities. Companies that are lucky enough to have resources like these give their workers a way to enjoy time together and create a happier workplace. For companies without these resources, the Internet is a cost-effective way for employees to share time together enjoying the entertainment it offers. Instead of feeling isolated in an office space, workers can connect online and have some fun whether they share the same office space or not. What company would ever want to discourage employees from enjoying being at work and building relationships with coworkers?

C. *Compare Exercises A and B with another student. How are they the same? How are they different?*

KEEPING TRACK OF SOURCES

Along with your notes, you will also need to write down specific information about each source, such as the author, date, title, publisher, and the **URL**—web address. Keeping track of this information is essential because you will need to list your sources on a designated page at the end of your paper. This page, a **reference page**, provides specific information about each source. In addition, if you decide to use any ideas or the exact words from a source in your paper, you will have to include a reference to the original source. This is called an **in-text citation**. You will learn more about citations in Unit 3 and the reference page in Unit 9.

Whether your teacher provides you with source materials or you find them on your own, you will need a place to keep your notes with the specific information about your sources so you can find it easily. There are several ways to keep track of your sources. As you learn more about keeping track of sources, you will develop the ones that work best for you.

Photocopies

Quite often your teacher will provide you with a photocopy of an article or text. If you do independent research, you can make a photocopy or printout of the source. The copy should include the title, author, date, and other information that you will need to reference in your writing assignment. Printouts from the Internet often include this information at the top or bottom of the page. You can also highlight sections of the text and handwrite notes in the margins.

Note Cards

Note cards are small, individual paper cards used to write specific information about sources. You can create a separate card for each source. On the card, write the title, author, date, and other information that you will need to reference in your writing assignment, as well as ideas or quotations you may decide to incorporate into your paper.

EXERCISE 5

A. Read the writing assignment and the note card. Then circle the information in the box that is included on the card.

author	date	month	publisher	year
country	day	page numbers	title	

Writing Assignment: Discuss useful, reliable online sources, and your reasons for choosing one.

(Front side)

Elaine Myers, M.D. and Cindy Das, M.D.
2012, January 12
"Web Advice Not Always Solid"
Health and Medicine Digest, magazine, pages 58–61

discusses types of health websites

Doctor on Call – lots of advertisements for medicines
– pages are full of pictures of medicines or people who feel sick
– do not know if site is nonprofit or commercial
– from the number of ads, site must make a lot of money
– diagnosis for symptoms, but with very few details or expanded
  explanations
– no credits or authors listed

(continued)

(Back side)

> Allain Clinic – clean pages, no advertisements or photos
> – non-profit website
> – neutral tone, sounds like a doctor assessing your symptoms
> – information doesn't quickly diagnose you with a serious condition
> – process of finding information feels calm and methodical
>
> "Allain Clinic is providing the general public with medical advice from a staff of highly-trained and experienced experts that is current, useful, and dependable." p. 61

B. *What is the article about on the front side of the note card? According to the notes, which website is better? What quotation does the student write down? Why do you think the quotation might be important?*

A Notebook

A special notebook used only for keeping information about sources will help you keep this information separate and easy to find. When it comes time to write your paper, it will be clear which ideas and words belong to each source and need to be properly cited.

EXERCISE 6

A. *Read the writing assignment and the excerpt from a notebook. Then circle the information in the box about the source that the student includes.*

author	date	month	publisher	year
country	day	page numbers	title	

Writing Assignment: How is new media affecting the way we communicate?

Clay Shirky, B.A. Yale University, Professor, New Media,
 Hunter College
2008
Here Comes Everybody
U.S.A.
The Penguin Press
- Shirky finds that communication tools, like cell phones and
   the Internet, are changing the way people gather and take
   action against injustices.

- Shirky example: woman who lost her cell phone . . . posted
   information online about missing phone/result: person who stole
   cell phone was found.

B. ***What is the book "Here Comes Everybody" about? What other information does the student note?***

The Computer and Web Resources

On your computer, you can create a Word document and type your information about sources. If you are using web sources, you can copy and paste the information into the document. One way to keep source information separate is to use a different font or color for notes you take about the ideas and exact words in the source.

Note: You can create a bookmark for websites that you use frequently or want to look at again. However, it is a good idea to also keep the information in another place in case the site goes offline or becomes unavailable.

Read the writing assignment and the document. Then circle the information in the box about the source that the student included.

author	date	month	publisher	year
country	day	page numbers	title	

Writing Assignment: What role does memorization play in learning?

Stanislas Dehaene, Ph.D., cognitive science, M.A., Applied Mathematics and Computer Science
1997
The Number Sense: How the Mind Creates Mathematics
U.S.A.
Oxford University Press

– Chinese have a greater ability for memorizing numbers in a two-second time span

– Chinese words for numbers are short, "4" is *si*; Many English words for numbers are longer, e.g., seven

EXERCISE 8

Work with another student. Discuss these questions:

- Which method for taking notes and keeping track of sources would work best for you? Why?
- What qualities make each source reliable? Useful for the writing assignments?

Guided Response Journals

As you know, a journal is a place to write your thoughts, ideas, and feelings. Guided response journals are an excellent way to make connections between source materials and your own knowledge and experiences. A response journal can also help you review exam materials and form opinions for writing assignments. Your journal may be private, or it may be shared with your classmates and teacher.

Guidelines for Writing a Guided Response Journal

- Write any ideas and thoughts that come to your mind about the topic.

- Use the personal pronoun *I* to express opinions, feelings, and questions about the topic. You can start your sentences with phrases such as:

  I think . . .   *I believe . . .*   *I don't know whether . . .*   *I wonder . . .*

- Include examples or brief stories from experience that connect with the topic.

- Do not worry about grammar or spelling mistakes.

WRITING TASK

Write a guided response journal entry.

A. *Think about what you have studied and practiced in this unit. What connections can you make to your own experiences and knowledge?*

Some examples may include . . .

- the challenges you face when looking for appropriate source materials.
- the note-taking system that works for you or that you would like to try.
- a comparison of two websites, such as the two you studied in Exercise 2.
- one of the example sources in this unit and why you would like to find out more about the topic.

B. *Find an article online, from a book, or from another print source about one of the sample writing topics from this unit:*

- Discuss how new media, such as smartphones, are affecting the way we communicate.
- Discuss the role memorization plays in learning.
- Discuss the advantages of electric cars.
- Discuss the benefits of learning a second language.

C. *Read the article and underline, highlight, or take notes. In your journal, or on a separate piece of paper, write a guided response journal entry about the article. Write for at least fifteen minutes. Follow the guidelines above. Then share your opinions and ideas with the class.*

Check Your Writing

Use this form to check your writing.

Guided Response Journal Checklist

Did you . . .

1. write for at least 15 minutes? ☐

2. write different ideas and thoughts about article? ☐

3. use the personal pronoun *I* to express your opinions, feelings, and questions about the topic? ☐

4. use phrases, such as *I believe . . . , I feel . . . , I wonder . . . , I don't know whether . . . ?* ☐

5. include examples or brief stories from your own life and experience that connect with the topic? ☐

6. Underline one or two ideas or feelings in your entry that are particularly meaningful to you.

Plagiarism, Quoting, and Paraphrasing

In academic writing, it is important to include information from outside sources and **cite** (give credit to) those sources. This shows that you have read and considered the opinions and ideas of others. In addition, citing sources indicates that you have broadened your knowledge and understanding about a topic.

You can incorporate information from outside sources into your writing by using quotations and paraphrasing. Any words or ideas you integrate into your writing from sources are given a citation— brief information about who the source is and where you found it. Then you will provide more detailed information about sources on a reference page at the end of your paper so that others can locate your original sources.

In this unit, you will learn about and practice . . .

- how to avoid plagiarism.
- how to use in-text citations correctly.
- when to use quotations and how to write them.
- how to paraphrase.

Warm Up

A. ***Work with another student. One of you is Student A, the other Student B. Follow the directions.***

1. Student A: Look at the quotation in Box 1. In your own words, tell Student B what it says. Try not to use any words from the original quote.

2. Student B: Look at the quotation in Box 2. In your own words, tell Student A what it says. Try not to use any words from the original quote.

"Any people anywhere, being inclined and having the power, have the right to rise up, and shake off the existing government, and form a new one that suits them better. This is a most valuable—a most sacred right—a right, which we hope and believe, is to liberate the world."
—Abraham Lincoln

Box 1

"I object to violence because when it appears to do good, the good is only temporary; the evil it does is permanent.
—Mahatma Ghandi

Box 2

B. *Work with another pair. Discuss these questions.*

- Was it difficult to explain the quotation in your own words? Why or why not?

- When you talked about the quotation, did you mention the originator of the quotation?

- In what situations do you usually acknowledge the originator of ideas or words that are not your own?

- If you were to write about the quotation in each box, what would be important to include? Why?

PLAGIARISM

"Plagiarism—n. the act of using someone else's words, ideas, or work and pretending they are your own."—from *Longman Dictionary of American English*

In informal conversations, we retell movies, stories, and things other people say all the time. We often acknowledge some specifics about these things, such as the title of the movie and perhaps the director, or the title of a book and its author, or the name of the person who said something.

When you write, you cannot use someone else's words or ideas and claim them as your own. Plagiarism is considered a serious offense, and many colleges and universities fail or expel students who plagiarize.

Here are some examples of **plagiarism**:

- Copying and pasting text from a source into your paper with no quotes and no acknowledgment of the source.

- Using someone else's ideas or exact words with no citation.

- Letting someone else write your essay and putting your name on it.

EXERCISE 1

Work with a group. Discuss these questions. Then share your answers with the class.

- Are there similar rules about plagiarism in your culture? What are they?

- In your culture, how do you include the words and ideas of others in papers you write for school?

- Why do you think some students plagiarize?

> ### Further Practice
>
> **Journal or Blog Topic**
>
> In your journal or on your class blog, write a paragraph to answer this question: Why do you think plagiarism is becoming a big problem in schools in the United States?

Ways to Prevent Plagiarism

Sometimes students do not understand what plagiarism is. Including others' ideas or words in a paper without acknowledging the source is a problem. It is every student's responsibility to follow the rules for acknowledging ideas and words that are not his or her own.

Guidelines to Preventing Plagiarism

- Always write down the name of your source when you are gathering information. *(See Part 3, Unit 2, for more about keeping track of sources.)*

- Give yourself enough time to gather information and write your essay. Not having enough time may lead you to copy or purchase someone else's essay. Many schools require students to submit their essays to turnitin.com, a software program that identifies plagiarized text.

- Always quote or paraphrase words that are spoken or written by others and cite them.

- Include a reference page at the end of your essay. Each of the sources cited in your essay is listed on this page, with the author's name, title of the source (book, magazine article, website, and so on), and date and location of the publication.

EXERCISE 2

Work with another student. Discuss these questions:

- What are some ways you have kept track of sources you use for research (note cards, notebook, computer) in English or your native language?

- What do you think is the best method for keeping track of sources? Why?

CITING SOURCES

When you write a paper, any information, ideas, opinions, or words that you use that are not your own must be properly cited in an **in-text citation** and again on a **reference page** so your reader can find the original source. You will learn how to write a reference page in Unit 9.

Different academic subjects require different **documentation** (citation) and **formatting styles**. A style called APA (for American Psychology Association) is generally used for psychology and the social sciences and MLA (Modern Language Association) for the arts, literature, and humanities. For the academic assignments in this part of *Writing Power*, you will use APA style.

Learning how to properly reference source materials is an important part of academic writing and is essential to avoid plagiarism.

In-text Citations

An **in-text citation** is abbreviated information about the source. This information is integrated into your sentences in different ways, depending on the sentence structure and what you are trying to say.

General format for in-text citations include:

- author's last name
- year of publication or n.d. (no date) if there is no date (common for online sources)
- (for a quotation) a page number or the paragraph number if there is no page number
- title of article or abbreviated title if author is unknown

Citations for Quotations with One Author

A **quotation** means using the exact words from the original source. When citing quotations, include the author's last name followed by the year of publication inside parentheses. After the quotation, include the page or paragraph number inside parentheses. Paragraph numbers are used for sources with no page numbers (common for online sources).

> ***Example:***
>
> Greer (2010) reported, "Yet as much as these technological tools have become commonplace on campus, there's still a caveat: The Internet can be misused, and missteps can be costly" (para. 2).

If the author is not mentioned with the quotation, include the author's name, year of publication, and page or paragraph number in parentheses at the end of the quotation.

> ***Example:***
>
> "Yet as much as these technological tools have become commonplace on campus, there's still a caveat: The Internet can be misused, and missteps can be costly" (Greer, 2010, para. 2).

Citations for Quotations with Two Authors

If there are two authors, include both last names. If the authors are cited at the end, separate their names with an **ampersand** (&).

> ***Examples:***
>
> Thompson and Yu (2011) stated "Students may not realize that whatever they post on the Web can never be erased" (p. 17).
>
> "Students may not realize that whatever they post on the Web can never be erased" (Thompson & Yu, 2011, p. 17).

Citiations with Author in a Paraphrase

In a paraphrase, use your own words to restate information or a quotation from a source. To cite a paraphrase, include the author's last name and year of publication.

> ***Examples:***
>
> Daley (2009) argued that the Internet is not owned by anyone and should therefore be free to all.
>
> The Internet is not owned by anyone and should therefore be free to all (Daley, 2009).

Citations with No Author in a Paraphrase

Websites may not include the author's name or a date. Include the title of the document or name of the organization in parentheses and the year (or n.d. if there is no date). If the title is long, shorten it to one or two words so it can be identified.

Example:

Scientists predict that by the year 2050 the world's population will reach 9 billion ("Future World," n.d).

The full title of the article is "Future World Population Estimates and Sustainable Resources," which is shortened to "Future World" in the citation.

EXERCISE 3

Work with another student. Compare the information in the citations. Then write your answers to the questions.

In-text Citation 1
According to the Pew Research Center, "Some 83% of American adults own cell phones and three-quarters of them (73%) send and receive text messages" (Smith, 2011, para. 1).

In-text Citation 2
According to a report from the Environmental Protection Agency, humans are almost solely responsible for the rise in greenhouse gases ("Climate Change," n.d.).

In-text Citation 3
Greer (2010) wrote about the potential and dangers the Internet has for students who will be entering the job market some day.

1. What information about the source is provided in citation 1? _____

2. What does *n.d.* mean in citation 2? _____ What other information

   is provided in the citation? _____

3. What type of source usually has *n.d.* in the citation? _____

4. Which citation only gives information about the source at the beginning of the

   sentence? _____ How would the citation appear if at the end of the

   sentence? _____

5. Why is there no page or paragraph number provided in citations 2 and 3?

   _____

A. *Use the information provided to rewrite the in-text citations in the correct format. Use the examples above to help you.*

1. Author: Wang
   Source: *The Internet: A Social Revolution*, page 32
   Date of Publication: 2007

   Citation: Wang stated that the Internet has caused more than one type of social revolution.

   In-text citation: _____

2. Author: None
   Source: Allain Clinic website
   Date of Publication: None

   Paragraph 1

   Citation: High cholesterol is connected to conditions such as heart attacks, strokes, and diabetes, but may be controlled with medication.

   In-text citation: _____

3. Authors: Elaine Myers, M.D., and Cyndy Das, M.D.
   Source: "Web Advice Not Always Solid" from *Health and Medicine Digest, I*
   Date of Publication: January 12, 2012

   Citation: "Consumers may not always realize that the credibility of health-related websites varies considerably."

   In-text citation: _____

4. Author: Clay Shirky
   Source: *Here Comes Everybody*
   Date of Publication: 2008

   Citation: Shirky gave the example of a woman whose cell phone was stolen, and because she posted information about the phone on the Internet the thief was caught.

   In-text citation: _____

5. Author: Galileo Galilei
   Source: *Dialogue Concerning the Two Chief Systems of the World*, no page number
   Date of Publication: 1632

   Citation: He supported the view of Copernicus that the earth revolves around the sun.

   In-text citation: _____

B. *Compare your citations with another student. Are they the same?*

USING QUOTATIONS

In writing, when you include the exact words spoken by another person or the exact words from a text you have read, you need to use **quotation marks** ("..."). The quotation marks should begin just before the first word of the quotation and end after the last word or the punctuation following the last word. In academic writing, quotations not only add interest but also, and more importantly, support your ideas, give your arguments substance, and make your writing credible. Often students are unsure of when to include a quotation, and some students use too many quotations. Your writing assignment is designed to express *your* ideas and thought-out arguments, so you must be careful to limit the number of quotations you use. You do not want to fill your paper with someone else's words and ideas instead of your own.

You should use a quotation from a source when . . .

- the author is highly regarded in and knowledgeable about the field.
- the author uses unique or special language to express an idea or thought.
- the author says something in a way that is better than your paraphrase.
- you want to use the exact spoken or written words from a source for emphasis.

Integrating Quotations

When you integrate quotations into your text, you want to carefully place them so your writing flows smoothly from one idea to the next.

Quotations can be integrated in several ways. You can include a full or partial quotation and place it at the beginning, middle, or end of a sentence. The quotation will be preceded or followed by a signal phrase, such as "As Jeff Greer, a writer for *U.S. News and World Report*," and/or a reporting verb, such as "pointed out." Partial quotations may be part of a sentence with no signal phrase or reporting verb. No matter how you integrate a quotation, the sentence must be grammatically correct and include a citation.

Integrated quotations . . .

- use quotation marks ("...") at the start and end of the quotation.
- include a comma after a signal phrase or reporting verb.
- begin with a capital letter except when it is a partial quotation.

Quotations in Texts

Notice the underlined signal phrases and bold-faced reporting verbs that accompany these examples.

Quotations after an Introductory Phrase

According to Greer (2010), "Some companies direct their own employees and interns to snoop[1] around and use all kinds of channels to get access to information" (para. 7).

In fact, as Jeff Greer (2010), a U.S. News and World Report *writer,* **pointed out,** *"Some companies direct their own employees and interns to snoop around and use all kinds of channels to get access to information" (para. 7).*

[1] *snoop*—to spy

Quotations preceded or followed by a Signal Phrase or Reporting Verb

Greer (2010) suggested, "Don't post what you are eating for lunch" (para. 12).

*"Don't post what you are eating for lunch," **suggested** Greer (2010, para. 12).*

Split Quotations

*"Some companies direct their own employees and interns to snoop around," **cautioned** Jeff Greer (2010), writer for U.S. News and World Report, "and use all kinds of channels to get access to information" (para. 7).*

Quotations with an Ellipsis (three dots . . . to show omitted words; a space goes before and after an ellipsis)

*U.S. News and World Report writer Jeff Greer (2010) **noted**, "Some companies . . . use all kinds of channels to get access to information" (para. 7).*

Quotations Longer Than 40 Words use block formatting *without* quotation marks. Notice the citation comes after the period of the last sentence.

Greer (2010) consulted with Brand-Yourself and Syracuse University to get strategies students can use to build their professional, online profile:

> *A big part of what both Brand-Yourself and Syracuse talk about is making a good impression online. That doesn't just mean smiling in your Facebook profile picture; it means showing that you're interested in your prospective field. Post links to interesting stories. Jump into debates and conversations when it's appropriate. Make LinkedIn[1] connections with recruiters and internship coordinators and join alumni networks, too. (para. 4)*

Partial Quotations inside a Paraphrase

*Students need to know that future employers may **"snoop around"** to find out as much information as they can about a prospective employee (Greer, 2010, para. 7).*

EXERCISE 5

A. **Read the quotations. Write the type of quotation from the list on pages 129–130. Then add the quotation marks and appropriate punctuation.**

1. _____

   Greer (2010) wrote There's much more to using social media tools than just quick updates and playful banter[2] among friends (para. 1)

2. _____

   There's much more to using social media tools than just quick updates and playful banter among friends pointed out Greer (2010, para. 1)

3. _____

   According to Greer (2010) There's much more to using social media tools than just quick updates and playful banter among friends (para. 1)

[1] LinkedIn—an online site people use to network with other professionals. People can post their resumes, professional profiles, and other work-related information.
[2] *banter*—playful conversation among friends

4. _____

There's much more to using social media tools commented Greer (2010) than just quick updates and playful banter among friends (para. 1)

5. _____

Greer (2010) emphasized that although most students use social networking for playful banter and keeping current with others, they could also take advantage of the other ways to use the media (para. 1)

6. _____

Greer (2010) stated There's much more to using social media tools than . . . playful banter among friends (para. 1)

B. *Discuss your answers with the class.*

Reporting Verbs and Signal Phrases

As you have just learned, **reporting verbs** introduce or follow a quotation and indicate the transition between your words and the quotation. **Signal phrases** such as *according to* or *in the words of* acknowledge the source. In APA style, reporting verbs and phrases are written in the simple past or present perfect. For example: *say* becomes *said* or *has said* and *write* becomes *wrote* or *has written*. There are many different reporting verbs. Deciding which ones to use will give your writing variety, provide emphasis, and help clarify the information you are quoting.

EXERCISE 6

A. *Work with another student. Check (✓) the reporting verbs and signal words and phrases you know. Look up the meanings of any words you do not know. Write the meanings in your notebook.*

Reporting Verbs				
☐ acknowledge	☐ ask	☐ comment	☐ note	☐ stress
☐ admit	☐ assert	☐ conclude	☐ point out	☐ suggest
☐ advise	☐ believe	☐ deny	☐ promise	☐ warn
☐ announce	☐ caution	☐ emphasize	☐ report	☐ wonder
☐ argue	☐ claim	☐ insist	☐ say	☐ write
Signal Phrases				
☐ According to	☐ [Affiliation, title, Name], noted	☐ As [name] [year] suggested	☐ In [Name]'s opinion	☐ In the words of [Name]

B. *On your own, read the quotations. Then on a separate piece of paper, rewrite each one, changing the quotation type and reporting verb or signal phrase. Be sure to properly cite the source. Use the Quotation Types and formats on pages 129–130 to help you.*

All quotations are from the article below. Paragraph numbers are in parentheses.

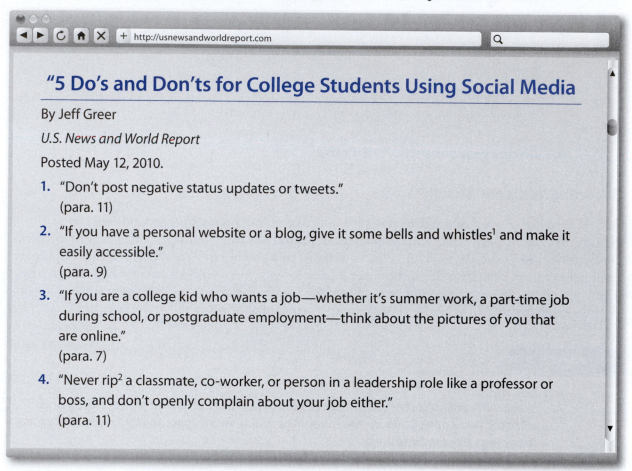

http://usnewsandworldreport.com

"5 Do's and Don'ts for College Students Using Social Media

By Jeff Greer

U.S. News and World Report

Posted May 12, 2010.

1. "Don't post negative status updates or tweets."
   (para. 11)

2. "If you have a personal website or a blog, give it some bells and whistles[1] and make it easily accessible."
   (para. 9)

3. "If you are a college kid who wants a job—whether it's summer work, a part-time job during school, or postgraduate employment—think about the pictures of you that are online."
   (para. 7)

4. "Never rip[2] a classmate, co-worker, or person in a leadership role like a professor or boss, and don't openly complain about your job either."
   (para. 11)

[1] *bells and whistles*—extra features to make something attractive or special
[2] *rip*—to say or write something negative about someone

C. *Work with another student. Check each other's quotations by answering these questions:*

- What type of quotation is each one?

- What are the signal phrases and reporting verbs? Are there quotation marks at the start and end of the quotation?

- Is there a comma before/after a signal phrase or reporting verb?

- Does the quotation begin with a capital letter if it is not a partial quotation?

- Is the source properly cited with the author's name, year of publication, and paragraph number?

- Are the commas and parentheses used correctly in the citation?

Paraphrasing

When you use ideas or information from source materials in your essay, use either a quotation or paraphrase. A **paraphrase** expresses the same ideas as the original source and includes a citation.

When you paraphrase, do not copy the exact words or phrases from the original source or use the same sentence structure. This would be considered plagiarism.

General Format for Citations with a Paraphrase

In a paraphrase, use your own words to restate information or a quotation from a source. To cite a paraphrase, include the author's last name and year of publication.

Examples:

Daley (2009) argued that the Internet is not owned by anyone and should therefore be free to all.

The Internet is not owned by anyone and should therefore be free to all (Daley, 2009).

Characteristics of a Paraphrase

A paraphrase should . . .

- contain the main ideas and important details of the original.
  Read the original material carefully and make sure you fully understand its meaning. Look up definitions to vocabulary words you do not know.

- be about the same length as the original.
  This is a general rule, but sometimes a paraphrase is longer or shorter. The important thing is not to leave out information or add ideas that are not part of the original material.

- use synonyms.
  Use different words from the original. Use a **thesaurus** (a book in which words are put in groups with other words that have a similar meaning) or dictionary to help you. Many word-processing programs also have this feature.

- use a different sentence structure from the original.
  Copying parts of sentences or using the same sentence structure from the original is considered plagiarism. Once you have read the original material, put it away. Then write what it is about in your own words. Re-ordering or re-organizing the ideas will help you. Later you can refer to the original to check that you have included all the ideas.

- use an in-text citation.
  You must include this information to avoid plagiarism.

Look at these examples of unacceptable and acceptable paraphrases for the quotation below.

Quotation

Thompson and Yu (2011) stated, "Students may not realize that whatever they post on the Web can never be erased" (p. 17).

Unacceptable: *Because the content on the Internet lasts forever, students may not be aware that they cannot remove anything they have put there.* **(No In-text Citation)**

Unacceptable: *Thompson and Yu (2011) said that students may not know that all the things they post online may never be erased.* **(Uses the Exact Words and Structure of the Original)**

Unacceptable: *According to Thompson and Yu (2011), the Internet provides students with a way that they can always be remembered.* **(Does Not Express the Ideas of the Original)**

Acceptable: *The Internet is permanent, so students who want to remove content, for example, their photos or comments, cannot. Students may not be aware of this (Thompson & Yu, 2011).*

Notice how the acceptable paraphrase is about the same length and expresses the same ideas as in the original and includes a citation. It also uses synonyms or words that have a similar meaning to those in the quotation, but are not exactly the same.

web → Internet

not realize → not be aware of

erase → remove

The sentence structure in the paraphrase is also different from the original. The paraphrase is two sentences but retains the ideas and important details of the original.

EXERCISE 7

A. Work with another student. Read the original passage and paraphrases and check (✓) acceptable or unacceptable. If it is unacceptable, write the reason.

Original
"Remember, just because your Facebook profile has privacy settings doesn't mean you're invisible online" (Greer, 2010, para. 7).

Paraphrase 1
Even though social media sites allow you to choose the information you want to make public, everything can be found on the web.

☐ Acceptable

☐ Unacceptable Reason: _____

Paraphrase 2
Social media sites allow you to keep your information as private as you want so you can be invisible online (Greer, 2010, para. 7).

☐ Acceptable

☐ Unacceptable Reason: _____

Paraphrase 3
Greer (2010) cautioned that it is important to be aware that anything you post online can be found even though social media sites provide ways for you to control the kind of information you make public.

☐ Acceptable

☐ Unacceptable Reason: _____

Paraphrase 4
Do not forget that just because you can choose privacy settings for your Facebook profile, it does not indicate you are completely invisible on the Net (Greer, 2010, para. 7).

☐ Acceptable

☐ Unacceptable Reason: _____

B. *Work with another pair and compare answers and reasons.*

Paraphrasing—Using Synonyms

Paraphrasing is one of the biggest challenges for language learners because it requires a large vocabulary. Keeping a separate vocabulary notebook can be helpful. Use a dictionary or thesaurus to help you find the appropriate synonyms or phrases you will need to complete the exercises in this section.

EXERCISE 8

A. *Work with another student. Read the original passage and the paraphrase. Match the synonym or phrase from the paraphrase to the original. Write the letter on the line.*

Original
"If you're a freshman, you probably aren't ready to commit to being a lawyer or marketing rep just yet, but you can use social media to interact with recent college graduates and professionals from multiple fields" (Greer, 2010, para. 5).

Paraphrase
Connecting with the university's former students or experts from various areas via the Internet is a good way for a new student who may not have decided on a career path to get started (Greer, 2010).

Original	Paraphrase
_____ 1. ". . . aren't ready to commit . . ."	**a.** a career path
_____ 2. ". . . recent college graduates . . ."	**b.** various
_____ 3. ". . . professionals . . ."	**c.** may not have decided on
_____ 4. ". . . multiple . . ."	**d.** university's former students
_____ 5. ". . . a lawyer or marketing rep . . ."	**e.** experts

B. *Work with another student. Read the original and the paraphrase. Identify synonyms and phrases in the paraphrase and match them to the original. Write your answers in the chart.*

Original
"This isn't a one-time thing when you are just looking for jobs," Klamm says. "It's more of an ongoing process. It's important that you have some type of presence at all times" (Greer, 2010, para. 6).

Paraphrase
Dan Klamm from Syracuse University's Career Services office advised students to always be actively present on the Internet in some way because job hunting does not just start and then stop but rather continues over a period of time (Greer, 2010).

Original	Paraphrase
presence	
at all times	
looking for a job	
a one-time thing	
ongoing	

Paraphrasing—Sentence Structure

When you write your paraphrase, changing the words is not enough. You will also need to change the sentence structure.

After you read the original and feel you have a solid understanding of the content, put it away. Take a minute and think about how you might tell someone about what you read. As your own way of organizing ideas starts to formulate how you would re-tell the original ideas, start writing your paraphrase.

EXERCISE 9

A. *Work with another student. Read the original passage and the paraphrases. Compare the structures in both paraphrases with the original. Then discuss these questions:*

- How are the structures similar to and different from the structures in the original?
- How does the organization of the original ideas change in paraphrase 1? Paraphrase 2?

Original
"This isn't a one-time thing when you are just looking for jobs," Klamm says. "It's more of an ongoing process. It's important that you have some type of presence at all times" (Greer, 2010, para. 6).

Paraphrase 1
Klamm noted that looking for a job does not happen one time. Finding a job is ongoing. It is key to have a presence all the time (Greer, 2010).

Paraphrase 2
Klamm advised students to always be actively present on the Internet in some way because job hunting does not start and then stop but rather continues over a period of time (Greer, 2010).

B. **On your own, write paraphrases for the quotations you wrote in Exercise 6B. Follow these steps:**

1. Look up the meanings to any words you do not know.

2. Select words and phrases and find synonyms to use for each.

3. Think about how you would tell someone about the passage in your own words. Experiment with different ways to re-organize or re-order the original.

4. On a separate piece of paper, write a paraphrase for the original.

WRITING TASK

Write one to two paragraphs about a topic using paraphrases and quotations.

A. **Review the information on quotations and paraphrases in this unit.**

B. **Choose one of these topics:**

- Give advice to classmates about how to create an online profile. Explain why maintaining it and building it are important for university admission and job hunting.

- Give advice to classmates about appropriate and inappropriate communication for a social or professional media site.

C. **Write one to two paragraphs about the topic you chose. Include in your paragraph(s) one quotation that you wrote in Exercise 6B and one paraphrase that you wrote in Exercise 9B. You may also choose to write a new quotation or paraphrase based on this passage:**

A big part of what both Brand-Yourself and Syracuse talk about is making a good impression online. That doesn't just mean smiling in your Facebook profile picture; it means showing that you're interested in your prospective field. Post links to interesting stories. Jump into debates and conversations when it's appropriate. Make LinkedIn connections with recruiters and internship coordinators and join alumni networks, too. (Greer, 2010, para. 4)

Check Your Writing

A. Use this form to check your paragraph(s), or exchange paragraphs with another student and check each other's writing.

Paragraph Checklist

Quotation

1. How did the quotation support the writer's point? (author highly regarded, unique language, used for emphasis) _____

2. What type of integrated quotation does the writer use (introductory phrase, split, ellipsis)? _____

3. The quotation uses quotation marks ("...") at the start and end of the quotation. ☐

4. The quotation includes a comma after a signal phrase or reporting verb. ☐

5. The quotation begins with a capital letter unless it is a partial quotation. ☐

6. The quotation includes an in-text citation. ☐

Paraphrase

7. How did the paraphrase support the writer's point? _____

8. The paraphrase expresses the main ideas and details from the original quotation. ☐

9. The paraphrase uses synonyms or phrases that are different from the original. ☐

10. The paraphrase uses different sentence structure from the original. ☐

11. The paraphrase includes an in-text citation. ☐

12. What changes do you suggest to improve the paragraph(s)?

_____

_____

B. Make changes to improve your paragraph(s). Remember to check your writing for grammar, spelling, and punctuation errors.

Summary Writing

Summary writing is one of the most important skills for academic studies, test taking, and the work world. Academic writing assignments often include summaries of important ideas from source materials to support the writer's point of view, provide evidence for arguments, and present different perspectives.

Writing a good summary involves having a solid understanding of the key concepts presented in the source materials. Writing summaries will help you review, condense, and reinforce the information you are studying.

In this unit you will . . .

- review the characteristics of a summary.
- identify key ideas in source materials.
- sort and select information for use in both a single source and an integrated summary.
- write a summary using information from two or more sources.

Warm Up

A. **Work in a group. Read these statements about summary writing. Mark each statement T (*True*) or F (*False*).**

_____ 1. A summary is about the same length as the original.

_____ 2. A summary is shorter than the original.

_____ 3. A summary may include sentences copied from the original.

_____ 4. A summary is written in your own words.

_____ 5. A summary may not include your own opinion.

_____ 6. A summary does not require information about the source.

_____ 7. A summary may include new updated information even if it is not included in the original.

_____ 8. A summary includes most of the details, examples, and descriptions of the original.

_____ 9. A summary includes the main points of the original.

B. **Check your answers at the bottom of the page. Then compare them with the class.**

Warm Up Answers
1. F, 2. T, 3. F, 4. T, 5. T, 6. F, 7. F, 8. F, 9. T

A SUMMARY FROM A SINGLE SOURCE

You may have practiced writing summaries from a single source. As you have just seen in the Warm Up, a good summary has some distinguishing characteristics.

EXERCISE 1

A. Preview the title of the online article. Discuss these questions with the class:

- What does *generation gap* mean?
- Based on the title, what do you think the article will be about?

B. Read the article.

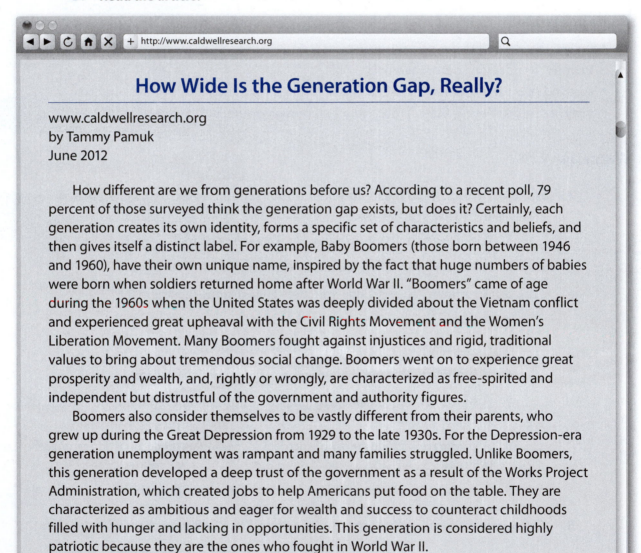

How Wide Is the Generation Gap, Really?

www.caldwellresearch.org
by Tammy Pamuk
June 2012

How different are we from generations before us? According to a recent poll, 79 percent of those surveyed think the generation gap exists, but does it? Certainly, each generation creates its own identity, forms a specific set of characteristics and beliefs, and then gives itself a distinct label. For example, Baby Boomers (those born between 1946 and 1960), have their own unique name, inspired by the fact that huge numbers of babies were born when soldiers returned home after World War II. "Boomers" came of age during the 1960s when the United States was deeply divided about the Vietnam conflict and experienced great upheaval with the Civil Rights Movement and the Women's Liberation Movement. Many Boomers fought against injustices and rigid, traditional values to bring about tremendous social change. Boomers went on to experience great prosperity and wealth, and, rightly or wrongly, are characterized as free-spirited and independent but distrustful of the government and authority figures.

Boomers also consider themselves to be vastly different from their parents, who grew up during the Great Depression from 1929 to the late 1930s. For the Depression-era generation unemployment was rampant and many families struggled. Unlike Boomers, this generation developed a deep trust of the government as a result of the Works Project Administration, which created jobs to help Americans put food on the table. They are characterized as ambitious and eager for wealth and success to counteract childhoods filled with hunger and lacking in opportunities. This generation is considered highly patriotic because they are the ones who fought in World War II.

It is not surprising then that research continues to highlight traits associated with each new generation. Millennials, or Generation Y, were born around 1990. They are more likely to have tattoos than Baby Boomers and Gen Xers born between 1961 and 1981. Millennials also show more overall openmindedness and tolerance of different lifestyles. Furthermore, Millennials use more technology than previous generations, and 75 percent use social media. However, even with these differences from generation to generation, the poll found that some things never change no matter how hard each generation tries to claim its own cultural and social norms. For example, more than 50 percent of the population surveyed still believe in the importance of marriage and want to own their own homes. Maybe the generation gap is more in our imaginations than we think.

B. *Check the meanings of any words you need to know to understand the main idea. Underline key words and phrases that relate to the main point of the article. Identify important information or examples that support the main idea. Mark them with a "*".*

C. *Work with another student. Compare the key words, phrases, important information, and examples you each underlined. Decide what the main idea is. Answer the questions to help you.*

1. How many people, according to the survey, believe there is a generation gap?

2. What are the specific generation groups mentioned in the article?

3. What are some examples used to show the similarities and differences of the generation groups?

4. What is the main point the writer makes about how people perceive the generation gap?

D. *Now read the two summaries.*

Summary 1

> In her article "How Wide Is the Generation Gap, Really?", Tammy Pamuk (2012) explores the question of whether or not the generation gap truly exists. She begins by reviewing two generations, the Baby Boomers and the Depression-era group, and how quite different they are in terms of certain values and attitudes that are often attributed to each. She continues by referring to surveys that support this view of how each new generation forms its own culture and social norms in contrast to previous generations. However, Pamuk brings in evidence that may show that each generation is not very different from the generation that precedes it. She concludes by noting that a recent poll indicates that despite the differences, big items such as marriage and home ownership are valued by the majority across all generations, and so the idea of this difference between generations is not as big as the polls would make you believe.

Summary 2

> Each new generation has its own characteristics. One example is the Depression-era generation: ambitious people who wanted wealth and success because of childhoods filled with hunger and few opportunities. In contrast are the Millennials who are more tech savvy—75 percent of them have social media pages. However, from generation to generation, individuals who were surveyed believed that the generation gap was a myth. Instead the surveys showed that despite each generation's particular characteristics, certain beliefs, such as getting married and owning a home, are still true.

E. *Work with another pair. Discuss the two summaries. Does each one have the characteristics of a good summary? Use the checklist to help you.*

The summary . . .	Summary 1	Summary 2
1. is shorter than the original text.	☐	☐
2. only includes the main ideas.	☐	☐
3. does not include small, unimportant details.	☐	☐
4. does not use exact, full sentences from the original text.	☐	☐
5. includes a reference to the original text.	☐	☐

INTEGRATED SUMMARIES

There are two types of summaries that are most commonly used in academic writing. The first type, and the one you just reviewed and practiced, is a **summary of one source**. The second type is called an **integrated summary**. For this type, you examine two or more sources about one topic and integrate them into a report or summary.

The information you might need to integrate may come from a lecture, a survey, a textbook reading, a discussion, or a research study. For example, you may be asked to show how the information from your professor's lecture and the information from your textbook or another reading relate to each other. You may be required to do this for exams with short essay questions or in longer academic essays. Very often, standardized tests require an integrated summary. In all of these situations, you will need to demonstrate your ability to synthesize various views about one topic and organize them in a cohesive piece of writing.

Understanding the Source Material

The first step in preparing to write an integrated summary is to have a thorough understanding of the information in your sources. Here are some things to consider.

Identify and learn new vocabulary.
Look up the meanings of any words or key terms you do not know. Write them in a special notebook to refer to later when you write your summary.

Think about how the sources are related to your writing topic.
Study the sources carefully. Think about how the ideas in the sources relate to the topic and each other. Do the sources show reasons, causes or effects, similarities or differences, problems or solutions, or the advantages or disadvantages of an issue, method, or product? Ask yourself questions such as: What happened? What was the cause? What was the effect? Who or what was involved? Where did it happen? Why did it happen? When did it happen?

Determine the author's opinion or attitude.
Look for words that show the opinion or attitude of the author(s) of the source. Reporting verbs such as *argue, explore, dispute, claim,* and so on will give you an idea of the writer's opinion. Determine whether the author agrees with, disagrees with, or is neutral about an issue, a piece of research, or cultural or social trend. Try to identify examples or details the author uses to illustrate various viewpoints.

> ### *Example:*
>
> *The woman, who is a victim of identity theft, is extremely upset and feels helpless—and rightly so. Identify theft is a devastating experience for the victim.*

In this example, *extremely upset* and *feels helpless* express the author's impression of the victim's feelings mentioned in the source; *and rightly so* indicates that the author thinks those feelings are justified. A *devastating experience* reflects the author's opinion about identity theft.

> ### *Example:*
>
> *The financial institution claims that it uses safe security systems and never discloses personal information. The issue of identity theft continues to . . .*

In the second example, the reporting verb *claim* means the statement is debatable and the content of the material will most likely present one or more points of view about an issue; the word *issue* indicates that the topic is controversial.

Take Notes

Identify the main points of the source and highlight or underline them. Then, without looking at the source, write on a separate piece of paper everything you can remember using your own words. Make sure your paraphrased passages use **synonyms** (different words) and sentence structures from the original. If you use key words or terms, make sure to use quotation marks.

> **Note:** *See Unit 3 for more on quotations and paraphrases.*

Organizing the Summary

Sort the information.

Once you understand the sources and have identified the main ideas, sort the various types of information according to how they relate to each other. For example, the information may explain causes and effects, similarities and differences, problems and solutions, or reasons why. You can use a graphic organizer or chart to help you.

> *Example:*

Source 1 Houston's Restaurant Workers	Source 2 AP Reporter	Same/Different
presents the issue of whether online communication is private or public	presents the issue of whether online communication is private or public	same
employees (restaurant workers)	employee (reporter)	same—employees
used social networking site made negative comments about employer was fired for online comments	used social networking site made negative comments about employer was given a warning by employer	same—used social networking sites same different

Make a simple outline.

After you sort the information, make a simple outline to organize the sequence of the information and determine how you will integrate the various sources. One way to order the information is to summarize the first source in the first paragraph. In the second paragraph, summarize information from the second source and show how it relates to the first. For example, if your essay is about whether online communication should be considered private or public, you could discuss how private, online conversations are perceived from both an employee's and employer's point of view. Your integrated summary will show both sides, one of which supports your thesis—the point you are trying to make.

Example:

Topic: Online Communication: Is it public or private?

I. Source about private online communication (paragraph 1)

   A. restaurant workers post negative comments about employer on private online chat

      1. coworker shares password with restaurant manager

      2. manager reads comment

   B. restaurant's reaction to negative comments and employee's response

      1. restaurant fires workers

      2. workers react; claim invasion of privacy

      3. workers sue employer

II. Source about another private online communication (paragraph 2)

   A. news reporter posts negative comments about news publisher on private online chat

      1. coworker shares password with employer, a well-known news service

      2. news service reads reporter's personal, private, online comments

   B. employer's reaction to negative comments

      1. news service strongly warns reporter against stating personal opinions online

      2. news service is worried about its "reputation as an unbiased news source"

   C. both reports emphasize issue of privacy online and that no current laws deal with the problem

---

Cite your sources.

Include citations of your sources. Information about the author, title, and other details usually appear in the first sentence of the summary section of each source. *(For more information about citing sources, see Unit 3.)*

A. *Read the writing topic and the titles of the sources. Then read the sample integrated summary.*

Topic: Employees have a right to say whatever they want on a private social networking site.

Source 1
"Privacy vs. Professionalism"
CNN.com/studentnews
2009

Source 2
"AP Reporter Reprimanded for Facebook Post"
By David Kravets
wired.com
2009

Atsuko Dan
April 28, 2012
Impacts of Social Networking
Professor Visser

In a CNN video report (2009), the issue of online privacy is challenged by two workers from Houston's Restaurant in New Jersey. The two workers posted negative comments about their work situation on their private, password-protected, social networking site. The workers made these comments not knowing that another worker had given the password to the restaurant manager, who then read their online chat. As a result, the restaurant fired the employees for what they stated was the workers' "unprofessional conduct" and for revealing company secrets. The workers were outraged and claimed that their privacy had been invaded. Finally, the workers argued that they had a right to voice their opinion in a private, online community.

According to an article by David Kravets (2009) in wired.com, another similar incident occurred, but with less severe consequences for a journalist employed by the major news service, the Associated Press (AP). Like the restaurant workers, the reporter made negative comments about his business on his social networking site and one of his coworkers provided his employer access to the comments. As a result, the reporter's employer, AP, gave the reporter a strong warning because publicly posting his personal opinions "may damage the AP's reputation as an unbiased source of news (para.6)." However, in this case, the reporter was not fired. Both reports emphasized the growing controversy surrounding the issue of online communication and privacy and that current laws do not exist to address the situation.

B. Work with another student. Answer these questions about the integrated summary. Write your answers on the lines.

Which paragraph presents only the main ideas from Source 1? _____

Which paragraph presents the main ideas from Source 2? _____

Underline the words, phrases, or sentences that show where the two sources are integrated.

Where is article 1 cited in the summary?

_____

Where is article 2 cited in the summary?

_____

How does the integrated summary provide support for the writing topic?

_____

_____

_____

EXERCISE 3

A. Preview the vocabulary from one source for an integrated summary. Check any new words or phrases in the dictionary and add them to your vocabulary notebook.

blanket policy	legislative	stance
disclose	overreach	The American Civil Liberties Union (ACLU)
invasion of privacy	overstep	veteran

B. Discuss the meanings with the class.

Note: *See Part 2, Unit 1 for more on Building Vocabulary.*

A. *Read source number 1.*

http://www.salon.com

Government Employer Asks Man for Facebook Login During Job Interview

By Adam Clark Estes
salon.com
2011

When do background checks go too deep? When is a routine security measure a total invasion of privacy? When Facebook is involved, suggests the American Civil Liberties Union (ACLU).

The ACLU recently sent a letter to the Maryland Department of Corrections in reference to a blanket policy requiring applicants to submit social media log-ins and passwords for routine background checks, reports the *Atlantic*'s Alexis Madrigal. The letter details the experience of Officer Robert Collins, a seven-year veteran of the department, who spoke out about the new policy after applying for a new position. In a statement for ACLU Maryland, Collins described his employer's request and his reaction:

> Here I am, a U.S. citizen who hasn't broken any laws, who hasn't committed any crime, and I have an employer looking at my personal communications, my personal posts, my personal pictures, you know, looking at my personally identifiable information . . . you know, where my religious, my political beliefs, my sexuality; all of these things are possibly disclosed on this page. It's an absolute total invasion, and an overreach, and overstep of their power.

It's unclear how long the policy has been in place, but the ACLU's stance is clear. Calling the state's request for such deep access for a routine background check a "frightening and illegal invasion of privacy" that raises "significant legal concerns," the ACLU draws attention to how little legislative attention has been paid to online privacy.

B. Work with another student. Discuss these questions:

1. Who are the people in the article?

2. What organization's or departments are mentioned in the article?

3. What problem is identified in the article? What words or phrases express the author's, the organization's, or the people's feelings, opinions, or position about the issue?

4. Where do the events in the article take place?

5. When did the events happen?

6. Why did the problem occur?

7. What were the effects of the situation?

C. On a separate piece of paper, make notes about the main ideas of the article. Then compare your notes with another student. To your notes, add any important information that is missing. Save your notes.

EXERCISE 5

A. Preview the vocabulary from a second source for an integrated summary. Check any new words or phrases in the dictionary and add them to your vocabulary notebook.

allegedly	complied (base form *comply*)	stunning
astounding	disregard	suing (base form *sue*)
cheerleader	reprimand	violate

B. Discuss the meanings with the class.

A. **Read source number 2.**

School Sued for Reading Student's Private Facebook Messages

By Wendy Davis
July 23, 2009
mediapost.com

Authorities at Pearl High School in Pearl, Mississippi, have allegedly joined the managers of a Houston's in New Jersey and officials from Bozeman, Montana, in demonstrating a stunning disregard of people's online privacy.

Mandi Jackson, a student at the school, says that a cheerleading coach, Tommie Hill, demanded that Jackson disclose her Facebook password.

Hill then allegedly logged in and retrieved private messages—not posts on her public wall, but confidential communications—between Jackson and another cheerleader and shared those with school officials. Jackson alleges that the school "publicly reprimanded, punished and humiliated" her for the contents of those messages. Among other measures, the school allegedly didn't allow her to participate in some school-sponsored events.

Jackson is now suing the school in federal court in Mississippi for violating her privacy rights.

Assuming her allegations are true, it's astounding that school authorities and their agents could have thought they had the right to intercept private messages between students.

It's not clear why Jackson complied with the request that she reveal her password, but she's not alone in doing so. Even adults have been pressured into disclosing passwords to private accounts.

In Bozeman, Montana, applicants for city jobs apparently revealed their user names and passwords to social networking sites in response to questions from the city, until officials put an end to the practice last month.

And in Hackensack, NJ, an employee at a Houston's told a manager the password to a private MySpace group that had been created by other employees to complain about the restaurant's management. Houston's fired two workers, who then sued. Last month they won their case when a jury in Newark, NJ, decided the restaurant violated federal and state privacy laws and awarded the former employees $17,000.

B. **On a separate piece of paper, create your own questions about Source 2. Use the questions in Exercise 4B to help you.**

C. **Work with another student. Exchange papers and answer each others' questions.**

D. **On your own, make notes about the main ideas of the article on a separate piece of paper. Then compare your notes with another student. Add any important information that is missing to your notes. Save your notes.**

Complete the chart with the main ideas from Source 1 and Source 2. Then use the chart to help you sort and organize your information.

	Source 1	Source 2	Same/Different
people	employees	student/employees	different
organizations			
problem			
words that express opinions or points of view			
where events occurred			
when events occurred			
cause(s) of the situation			
effect(s) of the situation			

Complete this outline for an integrated summary. Use your completed chart in Exercise 9 to help you.

Topic:

I. Invasion of privacy in State of Maryland, employee and ACLU protest

    A. Department of Corrections employee, Officer Collins

        1. Collins has to give logins to his Facebook account as part of a normal background check

        2. _____

    B. ACLU writes letter

        1. supports Collins: employers should not be able to view employees private, online communication

        2. _____

II. Similar incidents in other states

    A. State of Mississippi

        1. _____

        2. _____

    B. State of Montana

        1. _____

        2. _____

    C. State of New Jersey

        1. _____

        2. _____

    D.

WRITING TASK

Write an integrated summary of two articles.

    A. *Reread the two articles on pages 148 and 150.*

    B. *Use your notes, charts, and outline on pages 149–152 to help you write a summary that synthesizes information from both articles.*

Check Your Writing

A. *Use this form to check your summary, or exchange summaries with another student and check each other's writing.*

Summary Checklist

The summary . . .

1. is shorter than the original. ☐
2. does not include sentences copied from the original sources. ☐
3. does not include new information or the opinion of the student. ☐
4. includes references to the original sources. ☐
5. Were there any unimportant details included in the summary? If so, write a question mark (?) in front of them on the paragraph. _____
6. Which paragraph presents the main ideas from Source 1? _____
7. Which paragraph presents the main ideas from Source 2? _____
8. Where in the summary is the information from both sources integrated? _____ _____ Underline the words, phrases or sentences that show this.
9. Put an asterisk (*) next to one or two sentences in the summary that you particularly liked.
10. What questions do you have for the writer? Write them here.

    _____

    _____

11. What changes do you suggest to improve the summary?

    _____

    _____

B. *Make changes to improve your summary. Remember to check your writing for grammar, spelling, and punctuation errors.*

Further Practice

Journal or Blog Topic

Choose an interesting current news story. Read articles about the story from at least two different sources. Write an integrated summary in your journal or post it on your class blog. If you use the class blog, post comments on your classmates' summaries with your personal opinion about the news story.

Prewriting Techniques

Inspiration is a necessity for all great ideas. Sometimes it happens in an accidental way, and sometimes it happens through methodical exploration. As you probably know, **prewriting**, or brainstorming, is the method many writers use to generate ideas about their topics.

In an academic setting, your teacher will assign a writing topic based on something you have been studying or tell you to find your own topic, research it, and develop a thesis. Brainstorming is the first step in finding out what you already know and what you will need to research.

There are a number of ways you can begin to generate ideas about your topic. Regardless of the method you choose, be sure to keep an open mind as you are exploring your topic. In this stage of the writing process, all ideas are important. You never know when a small idea may turn out to be the centerpiece of your essay.

In this unit, you will practice the following prewriting techniques:

- using library resources
- freewriting
- using Internet key word searches
- listing
- clustering
- making a T-chart

Warm Up

A. **Work in a group. Look at the creations and inventions. How do you think the innovators developed their ideas? Write the numbers of the activities under each picture. Add more activities to the list if you can.**

1. took a walk

2. went to a museum

3. found a quiet place to think

4. did some drawing

5. did some brainstorming like clustering, or listing

6. listened to music

7. went to the library and browsed through books and did some research

8. talked to a librarian

9. did some freewriting

1. The first book, *The Diamond Sutra* (China, AD 868)	2. The piano (Bartolomeo Cristofori, 1710)	3. The printing press (Johannes Gutenberg, 1450)	4. The bifocal lens (Benjamin Franklin, 1780)	5. The alphabet (Sinai and Egypt, second millennium BCE)
_____	_____	_____	_____	_____
_____	_____	_____	_____	_____
_____	_____	_____	_____	_____
_____	_____	_____	_____	_____
_____	_____	_____	_____	_____

B. *Discuss these questions with your group:*

- Which activities from the list in Exercise A have you tried to get ideas for writing assignments?

- What are some other ways you gather and organize your ideas? Which ones have helped you the most to prepare for your writing assignments?

USING LIBRARY RESOURCES

Your school or public library is one of the most useful places to start searching for information and gathering ideas for writing assignments. A library is designed for researching, studying, thinking, and accessing information.

At the library you can . . .

- talk to a librarian and get suggestions about where to look for information.
- access the electronic data bases—digitized documents of academic journals, books, magazines, and so on.
- browse through the stacks (bookshelves), for books and reference materials.
- use computers, printers, and copiers.
- find a quiet area to study.

Look at this example from a student's notes about his visit to the library to do research for the writing topic: Should the postal service be discontinued?

Librarian's suggestions for areas to research	My notes & ideas
<u>Academic journal articles</u> research about postal service around the world research about technology and postal service	– government planning to close hundreds of post offices & eventually shut down the entire system (online article "Postal Service Going Bankrupt").
<u>Books</u> history of the postal service study of postage stamps & related items social & educational value connected to collecting stamps	– closing post office would leave many people with no way to send or receive letters. Not everyone can afford Internet, lives near library or has free access to Internet. – closing postal service means loss of many jobs (research study, Newton & Bai). How would this affect economy? Where would these people find other jobs?
<u>Online articles and websites</u> costs for postal service, operation, postal rates, printing postage job loss, businesses lose advertising in mail stamps & fundraising for cure for cancer movement National Postal Museum	– stamp collecting excellent way for young children (& adults!) to learn about history, geography, money, & different cultures (History of Philately, 2001). Some stamps help fund research for cure for breast cancer. If no postal service, no stamps.

EXERCISE 1

Visit your school, university, or city library. Start looking for ideas about the topic. Follow these steps.

Topic: The issue of safety and cell phone use while driving

1. Talk to the librarian. Get suggestions about where to find information; write them in your notebook.

2. Use the library database to search for information. Print out articles that you find.

3. Find and select books related to the topic.

4. Study the information you have found and take notes. Carefully document your sources and paraphrase any notes you take *(see Unit 2)*.

5. Write a paragraph about your library experience. How did it help you generate ideas about your topic? What difficulties did you encounter?

6. Bring your paragraph and your research notes to class; share them with your classmates. Compare your sources.

FREEWRITING

You may have practiced freewriting or journal writing in Part 1 as a way to increase your fluency in English. In this unit, you are going to practice freewriting as a fast and easy way to get your mind focused on an assigned topic. With **freewriting**, you do not have to worry about grammar or spelling. You simply write down everything that comes into your head about the topic, and you often write for a set amount of time. It is like a free-association exercise.

EXERCISE 2

A. ***On a separate piece of paper, write everything that comes into your head about this topic or a topic given to you by your teacher. Write for ten minutes without stopping.***

   Topic: Explain the advantages and disadvantages of electronic readers

B. ***Work with another student. Share your freewrites. Then, on a separate piece of paper, combine your ideas. Compare your list with the whole class. What other ideas can you add to your list? What opinions have you formed about the topic?***

USING INTERNET KEY WORD SEARCHES

You can do an Internet search using key words to help you generate ideas about and narrow any topic.

Look at this sample of the path a key word search took and the possibilities it presented. The student typed the word *communication* in the search box, and a list of related topics appeared. Then the student clicked on related subjects to open up more topics. This type of brainstorm is almost like a listing brainstorm, in which you list all of the ideas you can think of, but the Internet does it for you.

Notice the different areas of focus and points of view listed in the searches.

Searches of key word *communication*
types of communication	communication articles
communication skills	effective communication
importance of communication	interpersonal communication
	history of communication

Searches for *interpersonal communication*
definition of interpersonal communication	communication skills
nonverbal communication	theories

Searches for *non-verbal communication*
learning disorders/cues/nonverbal communication examples, skills, images, in gangs, activities, body language, activities/importance of in professional settings/kinesics examples/active/nonverbal communication percentage, articles, types, definition

A. Work in a group. Look at the broad topics. Choose one and brainstorm a list of topics you might find if you did a key word search about it.

- Careers in biology
- Public transportation
- Cultural identity theories
- Internet privacy

B. Use the topic your group chose in Exercise A. On your own, do a key word search using a search engine on the Internet. In your notebook, write a list of all the topics you find.

C. Compare your results to the list you created with your group. Which topics were on your brainstorm list? Which ones were not on your list? Were there any that were surprising?

D. Work with another student. Discuss any topics for which you could narrow the focus.

LISTING

When you **list,** you write down everything you can think of about a topic. You do not disregard any ideas. Listing is fast and easy and will help you see what you already know.

> **Note:** When you have a limited time to write, such as for an exam, making a brainstorm list is a good prewriting strategy to use because it can be done simply and quickly.

Look at this example of a five-minute brainstorm list about the topic "immunizations."

Immunizations

require every child to have

should every worker have them? College students?

which are most important? measles, mumps, rubella, meningitis, chicken pox,

small pox, vaccines that scientists are working on now

dangerous, side-effects, nausea, headache, are they safe . . . statistics?

unfounded fears of . . .

may cause autism, true or false? harmful to pregnant women?

are expensive but usually free at city clinics . . . make free for everyone?

polio vaccine/the history/Jonas Salk

what diseases eradicated because of vaccines? Where eradicated?

Work in a group. Follow these steps to make a brainstorm list:

1. Each person in your group needs four to six note cards or strips of paper.

2. On your own, make a brainstorm list about the topic "Advantages of Tablet Computers." Write for five minutes.

3. As you brainstorm, write down each idea, thought, or question you have on a note card or strip of paper. Try to write something on each one.

4. After five minutes, come together and spread all of your note cards or papers on a table. Sort them according to ideas. Discard any ideas that are the same.

5. With your group, discuss how the groups of ideas might be used in an essay.

CLUSTERING

Clustering is another way you can brainstorm ideas. Start by writing the topic in the center of your paper and circling it. Then write down all of the ideas you can think of around the center circle, and circle them, too. As you think of more ideas, circle them and connect them to the other circles with a line. When you finish, your paper will look like a graphic representation of ideas that are connected to your topic.

Example:

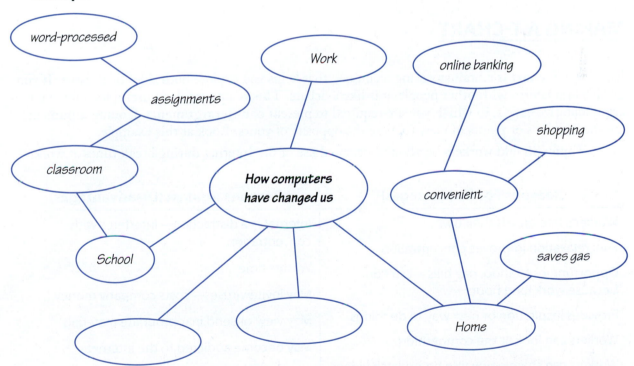

A. Look at the example cluster. Discuss these questions with the class:

- What is the main topic? Where is it written?

- How does the cluster represent the person's thoughts? In what order do you think the circles were written?

B. On your own, add your ideas to the blank circles. Continue adding more circles and ideas to the cluster. Then share your ideas with another student.

EXERCISE 6

A. Work with another student. Choose one of these topics to brainstorm about:

- How video games affect children
- Should information be controlled on the Internet?
- Why a college education is important

B. On your own, make a cluster about the topic on a separate piece of paper.

C. Compare your clusters. How are they similar? How are they different?

MAKING A T-CHART

Making a **T-chart** is a brainstorming technique that helps you explore both sides of an issue. If you do this brainstorm with other people, it is like a debate. This is a particularly useful technique for argumentative essays, in which you are required to present **counterarguments**. Counterarguments are the opinions or points of view that are the opposite of yours. Look at this example.

Topic: Should workers be allowed personal use of the Internet during break times at work?

Reasons For (Advantages)	Reasons Against (Disadvantages)
Worker's free time is their own.	Internet is a distraction—interferes with concentration
Fun, relaxation improves concentration	
Opportunities to shop, pay bills—can't do because work long hours	Wastes time
Provides inspiration or new way to do things	May invite viruses—costs company money
Workers can look at the competition	May view or send inappropriate materials
Workers can share enjoyable time; watch videos or play games	May become addicted to the Internet
	Personal things like emails, shopping, inappropriate workplace activity

A. *On a separate piece of paper make a T-chart to brainstorm the reasons for and against the topic.*

Topic: A college or university should have the right to deny a degree to any student who posts inappropriate content on the Internet.

Reasons For (Advantages)	Reasons Against (Disadvantages)

B. *Work in a group. Discuss these questions:*

- What is your opinion about the topic?
- Which reasons can you use to support your opinion?
- How might someone with the opposite opinion respond to yours?

WRITING TASK

Complete a prewriting brainstorm and use it to write an essay.

A. *Choose a topic from Exercise 1, 2, 4, 6, or 7. Reread your prewriting brainstorm about that topic. Then decide what else you want/need to know.*

B. *What opinion have you formed about your topic? Freewrite about your topic for ten minutes.*

C. *Use your prewriting brainstorm, freewrite, and notes to write a three to four paragraph essay about the topic. Remember to follow proper essay structure and format. (See Unit 1, page 99.)*

Check Your Writing

A. *Use this form to check your writing, or exchange essays with another student and check each other's writing.*

Essay Checklist

The essay . . .

1. follows the guidelines for formal register, structure, and format. ☐

2. focuses on one topic. ☐

3. includes an introduction with some general information about the topic. ☐

4. has a sentence in the introduction that expresses the writer's opinion. ☐

5. includes examples that support the writer's opinion. ☐

6. properly cites sources. ☐

7. Were there any sentences you didn't understand? If so, write a question mark (?) in front of them on the essay.

8. Do you have any questions for the writer? Write them here.

   _____

   _____

9. What changes do you suggest to improve the essay?

   _____

   _____

B. *Make changes to improve your essay. Remember to check your writing for grammar, spelling, and punctuation errors.*

Thesis Statements, Introductions, and Conclusions

Academic writing in English needs to be clear, concise, and direct. Course instructors expect writing assignments to have a clear focus or main point that is supported in a logical way.

Determining the focus for a piece of writing will be the key to successfully presenting your ideas clearly and logically. The way to do this is to introduce a central idea—or **thesis**—at the start of your essay. Your **thesis statement** usually expresses your opinion about an issue and states the main points you will use to support the opinion. In the body of your essay, each paragraph will develop and support one of those main points. Then, in the conclusion, you will restate your thesis and briefly summarize the main points.

In this unit you will learn . . .

- how to analyze an essay assignment and understand what the assignment requires.
- how to write an effective thesis statement.
- how to develop an introduction and conclusion for your essay.

Warm Up

A. *Choose one topic from the list below that you think is important. Write one sentence about why you think it is important. Compare your opinion with the class.*

education	health care	pollution
globalization	natural resources	poverty
global warming	over-population	racism

B. *Work with another student. Imagine you are going to write an essay about the topic you chose in Exercise A. Discuss what kind of information you could use to develop and support your opinion.*

UNDERSTANDING THE ASSIGNMENT

Before you begin any writing assignment, you must be sure that you understand what is required. Your assignment may ask you to explain a subject or an idea, analyze a concept or scientific evidence, or present an argument.

Often your assignment will be stated in the form of a *how* or *why* question.

Examples:

Write a five-paragraph essay that answers this question: "How have cell phones changed the way parents and children communicate?"

Write a five-paragraph essay that states and supports your opinion about this question: "Why is global warming such a controversial topic of date?"

Other times, an imperative verb form will direct you to write about the topic from a particular perspective. For example, you may be asked to *discuss* a topic or *explain* an idea.

Example:

We make decisions every day. Some are inconsequential, and others change us forever. Discuss a difficult decision you had to make. Be sure to include specific details to support your main point.

The verb *discuss* means *talk about*, so in your essay about an important decision you made, you might include answers to these questions:

- What was the decision? Why was it difficult?
- What were some of the things that you thought about before making the decision?
- How did you make the decision? How did the decision affect you?

EXERCISE 1

A. Write the meaning next to each verb in the chart. Check your meanings with the class. Follow the example.

Agree/Disagree	Show cause and/or effect	Discuss how A and B are same or different	Analyze *to examine or think about something*
Argue	Comment on	Define	List the steps
Compare	Evaluate	Explain (how)	Summarize

B. Choose a verb from the chart in Exercise 1A for each different aspect of nuclear power. Write the verb on the line. More than one verb may be appropriate. Follow the example.

   Comment on / Evaluate   the advantages of nuclear power

_____ nuclear power and another source of energy

_____ the risks of nuclear power

_____ how nuclear fusion works

_____ nuclear power is the answer to the energy crisis

_____ nuclear power plant disasters

C. Compare answers with another student. Are they the same? Discuss how the focus of a topic changes with a different verb.

THESIS STATEMENTS

As you learned in Unit 5, the prewriting stage helps you to generate ideas about the topic. When you have done that, you are ready to decide what the focus of your essay will be and what it is you want to say. A key part of expressing the controlling idea of your essay is to develop a **thesis statement**.

The thesis statement of an essay, like the topic sentence in a paragraph, presents the controlling idea and the writer's opinion or perspective about the topic. A thesis statement, then, may state the answer to a question, express an opinion about an issue, or suggest a solution to a controversial problem.

The thesis statement is one or two sentences in the introduction of an essay. In some cases such as personal essays or narratives, there is no explicit thesis statement but most academic essay assignments require a thesis. Developing a clear thesis statement will help you organize the body of your essay to best support the idea that you express in the thesis statement. Consider these characteristics of an effective thesis statement.

An effective thesis statement answers a question or addresses an issue.
A thesis statement does not simply state or announce the topic. For instance, *Letter Writing in the 21st Century* or *The Issue of the Death Penalty* does not express an opinion or perspective about the topic. Look at the writing assignment and the example. Notice how the thesis statement expresses the writer's opinion about the topic and answers a question.

Example:

Writing assignment: In the past, personal written communication was most often conducted through the mail service. The arrival of email has added another way in which to communicate. Comment on the effect this change has had on personal written communication.

Thesis statement: *Old-fashioned letter writing must be preserved to ensure alternative modes of communication, retain the human touch, and assure access to historical records.*

Question the thesis answers: Why is writing old-fashioned letters still important?

An effective thesis statement expresses a narrow topic.
Topics such as *globalization* or *poverty* are too general or broad to cover within an essay. Look at this topic. Notice how the writer narrowed it down into a single, focused, controlling idea expressed in the thesis statement.

Example:

Topic: Health care is a big issue around the world.

Health care

Poor areas

Low-cost community health programs

Care for the sick

Disease prevention programs

Proper training for health workers

Thesis statement: *Low-cost community health programs are needed in poor areas to care for the sick, provide disease prevention plans, and train health workers.*

An effective thesis statement clearly states the topic and a sharply focused controlling idea: it makes a claim, assertion, or expresses an opinion.

Examples:

Opinion

*Companies need to realize that workers **will be more productive, more creative, and happier** if allowed to freely use the Internet at the workplace.*

Assertion

*Low-cost community health centers **are urgently needed** in poor areas to care for the sick, promote disease prevention plans, and train more health workers.*

An effective thesis statement shows how the topic will be developed.

Notice how each underlined section in the second thesis statement above states an important point that will be developed to support the controlling idea of the entire essay.

An effective thesis statement is not simply a factual statement or statistic.

Facts and statistics are limiting and cannot be developed into a controlling idea. They can, however, play an important role in providing emphasis and support for your controlling idea.

Example:

Factual statement, not a thesis: *Fifty percent of the deaths in developing countries are caused by infectious diseases.*

Thesis statement: *Because fifty percent of deaths in developing countries are caused by infectious diseases, there is an urgent need for low-cost community health centers that care for the sick and promote disease prevention plans.*

An effective thesis statement uses specific language.

Words such as *good, bad, nice,* or *interesting* are too vague. Look at how specific language changes the focus in these two examples.

Examples:

Social media is an interesting way to keep in contact with friends who live far away.

Staying in touch with friends is easy with the fun, fresh options social media offers such as viewing family events, sharing favorite movies or music, or posting comments in one quick click.

Look at the sample essay assignment and three thesis statements. Which one do you think is the most effective thesis statement for the writing assignment?

Essay Assignment: *The death penalty is currently allowed in fifty-seven countries worldwide (infoplease.com, 2011). In a five-paragraph essay, discuss whether or not you think the death penalty should be abolished.*

Thesis Statement 1: *I will explain why the death penalty should not be allowed.*

Thesis Statement 2: *The death penalty is allowed in more than fifty countries around the world.*

Thesis Statement 3: *The death penalty is uncivilized and should be banned in every country because it is inhumane, does not deter crime, and kills innocent people.*

Thesis statement 1 expresses the writer's opinion—*ban the death penalty*—and a controlling idea—*to explain why the death penalty should not be allowed*. However, it is more like an announcement and does not state the major points that will develop the controlling idea.

Thesis statement 2 is a fact and does not make a claim or argument or answer the question, "Should the death penalty be allowed?"

Thesis statement 3 is an effective thesis statement. It expresses the writer's opinion and a sharply focused controlling idea—*the death penalty is uncivilized and should be banned*. In addition, it shows the plan for developing the thesis—the death penalty *is inhumane, does not deter crime, and kills innocent people*. It is clear to the reader that the writer will discuss three reasons why the death penalty should be banned. Each of these three reasons will be explained in the body paragraphs of the essay.

You can think of a thesis statement as an umbrella. The handle and the frame are the controlling idea, and each section of the top is an important idea that is developed to support the controlling idea of the entire essay.

Thesis Statement:
(states the controlling idea <u>and</u> how it will be developed)
*The death penalty is uncivilized and should be banned
in every country because it is inhumane, does not
deter crime, and kills innocent people.*

How the Controlling Idea Will Be Developed

Subtopic 1	**Subtopic 2**	**Subtopic 3**
is inhumane	*does not deter crime*	*kills innocent people*

Controlling Idea:
The death penalty should be banned.

A. *Work with another student. Read the thesis statements and check (✓) "Effective" or "Ineffective." If the thesis statement is not effective, write the reason from the list on the line. There may be more than one reason.*

> does not answer a question or address an issue
> does not show how the topic will be developed
> gives no clear opinion or claim
>
> is simply a fact or statistic
> language is vague
> topic is too broad

1. The graphics and characters in the video game *Trail of Glory* are really good.

   ☐ Effective   ☐ Ineffective

   Reason: _____

2. The benefits from playing video games outweigh the drawbacks by promoting pro-social behavior, reducing stress, and improving cognitive skills.

   ☐ Effective   ☐ Ineffective

   Reason: _____

3. There are many reasons why memory is vital to learning.

   ☐ Effective   ☐ Ineffective

   Reason: _____

4. Product A and product B may appear to be almost identical, but if you examine them closely you will find that product A is superior in design and performance.

   ☐ Effective   ☐ Ineffective

   Reason: _____

5. Sixteen percent of the children who participated in a study by the Kaiser Family Foundation said that their parents do not set any rules for using the computer, television, or video games (Rideout, Foehr, and Roberts, 2010).

   ☐ Effective   ☐ Ineffective

   Reason: _____

B. *Answer these questions about the thesis statements from Exercise A and discuss your answers with the class:*

- What is the controlling idea or opinion?
- What important points will the writer develop in the essay?

A. Choose one of these topics. What do you know about the topic? Do a prewriting brainstorm (see Unit 5 for more on prewriting techniques) about the topic.

- Behavior in the workplace
- Cell phones
- Online communication
- Tattoos
- Texting etiquette
- Time is money

B. Narrow the topic into a focused controlling idea. Draw a diagram like the umbrella on page 167.

C. Write a thesis statement.

D. Work in a group. Take turns reading your thesis statements aloud. For each statement, discuss these questions:

- What is the topic?
- What is the controlling idea?
- What opinion or point of view does the writer express?
- Which important points will the writer develop?

INTRODUCTIONS

Academic essays begin with an introductory paragraph. The **introductory paragraph** provides general or background information about the topic and then moves to the specific focus or purpose of the essay, the thesis. The thesis statement may be one or two sentences and is usually at the end of the introduction. Introductory paragraphs are usually shorter than body paragraphs and should capture the interest of the reader.

A. Read the sample introduction. Underline the background information. Double underline the thesis statement.

According to Internet World Statistics (2011), over 3 billion people use the Internet every day. They connect to the Internet on their home computers, portable devices such as smartphones or tablets, or at work. At work, companies worry that employees' productivity might be affected by their spending time on the Internet. However, the opposite may be true, according to a study by Dr. Brent Coker from the University of Melbourne (2009). Companies need to realize that workers will be more productive, more creative, and happier if allowed to freely use the Internet at the workplace.

B. Based on the thesis statement, what important points will the writer develop in the essay?

Hooks

An introduction should capture the reader's interest. To do this, writers use different techniques, or **hooks**, to begin their essays. Some types of hooks are:

- **an anecdote** a short story or narration that illustrates or exemplifies the main point.

Example:

All the students in the class were sitting in their seats silently taking a test—every one but Adam. Adam, a bright, energetic student, was shifting in his seat constantly. He would look up from his paper whenever he heard a page turn or another student cough or a truck honk its horn outside. Once again, Adam would not finish his test. He is failing because he is unable to focus or sit still for very long. Recently, Adam was diagnosed with Attention Deficit Hyperactivity Disorder (ADHD). However, this diagnosis does not mean Adam is destined for a lifetime of failure. With proper medication, school support, and counseling, Adam could graduate at the top of his class.

- **a surprising fact or statistic**

Example:

According to the U.S. Department of Education's website, 5 percent of all school children have learning disabilities (2011).

- **a famous quote or saying**

Example:

"I felt like an alien. I always felt like I never belonged to any group that I wanted to belong to." Steven Spielberg, movie producer and director, learning disabled, did not finish high school.

- **a thought-provoking question**

Example:

Can students with learning disabilities do as well as students without learning disabilities?

EXERCISE 5

A. **Work with another student. Look at the sample introductions. Identify the type of hook used in each one from this list. More than one type may be used.**

anecdote	surprising fact or statistic
famous quote or saying	thought-provoking question

Paragraph 1

How much more can our planet take? Each year another beautiful, natural waterway is devastated by an oil spill. Each year fuel emissions increase and contribute to climate change (Environmental Protection Agency, 2011). If we do not reduce our dependence on oil, we will destroy our precious Earth. Each person can do his or her small part to protect the planet by recycling, lowering electrical usage, and choosing fuel efficient transportation.

Hook: _____

Paragraph 2

Kofi was just old enough to reach into the big container of water with the plastic cup and get himself a drink. The water in the container was kept outside and was used for the animals, cleaning, cooking, and drinking. What Kofi did not know was that the refreshing drink of water was contaminated and could make him very ill, or worse. With an estimated 1.4 billion deaths each year caused by unsafe water (Unicef, 2005), it is the responsibility of the wealthiest nations to provide aid and education about low-cost methods for clean water such as the sari method, seeds from the moringa oleifera, or chlorine tablets.

Hook: _____

Paragraph 3

Recent reports have shown that 563 million pieces of mail are sent each day, compared to 294 billion emails (Postal Facts, 2011; Radicati Group, 2009). It is clear that the Internet has us corresponding and communicating with others more than regular mail ever has. Businesses and private citizens can make plans, set meetings, and get answers fast. However, the speed email offers does not necessarily make for better communication, especially when composing personal, heartfelt, or serious messages. In this regard, we should not let email automatically be the first choice when it comes to letter writing simply because it is convenient. When it comes to personal communication, we need to preserve old-fashioned letter writing to ensure that we maintain alternative modes of communication, retain the human touch, and assure access to historical records.

Hook: _____

B. *Discuss these questions about the sample introductions:*

- What is the topic?
- What is the controlling idea?
- Where in the introduction is the thesis statement?
- What background information is included?
- Based on the introduction what important points will each writer develop in the essay?

C. *On a separate piece of paper, use a different hook to rewrite the beginning of each introduction from Exercise A. Share your new hooks with the class.*

A. *Use the thesis statement you wrote in Exercise 3C to write an introductory paragraph. Remember to add a hook.*

B. *When you finish writing, check your introduction for the following:*

☐ The topic is narrowed down into a focused main idea.

☐ The paragraph includes a hook.

☐ The paragraph provides background information about the topic.

☐ The thesis statement states an opinion or addresses an issue.

☐ The thesis statement makes the intent or plan for the essay clear.

C. *Share your introductory paragraph with another student. Look again at the checklist in Exercise B, and discuss any missing parts.*

CONCLUSIONS

Good endings are as important as good beginnings. A **concluding paragraph** is usually shorter than a body paragraph, reviews the important points of the essay, and restates the thesis using different words. The concluding paragraph does not add new ideas. Often, the writer makes a final comment such as a recommendation, warning, or suggestion in order to leave a strong impression about the topic.

There are certain transitions or signal phrases that indicate the conclusion of an essay. They include:

All in all,	In closing,	To conclude,
Finally,	In conclusion,	To sum up,

EXERCISE 7

Read the introductory and concluding paragraphs from the sample essay "Free Workers to Surf." Then answer the questions.

Introduction

According to Internet World Statistics (2011), over 3 billion people use the Internet every day. They connect to the Internet on their home computers, portable devices such as smartphones or tablets, or at work. At work, companies worry that employees' productivity might be affected by their spending time on the Internet. However, the opposite may be true, according to a study by Dr. Brent Coker from the University of Melbourne (2009). Companies need to realize that workers will be more productive, more creative, and happier if allowed to freely use the Internet at the workplace.

Conclusion

In conclusion, the Internet is everywhere. At work, employees who have the freedom to access it during breaks will be more effective, innovative, and content. With advanced Internet safety software and Internet usage guidelines, companies can no longer deny workers a tool that has the potential to provide increased job satisfaction.

1. What is the thesis statement? Write it here.

   _____

2. What is the restated thesis in the conclusion?

   _____

3. Circle the transition word(s) that the writer used in the conclusion.

4. What are the 3 important points that are restated in the conclusion? Write them on the lines.

   _____

   _____

   _____

5. Compare the thesis statement in the introduction to the restated thesis in the conclusion. How does the writer restate the thesis? Underline words that are similar in the two statements.

6. What kind of final comment does the writer make in the conclusion—a warning, suggestion, recommendation, or opinion? Write your answer on the line.

   _____

EXERCISE 8

A. **Write a concluding paragraph based on your introductory paragraph from Exercise 6.**

B. **When you finish writing, check your introduction for the following:**

   ☐ The concluding paragraph uses a transition or signal word(s).

   ☐ The conclusion reviews the important points of the essay and restates the thesis.

   ☐ The restatement of the thesis uses words that are different from those in the introduction.

   ☐ The conclusion includes a final comment such as a recommendation, a warning, or an opinion.

C. **Share your concluding paragraph with another student. Look again at the checklist in Exercise B, and discuss any missing parts.**

WRITING TASK

Write an effective introduction and a matching concluding paragraph.

A. *Choose a different topic from Exercise 3—one you did NOT use to write a thesis statement. On a separate piece of paper, do a prewriting brainstorm about the topic.*

B. *On a new piece of paper, use your brainstorm to write an effective thesis statement. Then use your thesis statement to write an introduction. Include one of the types of hooks introduced in this unit.*

C. *Write a conclusion to match your introduction. Use one of the transitions from page 172.*

Check Your Writing

A. *Use this form to check your writing, or exchange paragraphs with another student and check each other's writing.*

Introduction and Conclusion Checklist

The introduction . . .

1. includes an effective hook. ☐

2. includes a thesis statement that refers to the topic and states an opinion. ☐

3. makes clear the controlling idea, intent, or plan for the essay. ☐

The conclusion . . .

4. uses an appropriate transition or signal word. ☐

5. reviews the important points and restates the thesis. ☐

6. restates the thesis using different words from those used in the introduction. ☐

7. includes a final comment such as a recommendation, a warning, or an opinion. ☐

8. What changes do you suggest to improve the paragraphs?

_____

_____

_____

B. *Make changes to improve your paragraphs. Remember to check your writing for grammar, spelling, and punctuation errors.*

UNIT 7

Essay Support

In short academic essays, each paragraph has a special job in developing and supporting the writer's **thesis**—the controlling idea of the entire essay. You can think of these supporting paragraphs as the sections of a bridge. Each section has unique dimensions that provide solid and stable support and connect section to section.

Writers develop their ideas in paragraphs using various organizational patterns and supporting details such as examples, illustrations, and narrations. Writers also use comparisons, definitions, classifications, personal experiences, descriptions, facts, or statistics to develop and support their ideas. In your previous writing classes, you may have studied and practiced using some of these.

In this unit, you will learn ways to develop your essays by . . .

- using appropriate patterns of organization to support your thesis.
- using relevant details to develop and support key ideas.
- using transitional markers, key words, pronouns, and synonyms to create cohesive paragraphs.
- using transitions to link paragraphs within the essay.

Warm Up

Check (✓) all the phrases that best describe the characteristics of a body paragraph. More than one answer is possible. Discuss your answers with the class.

1. Body paragraphs . . .
   ☐ focus on one controlling idea—a main point.
   ☐ focus on one or more main points.
   ☐ do not have to focus on a main point.

2. Body paragraphs . . .
   ☐ are indented.
   ☐ start with a lower case letter.
   ☐ use block formatting.

3. The first sentence in a paragraph . . .
   ☐ may introduce the topic of the paragraph.
   ☐ may introduce a new point the writer is making to support his or her thesis in the essay.
   ☐ may link the ideas from a previous paragraph to a new paragraph in an essay.

4. Body paragraphs . . .
   ☐ may define special terms.
   ☐ compare two things or people.
   ☐ tell a story.
   ☐ show cause and effect.

5. Sentences in a body paragraph . . .
   ☐ all relate to the main idea of that paragraph.
   ☐ support the main idea of that paragraph.
   ☐ may not all relate to the main idea of that paragraph.

6. The topic sentence of a body paragraph . . .
   ☐ includes the main idea of the paragraph.
   ☐ may introduce an important point of the thesis.
   ☐ may follow an introductory sentence.

ESSAY DEVELOPMENT

Patterns of Organization

In an essay, each **body paragraph** serves a special purpose in supporting and developing your thesis. For example, in a paper for a history class, you may want to show the causes and effects of a war or political movement. For a biology class, you may have to explain a process or classify and describe certain species in your paper. For a psychology course, you may be required to write a paper that defines and illustrates certain conditions or behaviors. In a business course, you may need to write about a marketing or customer problem and a solution to it. Choosing the appropriate pattern of organization will help you present your ideas and evidence logically and clearly from start to finish.

In your essay, you may use *one or more* of these patterns in the body paragraphs to support your thesis.

Narration tells a story of an event and how it happened in chronological order. A narration can be a whole essay, for example, about an important historical event, or just one or two paragraphs within an essay that illustrate or emphasize a point the writer is making. Sometimes narrations do not include a topic sentence because the main point is obvious or can be inferred from the details. Narrations usually include sensory details and descriptions that help the reader visualize the people and things in the story.

Persuasion presents an opinion about a debatable issue, such as *the death penalty*, and is supported by evidence to convince readers to agree with the writer's opinion about the issue. *(See Unit 8 for more on the persuasive essay.)*

Classification defines an object—a person, place, thing, or concept—and then breaks it down into separate parts or groups. It is organized in a way that shows a purpose. For example, a writer might rate cell phones by the features they offer. The distinct features of each cell phone, such as the camera, video, contact list, texting, calendar, alarm, and free applications, would be described.

Extended definition defines something in a more detailed way than what would be in a dictionary. In a paragraph or essay, a term or abstract concept such as *peace* or *freedom* is explained with examples, comparisons, and traits to illustrate the more subtle meanings associated with the word.

Process/Sequence explains a process, steps, or series of events, for example, *how stars are formed* or *the events that led to World War II.*

Cause/Effect shows the relationship between an event and its cause. *What are the effects of climate change? How is a lack of face-to-face communication changing us?*

Comparison/Contrast shows how two things or people are similar and/or different. For example, a writer might compare the leadership styles of two people in high positions or contrast a new trend or practice with a traditional one, such as human caregivers versus robot caregivers.

Problem/Solution explains a problem and a possible way or ways to solve the problem, such as *how not lose a job* or *how a company can train a team of workers to change.*

A. Work with another student. Read these body paragraphs. Identify the organizational pattern(s) each writer uses. Write them on the lines.

Paragraph 1

Although transportation centers, such as train or bus stations, must be high-tech, state-of-the art facilities that move travelers easily and efficiently to their new destinations, these modern spaces sometimes do little to inspire people to travel. For example, when Hanford Rail Station was rebuilt, it provided more services and features than the original station; however, the new station held travelers in a dark, cramped space with low ceilings. Travelers had to make their way through a confusing maze of aisles and passageways as they struggled to navigate their way to their trains. Travelers were focused less on starting an exciting journey and more on escaping from an unbearable space. Unlike this new ultra-modern space, the old station brought travelers into its grand, open, magnificent space and made them feel as if they were fearless explorers on their way to new adventures. Nonetheless, the old station lacked the infrastructure to accommodate modern travel. Now, once again, yet another station is being built to replace Hanford Station. Let us hope the designers and architects can design a space that can serve modern transportation needs while giving travelers a desire to venture out into the wide world and beyond.

Pattern(s): _____

Paragraph 2

The word *closure*, in the past, was mostly used to express its literal meaning—the closing of a building or factory or the end of a meeting. In the last several decades, however, the word has taken on a new meaning and is used to express an emotional or psychological process. In social, legal, or political contexts, when people talk about closure, they mean a person can stop thinking about or come to a resolution about a traumatic experience. For example, when a person dies, the funeral serves as a final act that gives closure to relatives and friends. They are able to express or finalize their grief for a loved one. In the case of a violent crime, victims usually have strong, unresolved feelings. In the courtroom, victims, or relatives of murdered victims, can make statements at the time of sentencing about the effect the crime has had on their lives. In this regard, closure may take on a larger significance. It not only gives victims a voice to end their lingering suffering as a result of the crime but also provides a way to influence the severity of the punishment.

Pattern(s): _____

Paragraph 3

    Giving workers access to the Internet during break times not only will make workers more productive (Coker, 2009) but also may result in more creative thinking. For example, a worker who is involved with product placement or marketing may see or hear something that sparks a new idea or way to promote new products while casually surfing the Net. With instant information on the Net, a company has to be ahead of the competition, not a step behind. Allowing workers to control where they want to travel on the Net may be one of the reasons a company keeps its competitive edge. The images, creative websites, videos, or music a worker clicks on may be the inspiration for a company's next product, ad campaign, or marketing strategy, all of which may have happened because an employee needed a few minutes of relief time from his or her normal work duties.

Pattern(s): _____

Paragraph 4

    People will argue that they have unlimited storage capacity for emails and so they will always have them. Is email storage permanent? Nobody can answer that yet. However, many people complain of the amount of email that accumulates in their inboxes and how it becomes a drudgery to continually have to delete or move it into folders. More problems develop when emails disappear into thin air or systems fail. For these reasons, the loss of special letters like the ones my grandfather wrote to my grandmother when he was stationed overseas during World War I, or the ones from my parents when I studied abroad, or the ones from my husband when we were dating, would be devastating. These letters are an archive of my family's history and will be passed down from generation to generation. I would not want to rely on or give a virtual container the control to manage my precious possessions. Besides, it is doubtful that a person's inbox or email account will be easily accessible to succeeding family members. Would you want to take that risk?

Pattern(s): _____

B. ***Work with another student. Read the paragraphs again and underline the topic sentences. Remember that not all paragraphs begin with a topic sentence.***

Developing and Supporting Ideas

As you develop and support your controlling idea from paragraph to paragraph in your essay, you need to provide enough details such as examples, explanations, facts, and statistics. Without adequate support, your ideas may be unclear and your reader may not take you seriously. Supporting details may include . . .

- **explanations or illustrations** to give reasons why something happened or describe how something works: *Because admissions officers are searching applicants' online activities, applicants need to think carefully about what they post on their social media pages.*

- **examples** to show what you mean or what something is like: *University life offers students numerous ways to expand their knowledge, explore new ideas, and make new connections with others. For example, many universities have blogs where students can write about their interests and current ideas and share them with other students and professors.*

- **facts or statistics** to strengthen a point and provide evidence: *According to the Pew Research Center (2011), more than 70 percent of adult Americans who own cell phones communicate by text messaging.*

- **anecdotes**, which are short interesting stories about a particular person or event. They can help emphasize or clarify the main idea.

- **descriptions** to give details about what someone or something is like: *Annie, a tall, energetic, seventeen-year-old, spent hours every evening simultaneously moving from homework to texting to posting on her social media pages.*

- **personal experiences** to connect the writer's experience to the main idea to make it easier to understand.

- **expert opinions** from people with special skills or knowledge to support the main idea: *In their study, Foerde, Knowlton, and Poldrack (2006), found that multitasking may be changing the way we learn and remember information.*

EXERCISE 2

Work with another student. Look back at the body paragraphs in Exercise 1. Find supporting details in sentences from each one and write them on the lines. Then write the type of supporting detail from the box. More than one answer may be possible.

anecdotes	expert opinions	personal experiences
descriptions	explanations or illustrations	
examples	facts or statistics	

Paragraph 1

Supporting details: _____

Type: _____

Paragraph 2

Supporting details: _____

Type: _____

Paragraph 3

Supporting details: _____

Type: _____

Paragraph 4

Supporting details: _____

Type: _____

> ## Remember
>
> Freewriting is a way to brainstorm about a topic. When you freewrite, you begin writing, and you continue writing as much as you can without stopping, usually for several minutes or more. You do not stop to correct grammar mistakes or rewrite sentences.
> *(For more about freewriting, see Part 3, Unit 5.)*

A. *Follow these steps to do a freewrite.*

1. Choose one of the topics.
   - a communication you received from someone or sent to someone, by letter, by phone, or by text
   - a gift you received or gave
   - an inappropriate or unusual method of communication

2. Consider how the topic has affected you. Was the experience positive or negative? What are some details you can include that would express how the experience affected you?

3. Begin your freewrite and write for thirty minutes.

B. *Exchange your freewrite with another student and read the freewrite. Answer the questions. Share your answers with your partner. Save your freewrite for use later in this unit.*

1. How did the experience affect the writer? What point does the writer make, or

   what kind of point *could* the writer make? _____

2. What kind of organizational pattern(s) could the writer use in the body of an essay?

   _____

3. What types of supporting details does the writer use? _____

4. What do you like about the freewrite? _____

Linking Ideas—Cohesive Paragraphs

All the sentences and paragraphs in a well-written essay should flow smoothly from one to the next. **Cohesive writing** means all the sentences or parts of sentences are logically connected. Ideas are presented in a logical order and show how they relate to each other and to the controlling idea of the essay. Ways to achieve cohesive paragraphs include . . .

- using transitional markers.
- repeating key words.
- using pronouns.
- using synonyms.

Transitional Markers

Linking words and phrases are sometimes called **transitional markers** or **connecting words**. They help clarify how the ideas within and between sentences relate to each other. Because many transitional markers have a similar meaning, writers use them in a variety of ways to make their writing more interesting.

Look at the variety of ways you can introduce an example in a paragraph.

Examples:

Hummingbirds can move in several different ways; **for instance**, *they can hover over a plant, fly backwards, and fly sideways.*

Hummingbirds can move in several different ways. **For example**, *they can hover over a plant, fly backwards, and fly sideways.*

Hummingbirds have the remarkable ability to move in several different ways. **Examples of this** *include hovering over a plant, flying backwards, and flying sideways.*

Hummingbirds have the remarkable ability to move in different ways. **To illustrate**, *they can fly above a flower and remain there for several minutes, unlike most other birds. They can also fly backwards and sideways.*

Transitional Markers
To add an idea
also, and, besides, equally important, first, furthermore, in addition, last, moreover, next, second, too
To show cause and effect
affect, as a result, because, causes, consequently, effect, is a consequence of, is a result of, is caused by, is due to, makes, produces, reason why, reason, resulted in, results from, since, so, therefore, thus
To show contrast
although, but, contrary to, despite, even though, however, in contrast, in spite of, nevertheless, nonetheless, on the contrary, on the other hand, regardless of, still, though, while, yet
To show comparison
alike, both, in the same way, likewise, same, similarly
To give examples
an example of this, for example, for instance, in the case of, to illustrate
To show emphasis
as a matter of fact, In fact, interestingly, naturally, of course
To show time
after, as soon as, as, before, first, immediately, meanwhile, next, since, then, upon, when, while

Transitional markers have special meanings, so it is important to choose the ones that express exactly what you are trying to say.

Notice in the examples how the correct transitional marker clarifies the relationship between ideas.

Examples:

Incorrect transition: *The field of robotics is moving into a new area with the invention of talking robots called "Lingodroids." There may be many uses for talking androids,* **and** *people, who work in jobs where the human touch is necessary, like caregivers, are concerned they may be replaced by machines.*

Correct transition: *The field of robotics is moving into a new area with the invention of talking robots called "Lingodroids." There may be many uses for talking androids;* **however**, *people who work in jobs where the human touch is necessary, like caregivers, are concerned they may be replaced by machines.*

One thing to keep in mind is that using too many transitional markers in your paragraphs will break up the rhythm and flow of your ideas. Deciding when and which expression to use is about finding the right balance. Reading regularly will help you get an understanding of when and how to use them.

EXERCISE 4

Look at the paragraphs in Exercise 1. Underline all of the transitional markers. When you are finished, compare your answers with the whole class. Which group found the most transitional markers?

Key Words, Pronouns, and Synonyms

In addition to transitional markers, writers use key words, pronouns, and synonyms to make their meaning clear and keep their readers interested in what they have to say.

Key Words

Key words are the important words used to express ideas about a significant point. Repetition of key words helps your reader follow your ideas easily. In the example, the words *leadership style* are an important part of the point the writer is making. Notice how *leadership style(s)* is repeated in the excerpt.

Example:

*Every leader is unique and develops a **leadership style** to suit the company environment, handle problems, or motivate and energize employees. However, if a leader changes jobs and moves into a new head position, this successful **leadership style** may become a disadvantage, according to Michael Watkins (2009) from Genesis Advisers, a leadership development firm. To help leaders make the necessary adjustments to their **leadership styles** in order to be effective in their new work environments, Watkins (2009) developed his "STARS" system, which breaks down the types of situations leaders may face in their new workplace into five areas — "start-up, turn around, accelerated growth, realignment, and sustaining success" (Watkins, 2009, p. 48).*

Pronouns (*this, that, these, those, he, she, they, their, our, it, who, which*)

Pronouns refer to words—**antecedents**—that were previously mentioned in a sentence or paragraph. Using pronouns is another way writers keep their ideas moving smoothly from sentence to sentence while relieving the reader of the monotony of overused words. Notice the difference in the way the sentences flow in these examples. *(See Part 2, Unit 2 for more about pronouns and antecedents.)*

Examples:

*Hummingbirds can move in several different ways; for instance, **hummingbirds** can hover over a plant, fly backwards, and fly sideways.*

*Hummingbirds can move in several different ways; for instance, **they** can hover over a plant, fly backwards, and fly sideways.*

*In this regard, **closure** may take on a larger significance. **Closure** not only gives the victim a voice but also an outlet.*

*In this regard, **closure** may take on a larger significance. **It** not only gives the victim a voice but also an outlet.*

Synonyms

Using **synonyms**, words with similar meanings, also adds interest and variety to your writing.

Example:

*The field of robotics is moving into a new area with the invention of talking **robots** called "Lingodroids." There may be many uses for talking **androids**; however, people who work in jobs where the human touch is necessary, like caregivers, are concerned they may be replaced by **machines**.*

EXERCISE 5

A. *Follow these steps to do a freewrite.*

1. Choose one of the topics.
   - On any given day, people spend time in different environments. Compare an old-fashioned, low-tech space to a modern, state-of-the-art, high-tech space.
   - Discuss the different features of cell phones.
   - Explain the ways social media are being used today.

2. Think about what you know about the topic. What opinion do you have about the topic? What are some details you can include that would help support your opinion?

> ### Remember
>
> - Use transitional markers to show how your ideas relate to each other.
> - Use key words, pronouns, and synonyms.

3. Begin your freewrite and write for thirty minutes.

B. *Exchange your freewrite with another student and read it. Answer the questions. Share your answers with your partner. Save your freewrite for use later in this unit.*

1. What point does the writer make, or what kind of point *could* the writer make?

   _____

2. What kind of organizational pattern(s) could the writer use in the body of an essay?

   _____

3. What types of supporting details does the writer include?

   _____

4. What are some key words in the freewrite? Underline any pronouns and synonyms the writer uses. What other places could the writer use pronouns and synonyms in

   the freewrite? _____

5. What do you like about the freewrite? _____

Linking Paragraphs—Creating Coherence

In an essay, paragraphs need to connect so that the various parts of the essay fit together well. When you begin a new paragraph, you are indicating that you are providing additional information. This new information must relate or respond to what has gone before. If the transitions from one paragraph to the next are illogical or abrupt, it will break the flow of your ideas and diminish the power of your writing.

Writers use all the ways you have practiced in this unit to move smoothly from beginning to end in an essay. These include using appropriate organizational patterns, using transitional markers, repeating key words, and using pronouns and synonyms. Notice how the use of key words makes the transition from paragraph to paragraph smooth and logical.

Example:

Paragraph 1

> *To help leaders make the necessary adjustments to their leadership styles in order to be effective in their new work environments, Watkins (2009) developed his "STARS" system, which breaks down the types of situations leaders may face in their new workplace into five areas—"start up, turn around, accelerated growth, realignment, and sustaining success" (Watkins, 2009, p. 48).*

Paragraph 2

> *The first area, "start up," looks at the pros and cons a new leader may find with a new company. A new company might have a lot of energy and ideas . . . (Watkins, 2009).*

In addition to using transitions, repeating key words, and using pronouns and synonyms, writers use restatement as a tool to create coherence in an essay. In this example, notice how the writer uses restatement as a way to make the transition from one paragraph to the next.

Example:

Paragraph 1

*With a handwritten letter, or even a word-processed one, the whole process is slower from start to finish . . . this time factor can be to people's advantage. Consider how lag time, or space between sending and receiving letters, may help diffuse strong emotions from being expressed like they might if the writers were sending off instant responses to emails in "real" time. Letters sent via traditional mail may serve to reconcile hurt feelings and repair relationships. **An old-fashioned letter gives two people that time and space to view a situation from a different perspective before responding.***

Paragraph 2

***Having some extra time to carefully consider a response is not the only advantage to using traditional mail to communicate.** There is no denying that . . .*

In this example, *having some extra time to carefully consider a response* is a restatement of *time and space to view a situation from a different perspective before responding.* This restatement makes a smooth transition from the first paragraph to the second.

EXERCISE 6

A. Read each thesis statement and the final parts of the paragraphs. Then use restatement to write a smooth transition to the next paragraph.

1. Thesis Statement: Companies need to realize that workers will be more productive, more creative, and happier if allowed to freely use the Internet at the workplace.

    End of Paragraph 1

    With safe systems and firm policies, workers should be able to use the Internet responsibly so they can return to their duties refreshed and ready to concentrate more fully.

    Restatement to begin Paragraph 2: _____

    End of Paragraph 2

    The images, creative websites, videos, or music a worker clicks on may be the inspiration for a company's next product, ad campaign, or marketing strategy, all of which may have happened when an employee needed a few minutes of relief time from his or her normal work duties.

    Restatement to begin Paragraph 3: _____

2. Thesis Statement: People should stop buying paper books and use e-readers because they are eco-friendly, improve the reading experience, and offer readers other options beyond simply reading a book.

End of Paragraph 1

If book lovers do not have to get in their cars and drive to the library or book stores, they will save on gas.

Restatement to begin Paragraph 2: _____

End of Paragraph 2:

E-readers have a variety of settings. For example, the font size can be made bigger so people with bad eyesight can read more easily. The font size can also be made smaller so more words appear on a page. Pages can be made brighter or dimmer depending on the reader's preference. All these features make reading easier and more convenient for book lovers.

Restatement to begin Paragraph 3: _____

WRITING TASK

Use one of your freewrite brainstorms from this unit to write an essay.

A. *Choose one of the topics you did a freewrite for in this unit. Go back and read your freewriting brainstorm about the topic. What else do you want/need to know? If you do more research, remember to check that your source is reliable.*

Exercise 3:

- a communication you received from someone or sent to someone, by letter, by phone, or by text
- a gift you received or gave
- an inappropriate or unusual method of communication

Exercise 5:

- On any given day, people spend time in different environments. Compare an old-fashioned, low-tech space to a modern, state-of-the-art, high-tech space.
- Discuss the different features of cell phones.
- Explain some ways social media is being used today.

B. *Write a thesis statement for your topic. (See Unit 6 for more about thesis statements.)*

C. *Write a four- to five-paragraph essay about your topic.*

Check Your Writing

A. *Use this form to check your writing, or exchange essays with another student and check each other's writing.*

Essay Checklist

The essay . . .

1. includes an introduction with a hook, general or background information, and a thesis statement that has one controlling idea. ☐

2. includes supporting sentences that all connect to the controlling idea. ☐

3. uses an appropriate organizational pattern or patterns. ☐

4. includes enough supporting details in each paragraph. ☐

5. links ideas appropriately and consistently using transitional markers, key words, pronouns, and synonyms. ☐

6. links paragraphs smoothly and logically. ☐

7. reviews the main points and restates the thesis in the concluding paragraph. ☐

8. Was any information missing or confusing to you? If so, write a question mark (?) in front of them on the paragraph.

9. What changes do you suggest to improve the essay?

_____

_____

B. *Make changes to improve your essay. Remember to check your writing for grammar, spelling, and punctuation errors.*

Organizing and Drafting

By this stage in the writing process, you will already have narrowed your topic and clarified the controlling idea of your essay. You will have done adequate research, brainstormed, and identified the supporting details you want to include in your essay.

At the organizing stage, you need to first think about the primary purpose of your essay. The organization of your essay will depend on this primary purpose. For example, if you are writing about a controversial issue, your primary purpose will be to persuade your reader to agree with your opinion or perspective. You might also encourage your reader to take a specific action. To support your thesis, you could use a number of organizational patterns in the body of your essay, such as explaining a problem and proposing a solution or explaining the causes and effects of a particular situation.

In this unit, you will focus on the persuasive essay. Your purpose is to convince or persuade your reader that your opinion about an issue is right. These issues include controversial ones such as the death penalty or freedom of speech. They might also be reactions to literary pieces or new research findings.

Warm Up

A. *Look at the pictures.*

B. *Work in a group. Discuss these questions:*

- How might the people in the pictures persuade you?
- In what other situations might you use persuasive speaking or writing?

Guilty or Innocent?

Buy or not?

Vote for me?

THE PERSUASIVE ESSAY

In your classes, you have probably practiced writing shorter academic essays that require little, if any, research. In a well-written persuasive essay, however, you need to clearly state an opinion about an issue and convince your reader that you are correct by supporting your opinion with solid evidence and logical reasoning. Presenting and supporting your opinion demand that you have a thorough understanding of the topic. Typically, an academic persuasive essay requires research. Additionally, this type of essay is generally longer and may use one or more organizational patterns to support the thesis. For example, in the body of this type of essay, a writer might use patterns such as cause and effect, advantages or disadvantages, or comparison/contrast to support the opinion.

EXERCISE 1

A. **Read the list of issues. Write your opinion about the issue and some reasons for your opinion.**

1. By the age of eighteen, everyone should have had to spend one year doing community service.

   Your opinion: _____

   Reasons: _____

2. Since the world is becoming a more global community, college students should be required to study abroad in order to better prepare them to become global citizens.

   Your opinion: _____

   Reasons: _____

3. Universities and colleges should be able to deny students from getting their degrees if they find inappropriate content on a student's personal social networking site.

   Your opinion: _____

   Reasons: _____

4. Because many people continue to work into their senior years, there should be a mandatory retirement age so that there will be more jobs for younger people.

   Your opinion: _____

   Reasons: _____

5. Students of any age should be permitted to have their cell phones in the classroom.

   Your opinion: _____

   Reasons: _____

B. **Work in a group. Discuss your opinions about the issues and the reasons for your opinions. Which issues do you know the most about? Did any of your opinions change as a result of your discussion? What caused you to change your opinion?**

The Art of Persuasion

Convincing others that your opinion is right is not simply a matter of feeling passionate about an issue. You need to show your **reasoning**—the logical process you used to form your opinion or judgement about the issue—with arguments that support your position and evidence that is based on your research. To be convincing, arguments must be **logical**, or sound. That is, they must clearly demonstrate what is true or false. Arguments that are not logical are called **flawed** or **faulty**. Look at these examples.

Example:

Teenagers are immature. Joan is a teenager. Joan will not be able to follow the rules for appropriate Internet use at her school.

This argument is not logical or convincing because it is a **generalization**—not all teenagers are immature.

Example:

The movie The Vampires of Park Pleasant is a fantastic film because it has grossed over $240 million dollars in worldwide distribution sales.

The argument is faulty because the money a movie earns is not a basis for evaluating its qualities as a good film.

Example:

Senator Shelton is an ineffective politician. He plays guitar and sings in a band.

This is a faulty argument and would not be convincing because it focuses on abilities that are not relevant to his abilities as a senator.

Example:

People who think that students should not have to learn another language just because they probably will not have to speak another language in their home country are simply stupid.

This is an ineffective argument because it is not based on evidence and could offend the reader by making a harsh judgment and using insulting language.

Example:

In a survey conducted by Kaplan Educational Services (2011), law school admissions officers reported they had not accepted certain students, even those with high test scores, if they found the students had posted unethical material on the Internet. In an instance like this, law schools should be able to view an applicant's online activity when deciding whether or not to accept him or her.

This is a sound argument. It is based on evidence. It provides facts and includes an example.

Ways to Develop and Support an Argument

Arguments need to be well-developed and supported. You need to show your reader that you have carefully considered and evaluated the evidence you have selected to support your opinion. Here are some different ways a writer might support an argument.

- **Personal experience** describes in detail relevant experience.

- **Logical reasoning** uses various methods that demonstrate logical thinking.
  - *Inductive* reasoning starts with specific case(s) and moves to general rule(s).
  - *Deductive* reasoning starts with more general rule(s) and moves to specific examples.
  - *Cause and effect* explains the causes and/or effects of a particular situation.

- **Analogy** demonstrates how two unlike subjects, such as the stages of life and a tree, are similar.

- **Statistics, facts, examples** provide concrete evidence to support an opinion.

- **Expert opinions** offer the perspective of individuals who are considered experts about an issue or topic.

- **Emotional appeal** creates a strong connection between the reader and the topic and appeals to a shared sense of beauty or ethics.

EXERCISE 2

Read these arguments. Circle "Yes" if you think the arguments are convincing or "No" if they are not. Write the reason for your answer. Then compare answers with another student.

Paragraph 1

According to our constitution, freedom of speech is the right of every man, woman, and child. That means that even opinions that most people would consider to be biased, ignorant, hurtful, and untrue can be expressed without punishment. Because of this, it is likely that most people will post derogatory remarks on their Facebook® pages without thinking about how it may affect their jobs and personal relationships.

Yes / No

Reason: _____

Paragraph 2

I recently participated in a volunteer program called "adopt a grandparent," in which I had to visit with an elderly gentleman who did not have a family. At first, I was not happy about having to get up on Saturday mornings to talk to an old person I did not know. To my surprise, I have not only gained a new friend, but have also learned more about how life was sixty to seventy years ago than I ever could have from a textbook. I never would have had this opportunity if my school had not required that I do thirty hours of community service. If students are not required to participate in community service, most will have no incentive to do it on their own.

Yes / No

Reason: _____

Paragraph 3

It is unbelievable that some people are so dense that they cannot see how living in another country and learning about other cultures will broaden a student's perspective and understanding of others. This opportunity should be available and affordable for all students, and governments and universities should be required to find ways to make it happen.

Yes / No

Reason: _____

Counterarguments and Refutation

When preparing to write a persuasive essay, you need to consider both sides of the issue. The arguments against your opinion are called **counterarguments**. A counterargument presents an opposing opinion and the argument that supports it.

In a persuasive essay, it is important to present the counterarguments. This shows that you have considered the issue from all sides. Then you can **refute**—prove that a statement or idea is not correct or fair—the opposing opinion.

A good strategy for organizing your ideas before you start writing is to sort all of the arguments related to an issue: those with which you agree and disagree.

EXERCISE 3

A. *Read the blog posting from students discussing various views about a topic.*

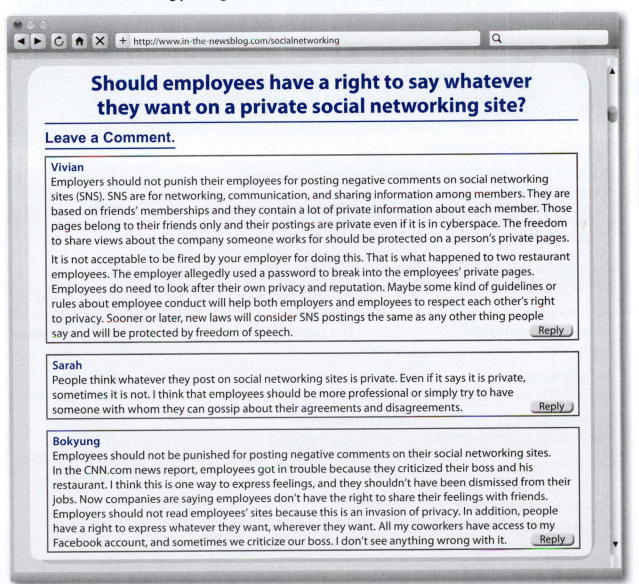

http://www.in-the-newsblog.com/socialnetworking

Should employees have a right to say whatever they want on a private social networking site?

Leave a Comment.

Vivian

Employers should not punish their employees for posting negative comments on social networking sites (SNS). SNS are for networking, communication, and sharing information among members. They are based on friends' memberships and they contain a lot of private information about each member. Those pages belong to their friends only and their postings are private even if it is in cyberspace. The freedom to share views about the company someone works for should be protected on a person's private pages.

It is not acceptable to be fired by your employer for doing this. That is what happened to two restaurant employees. The employer allegedly used a password to break into the employees' private pages. Employees do need to look after their own privacy and reputation. Maybe some kind of guidelines or rules about employee conduct will help both employers and employees to respect each other's right to privacy. Sooner or later, new laws will consider SNS postings the same as any other thing people say and will be protected by freedom of speech.

Reply

Sarah

People think whatever they post on social networking sites is private. Even if it says it is private, sometimes it is not. I think that employees should be more professional or simply try to have someone with whom they can gossip about their agreements and disagreements.

Reply

Bokyung

Employees should not be punished for posting negative comments on their social networking sites. In the CNN.com news report, employees got in trouble because they criticized their boss and his restaurant. I think this is one way to express feelings, and they shouldn't have been dismissed from their jobs. Now companies are saying employees don't have the right to share their feelings with friends. Employers should not read employees' sites because this is an invasion of privacy. In addition, people have a right to express whatever they want, wherever they want. All my coworkers have access to my Facebook account, and sometimes we criticize our boss. I don't see anything wrong with it.

Reply

B. Complete the T-chart with the arguments and counterarguments from the blog postings in Exercise A. Add your own arguments if you can.

For	Against

C. Work with another student. Compare your charts. Answer these questions:

- What is your opinion about the issue?
- Which arguments in the blog postings are based on personal experiences? Facts or statistics? An emotional response?
- Which arguments do you think are weak or cannot be supported?
- Is there enough information to argue the points effectively?
- In what order would you present the arguments? Why?

Persuasive Essay Patterns

The chart shows three different patterns of organization for persuasive essays.

Pattern A	Pattern B	Pattern C
Introduction -hook -explanation of the issue -thesis statement	Introduction -hook -explanation of the issue -thesis statement	Introduction -hook -explanation of the issue -thesis statement
Body Paragraph 1 counterargument(s) and refutation	Body Paragraph 1 reason 1 and supporting details	Body Paragraph 1 counterargument 1; refutation with supporting details
Body Paragraph 2 reason 1 and supporting details	Body Paragraph 2 reason 2 and supporting details	Body Paragraph 2 counterargument 2; refutation with supporting details
Body Paragraph 3 reason 2 and supporting details	Body Paragraph 3 counterarguments and refutation with supporting details	Body Paragraph 3 counterargument 3; refutation with supporting details
Conclusion • restatement of your thesis • summary of your points • final comment	Conclusion • restatement of your thesis • summary of your points • final comment	Conclusion • restatement of your thesis • summary of your points • final comment

Work in a group. Look at your T-chart from Exercise 3B. Choose one of the essay patterns from the chart on page 194. Use the information from your notes to make a chart for the essay pattern your group chose.

OUTLINES

After you have brainstormed and sorted your ideas, putting them into a simple outline will help you make a clear plan for organizing your essay. Remember that your outline is not written in stone! You can continue to make any additions or changes as you refine the ideas you want to include.

EXERCISE 5

A. **Read the writing assignment for a persuasive essay and a student's notes about the topic.**

Writing Assignment: In the past, personal written communication was most often conducted through the postal service. The arrival of email has added another way in which to communicate. Which is better: personal written communication delivered through the postal service or by email?

For email	Against email
-more convenient	-handwritten message more significant—more care given, takes more time to write/send
-only needs computer and Internet, won't run out of stamps or paper	-type of paper or stamp carries meaning
-benefits business correspondence; can make plans, set meetings, get answers fast	-more time between responses can heal hurt feelings, repair relationships
-better for the environment, no paper, no loss of valuable trees	-letters can be read in any location
-unlimited storage capacity, does not take up space	-letters have the human touch
-letters use paper, trees cut down, pollute the air	-email uses an energy source contributes to greenhouse gases
	-email needs Internet access
	-emails may disappear or get deleted, storage may not be permanent
	-letters can be passed down from generation to generation

I. Introduction

    A. Hook: statistic about the number of emails sent each day compared to letters

    B. Explanation of the issue

    C. Thesis statement

II. Body Paragraph

    A. Counterargument 1: emails more efficient/only Internet and computer

    B. Refutation

        1. letters carry more significance

        2. letters require more care, choosing paper, stamps, etc.

        3. extra time between letters can heal hurt feelings/heal relationships

III. Body Paragraph

    A. Counterargument 2: paper products cause greenhouse gases and harm the environment

    B. Refutation

        1. email uses energy sources, too

        2. letters can be read anywhere/no need for Internet access

        3. letters are tangible, so the reader feels closer to the letter sender

IV. Body Paragraph

    A. Counterargument 3: _____

    B. Refutation

        1. _____

        2. _____

V. Conclusion

    A. Restatement of the thesis: _____

    B. Summary of the main points _____

    C. Final comment _____

C. *Work with another student. Discuss these questions:*

- Based on the partial outline in Exercise B, what is the student's opinion about the topic? How do you know?

A. *Read the student's persuasive essay.*

Bao Wu

April 5, 2012

English 104

Professor Poole

Lasting Letters

Recent reports have shown that 563 million pieces of mail are sent each day compared to 294 billion emails (Postal Facts, 2011; Radicati Group, 2009). It is clear that the Internet has us corresponding and communicating with others more than regular mail ever has. Businesses and private citizens can make plans, set meetings, and get answers fast. However, the speed email offers does not necessarily make for better communication, especially when composing personal, heartfelt, or serious messages. We should not let email automatically be the first choice when it comes to letter writing simply because it is convenient. When it comes to personal communication, we need to preserve old-fashioned letter writing to ensure that we maintain alternative modes of communication, retain the human touch, and assure access to historical records.

Many people will never send a letter via "snail mail"[1] again and, in some ways, who can blame them? With email, all a person needs is an Internet connection and keyboard, followed by a click on *send*. In seconds, the message is sent and received. Sometimes, though, that is all the message conveys—an efficient communication or prompt reply. A handwritten letter, by today's standards, is anything but, and that is exactly why it has the potential to carry more significance. With a handwritten letter, or even a word-processed one, the whole process is slower from start to finish. First, the writer has to set aside time to choose the proper stationery. For some, the style and weight of the paper they select also carries a message—formal, informal, fun, or serious. Then, upon finishing the letter, there is the envelope that has to be addressed, stamped, and

[1] snail mail: mail that is delivered the traditional way through the post office

(continued)

physically carried to a mailbox. Additionally, this time factor can be to people's advantage. Consider how the lag time, or space between sending and receiving letters, may help diffuse strong emotions from being expressed like they might if the writers were sending off instant responses in emails in "real" time. Letters sent via traditional mail may serve to reconcile hurt feelings and repair relationships. An old-fashioned letter gives two people that time and space to view a situation from a different perspective before responding.

Having some extra time to carefully consider a response is not the only advantage to using traditional mail to communicate. There is no denying paper production causes greenhouse gases, but so does the power needed to send the increasing amount of spam email, according to a new report from McAfee and ICF International (2009). Both modes of communication contribute to our carbon footprint, and we need to be mindful of "Going Green" practices. One of the pleasures of letters, though, is being able to read them again and again over the years, and that does not take more paper or a power source. An inbox, however, needs an Internet connection, and emails can only be read in locations where it is available via a computer, e-reader, or smartphone. Letters, however, can be kept in any room, drawer, or a special box and shared with others. The letter holder controls the conditions and environment for reading. In addition, the letter itself is tangible. The act of unfolding the letter and touching the same paper that the sender had touched can make the reader feel closer and more intimately connected to the writer. None of this is possible with a virtual storage space. Even printed out emails don't have that human touch.

People will also argue that there is unlimited storage capacity for emails, and so they will always be able to have them. Is email storage permanent? Nobody can answer that yet. However, many people complain of the amount of email that accumulates in their inboxes and how it becomes a drudgery to continually have to delete or move it into folders. More problems develop when emails disappear into thin air or systems fail. The loss of special letters like the ones my grandfather wrote my grandmother when he was stationed overseas during World War I, or the ones from my parents when I studied abroad, or the ones from my husband when we were dating, would be devastating. These letters are an archive of my family's history and will be passed down from generation to generation. For these reasons, I would not want to rely on or give a virtual container the control to manage my precious possessions. Besides, it is doubtful that a person's inbox or email account will be easily accessible to succeeding family members. Would you want to take that risk?

In conclusion, the truth is, I could not live without my computer and could not live without email, but this does not mean that sending letters by traditional mail should become obsolete. It is a way of communicating that simply cannot be captured with all of our splendid technology. Writing letters forces us to slow down and consider our audience and expression of our ideas more carefully. Receiving letters gives us "live" documents that bring us closer to others. Finally, we need to be able to save letters safely to make it possible for them to become a repository of important events and memorable moments that become part of a family's legacy. If we let this practice disappear because it takes time, we will change the way we communicate and remember our past forever and not necessarily for the better.

References

The carbon footprint of spam report. Retrieved June 1, 2011 from
    http://img.en25.com/Web/McAfee/CarbonFootprint_web_final2.pdf

Postal facts. Retrieved June 1, 2011 from
    http://www.usps.com/communications/newsroom/postalfacts.htm

The Radicati group, Inc. releases "Email statistics report, 2009-2013." Retrieved June 1, 2011 from
    http://www.radicati.com/wp/wp-content/uploads/2009/05/e-mail-statistics-report-2009-pr.pdf

B. *Complete the outline in Exercise 5B with information from the essay.*

C. **Work with another student. Discuss these questions. Write your answers on the lines.**

1. How many paragraphs are in the essay? _____

2. What kind of hook is used in the introduction? _____

3. What is the thesis statement? _____

4. According to the thesis statement, what will the first body paragraph be about? What will the second body paragraph be about? What will the third body paragraph be about? _____

5. What counterarguments are addressed? _____

6. What types of supporting evidence does the writer use? _____

7. Underline the restated thesis statement in the conclusion. It may be more than one sentence. How is it different from the thesis statement in the introduction?

    _____

8. What kind of final comment does the writer use in the conclusion (warning, suggestion, recommendation, question)? _____

9. Which pattern of organization does the writer use—A, B, or C? _____

WRITING TASK

Follow these steps to write a first draft of a persuasive essay:
- Select a topic and brainstorm about it.
- Research and take notes.
- Organize and sort ideas.
- Write an outline.
- Write a first draft.

A. **Work with another student. Read the list of topics for a persuasive essay.**

- If a college or university becomes aware of inappropriate content posted by or about a student on the Internet, should the school have the right to deny that student a degree?

- Many colleges view applicants' social networking pages to help them determine whether or not to accept an applicant. Do you think admissions officers should be allowed to view applicants' pages?

- Should employers have the right to view prospective employees' online sites when hiring?

- Should high schools have the right to expel any student found to have posted inappropriate content on the Internet?

- Should employees have a right to say whatever they want on a social networking site?

- Should employers restrict workers' access to the Internet at the workplace?

- Which are better, digital readers or paper books?

- Should the post office be closed down?

B. *Choose a topic from the list above. Use one of the brainstorming techniques from Unit 5 to brainstorm about the topic. Think about what other information you need.*

C. *Research your topic. Make sure your sources are reliable. Take good notes and write detailed information about your source(s).*

D. *Sort and organize your ideas into a T-chart of* **for** *and* **against** *ideas.*

E. *Write a thesis statement for your essay.*

F. *Choose one of the patterns for a persuasive essay from the chart on page 194. Use your notes to make an outline.*

G. *Use your outline to write the first draft of your essay.*

Notes:
- Keep the first draft of your essay to use in Unit 9, Revision and Reference.
- Remember that you can change or add information to your outline and your essay as you write.

Check Your Writing

A. *Use this form to check your writing, or exchange essays with another student and check each other's writing.*

Essay Checklist

The essay . . .

1. states and supports a clear opinion about the topic. ☐

2. follows one of the patterns for the essay type. ☐

   circle one: A   B   C

3. has a thesis statement that states the controlling idea of the essay. ☐

4. includes enough supporting details. ☐

5. presents counterargument(s) and refutation(s). ☐

6. cites sources. ☐

7. has a conclusion that restates the thesis statement. ☐

8. Were there any faulty arguments? If so, write a question mark (?) in front of them on the paragraph.

9. Underline one or two sentences in the essay that you thought were interesting.

10. Do you have any questions for the writer? Write them here.

   _____

   _____

11. What changes do you suggest to improve the essay?

   _____

   _____

   _____

B. <u>Do not rewrite your essay yet.</u> *Check your writing for grammar, spelling, and punctuation errors, and make notes for possible changes to make in Unit 9.*

Revision and Reference

Revision is usually the final step of the writing process. In this step, you examine your work again with a critical eye to make sure your essay is focused, organized, well-developed, and accurate. Then you make any necessary changes to refine and polish your writing. In academic writing, you may write two or more drafts before you turn in your final work to your teacher.

> **Important Note:** For this unit, you will need the first draft of your essay from Unit 8 or the first draft of another essay.

Warm Up

> "I'm not a very good writer, but I'm an excellent rewriter."
> – James Michener, Pulitzer Prize–winning novelist

A. *Read the statements. Based on your experience, write **T** next to the statements that are true and **F** next to the statements that are false. Write **S** next to the statements if they are sometimes true.*

1. When I am writing my first draft, . . .

    _____ I ask for help if I am having a problem.

    _____ I use the notes from my research.

    _____ I usually spend ninety minutes or more, including prewriting.

    _____ I change, add, or delete sentences.

2. After I finish my first draft, . . .

    _____ I change, add, or delete sentences.

    _____ I ask someone other than my teacher to read it and give me feedback.

    _____ I do not read it before I hand it in to my teacher.

    _____ I check it for errors and make corrections.

    _____ I review it and hand it in to my teacher.

B. *Compare answers with another student.*

C. *Work with another student. Talk about what each step of the writing process means to you. Then discuss the questions. Use the steps in the box to help you.*

> choosing an organization pattern   organizing   researching
> drafting   prewriting   writing a thesis statement

- What step of the writing process has typically been the easiest for you? Why?
- What step has typically been the most challenging? Why?
- What are some other challenges you face in the writing process?

REVISION STRATEGIES

Revision is an essential part of the writing process. In this step, you take a fresh look at your work in order to make it more interesting, cohesive, and coherent for your reader.

The process of revision may involve . . .

adding
moving
deleting
rewriting
} words, phrases, paragraphs, or entire sections of a piece of writing.

Writers use several strategies to help them in the revision step of the writing process. These strategies may include . . .

- **Self-reviews**—using a checklist to carefully examine each component of your essay

- **Feedback from a teacher and peers**—considering responses from your readers and their suggestions for improving your essay

- **Proofreading**—correcting your grammar, spelling, and punctuation errors; usually the last step of the revision process

> **Note:** During the revision step of the writing process, writers usually start by rewriting sentences and paragraphs and leave proofreading until they have made all their changes. However, some writers rewrite and proofread at the same time.

Self-Reviews

Often students consider an essay ready to hand in as soon as they have finished writing their first draft. However, before you give your paper to your teacher or share it with your classmates, you need to check it carefully to make sure that you have included all the essential parts of an essay. You want to be certain that your ideas are well-organized, well-developed, and clearly expressed. You also want to check for and correct errors in grammar, spelling, and punctuation.

Use your essay draft from Unit 8 or another essay. Read your essay carefully and complete the Self-Review Checklist.

Self-Review Checklist

The introduction . . .

- includes an effective hook. ☐
- includes enough background information about the topic. ☐
- has a thesis statement that states the controlling idea, the main points, and the intent for the essay. ☐

The body paragraphs . . .

- each contain a topic sentence. ☐
- use appropriate patterns of organization (problem/solution, cause/effect, comparison/contrast, and so on) to develop and support the thesis statement. ☐
- have relevant details and examples to develop the main idea of the paragraph. ☐
- include key words, pronouns, and synonyms to connect the ideas between sentences. ☐
- include counterarguments to present different viewpoints about the issue (for a persuasive essay). ☐

The conclusion . . .

- restates the thesis using different words from those in the introduction. ☐
- briefly reviews the main points. ☐
- makes a final comment, such as a recommendation, warning, or suggestion. ☐
- does not introduce new ideas. ☐

The essay . . .

- includes a balance of original ideas, paraphrases, and quotations. ☐
- includes effective transitions that connect the body paragraphs. ☐
- has properly cited sources. ☐
- was checked for grammar, spelling, and punctuation errors. ☐

Peer Response

In addition to suggestions from your teacher about how to improve your writing, help and feedback from a **peer**—a classmate or another student—can be valuable.

A peer can tell you whether your writing was interesting and whether there were any sections or sentences that were unclear. In addition, a peer can give you suggestions for additional points to include.

You may have already participated in this kind of review for other writing assignments in this course.

EXERCISE 2

A. *Imagine that the first draft of the essay below is from a classmate. Read the essay.*

Min Cao
September 24, 2011
English 101
Professor Clarke

Book buyers are never going to give up reading, but will they ever consider changig from paper books to electronic readers? Many book lovers says they are too attached to their paper versions to ever switch to thin, light, e-readers. However, they are being unreasonable! Don't they care about the planet? Paper books are destroying our forests and polluting our air. People should stop buying paper books and use e-readers because they are eco-friendly, improve the reading experience.

There is no doubt that paper books all have a special place in our upbringing. However, producing paper causes greenhouse gases that pollute our air. The world population is now over 7 billion people and so the demand for paper will keep growing. Trees are part of our beautiful parks and are enjoyed by everyone. Trees offer shade on hot days and a cool breeze. Many trees are cut down each year reducing the number and variety of species. Forests should be protected because they provide oxygen for our planet. The wildlife is also severally affected and threatens their ability to survive. E-readers can help reduce our dependence on paper. One e-reader can hold hundreds of books and use minimal energy, so they help keep emissions that are harmful to the environment low. If more people use e-readers, libraries may need less space to store books, which means less space to heat and less pollution. If book lovers do not have to get in their cars and drive to the library or book stores, they will save on gas.

E-readers may make it easier and more fun for people who would not normally pick up a book, to try reading more. E-readers have a variety of settings. For example, the font size can be made bigger, making it possible for people with bad eyesight to read more easily. Upon using her e-reader for the first time, eighty-five-year-old Carolyn Cory exclaimed, "I can read so many more books now because I can make the words bigger." The font size can also be made smaller, so more words appear on a page. Pages can be made brighter or dimmer depending on the reader's preference. all these features make reading easier and more convenient for book lovers. Even more important is the finding in a study by Scholastic (YEAR), a publishing and education company, that 57 percent of children between the ages of nine and seventeen would like to use electronic readers and a third said they would be likely to read more if they had e-readers readers.

Finally, new versions of e-readers are in color and can connect to the Internet. This can make reading a whole new experience. Readers can check their email, do some shopping, or update their social networking sites. Not only that, on e-readers with the Internet, book lover can follow links and watch videos. According to a study by researchers Small, Moody, Siddarth, and Bookheimer (2008), senior citizens who surf the web may improve cognitive processes. Not only will e-readers engage users, but with Internet capabilities, it may also increase brain functions.

In conclusion, e-readers offer more pluses than minuses. They reduce the need for paper, so our forests can be preserved and our environment is cleaner. They may also increase brain power. The choice seems obvious, don't you think?

B. *Read the essay again. Circle any errors and underline any sentences or sections you don't understand. Mark any suggestions or ideas to improve the essay.*

C. *Complete the Peer Response Form for the essay in Exercise 2A.*

Peer Response Form

Your name: _____ Writer's name: _____

Date: _____

1. What is the controlling idea of the essay? _____

2. What kind of hook does the writer use? Is it effective for capturing the reader's attention?
   _____

3. Is there a clearly written thesis statement? According to the thesis statement, what specific
   areas or main points will the essay include? _____

4. What organizational patterns does the writer use in the body paragraphs?
   _____

5. Do the body paragraphs develop and support the thesis statement in a clear, logical way?
   _____

6. Are there enough reasons, details, and explanations in each of the body paragraphs?
   _____

7. What other details, explanations, or reasons could the writer add to support the thesis?
   _____

8. Is there any part of the essay that confuses you? Why? _____
   _____
   _____

9. What questions do you have about the essay? What is missing or unclear? What needs to be
   added, deleted, or moved? _____
   _____
   _____
   _____

10. What do you like about the essay? _____
    _____

11. What other suggestions do you have to improve the essay? _____
    _____

D. *Compare forms with another student. Discuss any differences.*

Work with another student. Exchange the first draft of your essay from Unit 8 or another essay. Complete the Peer Response Form for your partner's essay. Then discuss your suggestions with your partner.

Peer Response Form

Your name: _____ Writer's name: _____

Date: _____

1. What is the controlling idea of the essay? _____

2. What kind of hook does the writer use? Is it effective for capturing the reader's attention?
    _____

3. Is there a clearly written thesis statement? According to the thesis statement, what specific areas or main points will the essay include? _____

4. What organizational patterns does the writer use in the body paragraphs?
    _____

5. Do the body paragraphs develop and support the thesis statement in a clear, logical way?
    _____

6. Are there enough reasons, details, and explanations in each of the body paragraphs?
    _____

7. What other details, explanations, or reasons could the writer add to support the thesis?
    _____

8. Is there any part of the essay that confuses you? Why? _____
    _____
    _____

9. What questions do you have about the essay? What is missing or unclear? What needs to be added, deleted, or moved? _____
    _____
    _____
    _____

10. What do you like about the essay? _____
    _____

11. What other suggestions do you have to improve the essay? _____
    _____

REVISING YOUR FIRST DRAFT

After you have completed a self-review and a peer response, you are ready to begin revising your first draft.

In your revision, you may do all or some of the following:

add
move
delete
rewrite
} words, phrases, paragraphs, or sections of your essay.

EXERCISE 4

    A. **Work with another student. Look at these revisions to the sample first draft from Exercise 2.**

        Notice the following revisions:

- Added words, phrases, and so on, are highlighted.
- Deleted words, phrases, and so on, are crossed out.
- Moved words phrases, and so on, have [brackets].

    B. **Did the writer include any of your suggestions from the peer response in Exercise 2B? Tell the class which ones.**

Book buyers are never going to give up reading, but will they ever consider changing from paper books to electronic readers? Many book lovers say they are too attached to their paper versions to ever switch to thin, light, e-readers. However, they are being unreasonable! Don't they care about the planet? However, producing paper books are destroying our forests and pollutes our air. People should stop buying paper books and use e-readers because they are eco-friendly, improve the reading experience, and give readers options.

There is no doubt that paper books all have a special place in our upbringing. However, producing paper causes greenhouse gases that pollute our air. The world population is now over 7 billion people (source) and so the demand for paper will keep growing (source). Trees are part of our beautiful parks and are enjoyed by everyone. Trees offer shade on hot days and a cool breeze. Many trees are cut down each year reducing the number and variety of species. Forests

~~should be protected~~ not be cut down ~~because they provide oxygen for our planet.~~ ~~The wildlife is also severally affected and threatens their ability to survive.~~ E-readers can help reduce our dependence on paper. One e-reader can hold hundreds of books and uses minimal energy, so it helps keep emissions that are harmful to the environment low. Moreover, if more people use e-readers, libraries may need less space to store books, which means less space to heat and less pollution. Book lovers also benefit because they do not have to get in their cars and drive to the library or book stores, so they save money on gas and pollute less. The same is true for homeowners who may not have enough room for books. Some homeowners even rent storage space for their boxes of books because they do not have room for them in their houses. E-readers, help the environment, reduce energy costs, and save space . ~~If book lovers do not have to get in their cars and drive to the library or book stores, they will save on gas.~~

E-readers may make it easier and more fun for people who would not normally pick up a book, to try reading more. E-readers have a variety of settings. For example, the font size can be made bigger, making it possible for people with bad eyesight to read more easily. Upon using her e-reader for the first time, eighty-five-year-old Carolyn Cory exclaimed, "I can read so many more books now because I can make the words bigger." For readers who do not want to turn as many pages, the font size can also be made smaller, so more words appear on a page. Furthermore, pages can be made brighter or dimmer depending on the reader's preference. An e-reader is especially helpful to the person who cannot carry a heavy load. Often, book lovers walk out of a library or book store with an armload of books. E-readers, on the other hand, can hold hundreds of books and never weigh more. In addition, they can fit easily into a small bag so they can be transported anywhere. ~~all these features make reading easier and more convenient for book lovers~~. Even more important is the finding in a study by Scholastic (2010), a publishing and education company, that 57 percent of children between the ages of nine and seventeen would like to use electronic readers and a third said they would be likely to read more if they had e-readers ~~readers~~. [All these features make reading easier and more convenient for book lovers.]

(continued)

Finally, new versions of e-readers are in color and can connect to the Internet. This can make reading a whole new experience. Readers can check their email, do some shopping, or update their social networking sites. Not only that, on e-readers with the Internet, book lovers can follow links and watch videos. Detractors will say that all of these features are distracting and do not lead to deep, thoughtful reading (Carr, 2008). However, according to a study by researchers Small, Moody, Siddarth, and Bookheimer (2009), senior citizens who surf the web may improve cognitive processes. Not only will e-readers engage users, but with Internet capabilities, they ~~it~~ may also increase brain functions.

In conclusion, e-readers offer more pluses than minuses. They reduce the need for paper, so ~~our forests can be preserved and~~ our environment is cleaner. They make reading more accessible for some people while saving money and storage. They may also increase brain power. ~~The choice seems obvious, don't you think?~~ With all these benefits, why not become a 21st century reader and make the change to an e-reader?

EXERCISE 5

Use the Peer Response Form and any other suggestions you have received to begin revising your essay from Unit 8 or the essay you have used for this unit. Follow these instructions. Try to use as many as you can:

1. Move one or more phrases, sentences, or sections.

2. Rewrite or change one or more sentences.

3. Add one or more sentences.

4. Delete one or more sentences.

5. Read your second draft. How have these changes improved your essay?

   _____

   _____

   _____

Proofreading

Often, writers wait until after they have finished revising the content—**what** they are writing—before they concentrate on proofreading or correcting grammatical, spelling, punctuation, and formatting errors. In the proofreading stage of the process, the focus shifts to *how* the ideas are expressed. Trying to look at both aspects at once—the **what** and the **how**—of your writing can be challenging. Writers often find that they overlook significant errors when they try to edit and proofread at the same time. Once you are satisfied with the content, you can begin to focus on the details of how you have expressed yourself—your grammar, spelling, and punctuation.

Even though you are still learning English, you can find and correct many different types of errors. Here are some useful proofreading tips.

Guidelines for Proofreading

- If you used a computer to type your essay, use the spell check feature first. Then proofread it yourself.

- Read each sentence aloud slowly, one at a time.

- Read the essay once, focusing just on grammar and spelling.

- Read it again, focusing on punctuation.

- Read backwards—that is from the end to the beginning of the essay. This will help you focus on each word.

- Proofread one more time. You'll be surprised how many more errors you find.

One useful strategy for proofreading is to read one line at a time. You do this by covering your essay with another piece of paper. Then slowly move the paper down the page one line at a time. Reading one line at a time can help you find errors you miss when you are looking at the whole page.

EXERCISE 6

A. *Cover your revised essay with another piece of paper. Move the paper down to show the first line of your essay. Read it carefully. If you find a mistake, underline it. Then move the paper down to show the next line. Read it carefully. If you find a mistake, underline it. Repeat for each line.*

B. *Read the essay again without covering it with the paper. Use this proofreading checklist to look for grammar, spelling, and punctuation errors. Correct as many mistakes as you can.*

Proofreading Checklist

Language Use

- The essay uses appropriate language (formal register, no abbreviations or contractions). ☐

Grammar and Structure

- All sentences are complete sentences. ☐

- The subjects and verbs in all sentences agree. ☐

- Verb forms are used correctly. ☐

- Pronouns agree with their antecedents. ☐

- Gerunds and infinitives are appropriately used. ☐

- Articles are correctly used. ☐

- Sentences have parallel structure. ☐

- The first line of each paragraph is indented, or there is an extra line between paragraphs. ☐

Punctuation

- Each sentence ends with appropriate punctuation. ☐

- Apostrophes are used correctly to show possession. ☐

Spelling

- Names of people and places are spelled correctly. ☐

- Words that sound alike but have different meanings and spellings are correctly used (words such as *their/there, two/to/too, site/sight/cite*). ☐

Note: What kinds of mistakes do you often make? To create your own proofreading checklist, use the one above and add your most common errors. You can continue to use your personal proofreading checklist to help you find and correct errors in your future writing.

WRITING A REFERENCE PAGE

A **reference page** is a separate page at the end of your essay that includes more detailed information about the source(s) you used. When you finish revising your essay and know which sources you will include, you are ready to write a reference page. A reference page is sometimes called a **bibliography** or **works-cited page**. The information is always formatted in the same way. The reference page in this unit follows APA style.

Each type of source—book, periodical, or online article—you use requires specific information and formatting for the reference page.

These are examples of general entries for a reference page.

Print Sources

Books

Each reference to a book requires:

- Name of the author or authors and publication date
- Title of the book
- Location of the publisher
- Name of publisher

Example entry for book with one author:

Author   Year   Title   Location   Publisher

Turkle, S. (2011). *Alone together.* New York: Basic Books.

Example entry for book with more than one author:

Ampersand

Lee, S., McCann, D., & Messenger, J. C. (2007). *Working time around the world: Trends in working hours, laws, and policies in a global comparative perspective.* USA/Canada: Routledge.

Guidelines for Referencing Books

- **Alphabetize** authors by last name and use an ampersand (&) before the last author listed (format used for periodicals and online sources as well).

- **Capitalize the** last name and first initial of author(s), first letter of first word in title, first letter after a colon in title, cities, and publisher.

- **Place parentheses** around the year of publication.

- **Italicize** the title of book.

- **Use a colon** after the place where the book is published.

- **Periods** follow the author's first initial, date, title, and publisher.

Periodicals (Journals, Magazines, Newspapers)

Each reference to an article in a periodical requires:

- Author or Authors
- Year and month of publication, also the day if it is a weekly magazine
- Title of the article
- Title of periodical
- Volume number and issue (if included) for magazine or journal
- Page numbers

Example entry for reference page:

Author   Date   Title of article   Periodical   Volume/Issue   Page numbers

Dalton, C. (2011, February 21). Wired for distraction. *Time Magazine.* (177)7, 55-56.

Guidelines for Referencing Periodicals

- **Capitalize** the last name and first initial of author(s), months of the year, first letter of first word of title, and publication.

- **Place parentheses** around the date of publication and volume.

- **Commas** follow the author's last name, year of publication, and issue.

- **Italicize** the name of the periodical.

- **Periods** follow the author's first initial, date, title, name of periodical, and page(s).

Online Sources

Each reference to online sources requires the following, depending on the source type:

Online – periodical	Website page (no author)	Website page (authored by an organization)
• Author or authors • Date of publication (year, month, day) • Title of the online article • Name of periodical • Volume number and issue (if available) • Date article was retrieved • URL of article	• Name of page • Date of publication or n.d. (no date) if no date • Date page was retrieved • URL of source	• Name of organization • Title of page • Date of publication or n.d. (no date) if no date • Date page was retrieved • URL of source
If a source was accessed from a university website, write the name of the university after the retrieval date.		

Example entry for a periodical website page:

Author   Date   Title

Greer, J. (2010, May 12). 5 do's and don'ts for college students using social media.

Publication   Date retrieved

U.S. News and World Report. Retrieved November 10, 2011 from http://www.usnews.com/education/articles/2010/05/12/5-dos-and-donts-for-college-students-using-social-media

Guidelines for Referencing a Periodical Website Page

- **Capitalize** the last name and first initial of author(s), names of months, first letter of title, first letter of first word after a colon, name of publication, and the first letter of the word *Retrieved*.

- **Place parentheses** around the date of publication.

- **Commas** follow the author's last name, year of publication, the day of retrieval—for example, November 10, 2011.

- **Italicize** the name of the periodical.

- **Periods** follow the author's first initial, date, title, name of periodical.

- **URLs** that need two lines are broken before or after slash marks.

Example of entry for website page with no author:
Internet users in the world distribution by world regions. (2011). Retrieved October 15, 2011 from http://www.internetworldstats.com/stats.htm

Guidelines for Referencing a Website Page with No Author

- **Capitalize** the names of months, first letter of title, and the first letter of the word *Retrieved*.

- **Place parentheses** around the date of publication.

- **Commas** follow the day of retrieval—for example, November 10, 2011.

- **Italicize** the title of the page or document.

- **Periods** follow the title of the page or document and the date of publication if available.

- **URLs** that need two lines are broken before or after slash marks.

Example entry for website page with no author from a university website:
The Melbourne Newsroom. (2009). *Freedom to surf: Workers more productive if allowed to use the Internet for leisure.* Retrieved October 16, 2011, from the University of Melbourne website: http://newsroom.melbourne.edu/news/n-19

Note: The guidelines to reference a university website are similar to the guidelines for referencing a website page with no author. However, the name of the university follows the retrieval date and precedes the URL.

Reference Page Format

A reference page has a special format. To format a reference page you . . .

- center the title of the document—*References*—at the top of the page.

- list your sources alphabetically by the author's last name, the name of the online page, or name of the organization if there is no author.

- start each entry by the left margin and double space each entry.

- indent the subsequent lines five spaces (hanging indent). Word processing programs can be set to do this automatically.

Look at the reference page for the model essay in Unit 1.

References] (centered)

(alphabetical order) [*Internet users in the world distribution by world regions.* (2011). Retrieved October 15, 2011 from http://www.internetworldstats.com/stats.htm

(left margin) [Lee, S., McCann, D., & Messenger, J. C. (2007). *Working time around the world: Trends in working hours, laws, and policies in a global comparative perspective.* USA/Canada: Routledge.

(indented) [*the world: Trends in working hours, laws, and policies in a global comparative perspective.* USA/Canada: Routledge.

(double-spaced) [

The Melbourne Newsroom. (2009). *Freedom to surf: Workers more productive if allowed to use the internet for leisure.* Retrieved October 16, 2011, from the University of Melbourne website: http://newsroom.melbourne.edu/news/n-19

EXERCISE 7

Look again at the reference page above. Which type of source does each entry represent? Discuss your ideas with another student.

A. *Follow these steps to write two entries for a reference page for the sources cited in the sample revised essay in Exercise 4. Use the guidelines for writing reference entries on pages 215–217 to help you.*

1. Identify the type of source (book, article from a periodical, online).

   Reference 1 _____

   Nicholas Carr

   July/August 2008

   Is Google Making Us Stupid?

   The Atlantic

   Retrieved November 10, 2011

   http://www.theatlantic.com/magazine/archive/2008/07/
   is-google-making-us-stupid/6868/

   Reference 2 _____

   G. Small, T. Moody, P. Siddarth, and S. Bookheimer

   (2009)

   Your Brain on Google: Patterns of cerebral activation during internet searching

   The American Journal of Geriatric Psychiatry, Volume 17, Issue 2, pages 116–26

   Retrieved November 6, 2011

   http://search.proquest.com/docview/195989662?accountid=14068

2. Before you write, put the sources in alphabetical order by the author's last name or title of document or page, if there is no author.

3. Center the title *References* at the top of a sheet of paper.

4. Write the first line of the first entry by the left margin. If there is more than one line, skip one space and write the next line(s) by indenting five spaces. Word processing programs can be set to do this automatically.

5. Double space all entries.

6. Check to make sure each entry has the correct spelling, capitalization, periods, commas, parentheses, italics, and URLs.

B. *Compare your reference page with another student.*

Follow the steps in Exercise A to write a reference page for the essay you revised in Exercises 5 and 6. Then give your completed essay to your teacher.

References

Bandes, S. (2009). Victims, "Closure," and the Sociology of Emotion. *Law and Contemporary Problems* (72)2, 1-26.

Carr, N. (2010). *The Shallows: What the Internet Is Doing to Our Brains.* New York: Norton.

The Death Penalty Worldwide. (2007). Retrieved July 20, 2012 from http://www.infoplease.com/ipa/A0777460.html/

CNN Student News. (2009, May 5). Privacy vs. Professionalism. Retrieved August 6, 2012 from http://edition.cnn.com/2009/LIVING/studentnews/05/04/transcript.tue/index.html#three

Dehaene, S. (1997). *The Number Sense; How the Mind Creates Mathematics.* New York: Oxford University Press.

Environmental Protection Agency. (2012). *Climate Change—Greenhouse Gas Emissions.* Retrieved April 5, 2011 from http://www.epa.gov/climatechange/emissions/index.html

Environmental Protection Agency. (2012). *Climate change indicators in the United States.* Retrieved August 6, 2012 from http://www.epa.gov/climatechange/science/indicators/

Environmental Protection Agency. *Emission Facts: Average Annual Emissions and Fuel Consumption for Cars and Light Trucks.* (2000, April). Retrieved August 6, 2012 from http://www.epa.gov/oms/consumer/f00013.htm

Foerde, K., Knowlton, B. J., & Poldrack, R. A. *Modulation of competing memory systems by distraction.* PNAS 2006 103 (31) 11778-11783; published ahead of print July 25, 2006, doi:10.1073/pnas.0602659103.

Grant, A. (2011, September). Hummingbird Flight Secrets Revealed. *Discover Magazine.* Retrieved August 6, 2012 from http://discover.coverleaf.com/discovermagazine/201109?pg=14#pg14

Greitemeyer, T. and Osswald, S. (2010, February). Effects of prosocial video games on prosocial behavior. *Journal of Personality and Social Psychology.* 98(2), 211-221.

Growing Old in America: Expectations vs. Reality. (2009, June 29). Retrieved July 20, 2012 from http://pewresearch.org/pubs/1269/aging-survey-expectations-versus-reality

International Labour Office, Geneva. (2007, May). *Working time around the world: Main findings and policy implications.* Retrieved July 20, 2012 from http://www.ilo.org/wcmsp5/groups/public/---dgreports/---dcomm/documents/publication/wcms_082838.pdf

Kaplan Test Prep. (2011, October 11). *Kaplan Test Prep Survey Finds That Among Law School, Business School and College Admissions Officers, the Prevalence of Googling Applicants is Highest at Law Schools – By Far.* Retrieved August 6, 2012 from http://press.kaptest.com/press-releases/kaplan-test-prep-survey-finds-that-among-law-school-business-school-and-college-admissions-officers-the-prevalence-of-googling-applicants-i

Ketchum, J., Adams, F., Bloch, A. (2011, October.) *Accretion of Rocky Planets by Hot Jupiters.* The Astrophysical Journal Letters (741)1.

Kravets, D. (2009, June 9). AP reporter reprimanded for facebook post. *Wired.* Retrieved September 29, 2011, from http://www.wired.com/threatlevel/2009/06/facebooksword/

McAfee. (2009). *The carbon footprint of email spam report.* Retrieved June 1, 2011 from http://img.en25.com/Web/McAfee/CarbonFootprint_web_final2.pdf

National Center for Education Statistics. (2011). *Students with Disabilities.* Retrieved July 20, 2012 from http://nces.ed.gov/fastfacts/display.asp?id=64

National Science Foundation. (2007, May 7). *Scientists Offer New View of Photosynthesis.* Retrieved July 20, 2012 from http://www.nsf.gov

Ornes, S. (2011, September). Robots Invent Their Own Language. *Discover Magazine.* Retrieved August 6, 2012 from http://discovermagazine.com/2011/sep/16-robots-invent-their-own-language/

Partisan Polarization Surges in Bush, Obama Years. *Trends in American Values: 1987-2012.* (2012, June 4). Retrieved August 6, 2012 from http://www.people-press.org/2012/06/04/section-2-demographics-and-american-values/

Preventing Diarrheal Disease in Developing Countries: Safe Storage of Drinking Water. (2009, January).Retrieved August 6, 2012 from http://www.ehproject.org/PDF/ehkm/safe-storage2009.pdf

Radicati Group, Inc. (2009). *The Radicati Group, Inc. releases "Email statistics report, 2009-2013."* Retrieved June 1, 2011 from http://www.radicati.com/wp/wp-content/uploads/2009/05/e-mail-statistics-report-2009-pr.pdf

Ravnskov, Uffe. (n.d.). *The Cholesterol Myths.* Retrieved July 20, 2012 from http://www.ravnskov.nu/cholesterol.htm

Rideout, V., Foehr, U., and Roberts, D. (2010, January). *Generation M2. Media in the Lives of 8- to 18-Year-Olds. A Kaiser Family Foundation Study.* Retrieved August 6, 2012 from http://www.kff.org/entmedia/upload/8010.pdf

Scholastic Inc. (2010). *New Study on Reading in the Digital Age: Parents Say Electronic, Digital Devices Negatively Affect Kids' Reading Time.* Retrieved October 26, 2011 from http://mediaroom.scholastic.com/node/378

ScienceDaily.com. (2011, October 4). *2011 Nobel Prize in Physics: Discovery of Expanding Universe by Observing Distant Supernovae.* Retrieved August 6, 2012 from http://www.sciencedaily.com/releases/2011/10/111004091704.htm

Share the World's Resources. (n.d.). *Inequality in access to water.* Retrieved July 20, 2012 from http://www.stwr.org/land-energy-water/key-facts-water.html#_ftn8

Shirky, C. (2008). *Here Comes Everybody.* New York: The Penguin Press.

Smith, A. (2011). *Americans and text messaging.* Retrieved from http://pewinternet.org/Reports/2011/Cell-Phone-Texting-2011.aspx?src=prc-headline

UNICEF. (2005). The state of the world's children. Retrieved July 20, 2012 from http://www.unicef.org/sowc05/english/sowc05.pdf

Watkins, M. (2009, January). Picking the Right Transition Strategy. *Harvard Business Review.* Retrieved August 6, 2012 from http://hbr.org/2009/01/picking-the-right-transition-strategy/ar/1

What are the radiation risks from CT? (2009). Retrieved July 20, 2012 from http://www.fda.gov/Radiation-EmittingProducts/RadiationEmittingProductsandProcedures/MedicalImaging/MedicalX-Rays/ucm115329.htm

World Health Organization. (1999). *World Health Organization Report on Infectious Diseases.* Retrieved August 6, 2012 from http://www.who.int/infectious-disease-report/pages/textonly.html

Worldwatch.org. (2011). *U.N. Raises "Low" Population Projection for 2050.* Retrieved July 20, 2012 from http://www.worldwatch.org/node/6038

Social and Professional Writing

Introduction

There are many opportunities to write in English outside of school, such as writing emails, memos, or reports or memos for your job, or business letters to companies and service providers. You may also write on online sites for different reasons, such as to share information and opinions, respond to articles and blogs, network with professional colleagues, or socialize with family and friends. Job applications require specialized types of writing as well.

Business letters and memos are more formal than social writing and have specific formats, organization, language patterns, and vocabulary. In Part 4, you will practice skills necessary for writing in both social and some professional contexts. These units can be completed in any order, and you may want to focus on those that are most interesting and useful to you. These writing and language skills are for practical use both in and out of school.

Skills practiced in this section include:

- Professional Networking
- Opinion Writing
- Business Correspondence
- Cover Letters and Résumés
- Speech and Presentation Writing

Professional Networking

Professional networking is a form of meeting and communicating with other professionals. Correspondence mostly takes place between people online. A professional networking site helps people connect to one another. You might use the site: (a) to look for work, (b) to find and recruit an employee, (c) to learn about the latest developments in your field of interest, or (d) to discuss ideas about your area of professional interest with like-minded people. The largest professional networking website in the world at present is LinkedIn®, which is free to join.

Having a professional online presence is rapidly becoming essential for anyone engaged in a job search. Many companies check online profiles before contacting potential job candidates, so having a well-written professional profile is something that can set you apart from other job applicants.

In this unit, you will . . .

- learn about online professional networking sites.
- learn about the essential elements of a professional profile.
- write a summary of yourself for a professional networking site.
- write a recommendation for a colleague.

Warm Up

A. Work in a group. Discuss these questions:

- What are three of the best and three of the worst jobs in the world, in your opinion? Why?

- Do you know any people who love their job? Describe what they do and why they like it.

- If you could have any job in the world, what would you like to do? Why?

- What is most important to you in a job? Why?
  - a high salary
  - job satisfaction
  - working with a good team
  - something else

- What kind of employee are you (or would you be)? Describe some strengths and weakness you have as a worker.

B. Freewrite for five minutes about one of the topics in Exercise A.

A. *Read the survey questions and write your answers in the "Me" column. Then move around the room and interview your classmates. Find one person who answers "Yes" for each question, and write the person's name. When someone says "Yes," ask that person two follow-up questions of your own and briefly note the answers.*

Internet User Survey			
Find someone who . . .	**Me**	**Classmate's name**	**Notes**
1. uses a social network such as Facebook®.			
2. uses a professional network such as LinkedIn®.			
3. has taken an online course or attended an online lecture to learn more about a subject.			
4. reads blogs to learn more about personal or professional interests or specialization.			
5. has an online résumé or professional profile.			
6. has his / her own Website.			
7. takes part in online discussions to develop personal or professional knowledge.			
8. Compare answers with another student. Then use this space to write two or three interesting things you learned about your classmates while you did this survey.			

_____

_____

_____

_____

B. Complete the sentences. Then share them with the class.

1. _____ very is similar to me. We both _____.

2. Neither _____ nor I _____.

3. The person I spoke to who has the most knowledge about professional networking sites is _____. He / She _____.

4. Someone who uses the Internet to develop his / her professional area of specialization is _____. He / She _____.

5. No one I spoke to _____.

6. _____ is someone who makes a lot of effort to learn more about his / her area of specialization by using the Internet.

C. On a separate piece of paper, use the information from Exercises A and B to write a paragraph about the ways your classmates use professional networking. Use sentences similar to the ones in Exercise B, and include some of the interesting comments from question 8 of the survey in Exercise A.

PROFESSIONAL NETWORKING—INFORMATION AND SUMMARIES

On social networking sites, most users include personal information—name, gender, age, hobbies, interests, and so on. Most users upload photos as well.

However, on professional networks, users tend to include only information that will be of interest to potential employers, employees, and other professionals. To use professional networking sites effectively, consider why you are using that site. How would you like other people in your chosen profession to think about you? Remember that how you present yourself may make the difference between getting a job or not!

What to Include on a Professional Networking Site

A typical professional site includes . . .

- your full name.
- your current work position, if any, with your job title, name of company, and start date.
- the last few relevant job positions you've held, with dates.
- information about your education. Only list your high school if you have not attended college or a university.
- a professional summary.

It may also include . . .

- a current photo of yourself.
- a résumé, or a link to a résumé.

Note: If you upload a photo, make sure it looks professional: a nice clear picture of your face against a simple background. You should be wearing formal business clothes, such as a suit.

On most professional networking sites, you can also provide your full résumé. *(See Unit 4 for more on résumés.)* Remember that many recruiters may use a search engine to identify all the people on the network who have a specific certificate or who know someone that they know. Therefore, it is important to mention *all* your jobs, certificates, and professional details on your résumé, if possible.

Be careful of spelling mistakes! Proofread everything on your page carefully. Finally, to show that you are professional, update your profile regularly with a status.

EXERCISE 2

A. **Work with another student. Choose a job from your area of specialization or one of your own ideas. Imagine you are employers interested in recruiting someone. Discuss which information you think should be included on a professional networking site for the job you chose. On each line, write "D" for Definitely, "NS" for Not Sure, or "DN" for Definitely Not.**

____ first name and last name

____ current city and home address

____ hometown

____ email address

____ cell phone number

____ name of employer or school

____ names of all former employers

____ name of high school or university

____ current job title

____ photo

____ letter of recommendation from teachers

____ letter of recommendation from employers or colleagues

____ information about the family

____ key skills and knowledge areas

____ hobbies or interests

____ religion and political party or views

____ personal blog URL

____ a statement of personal philosophy

____ names of favorite books, movies, and music

____ a brief summary of who the person is and what makes him or her special

____ a professional résumé

____ university grades

____ favorite quotes

____ a statement of professional philosophy

B. *Imagine that your company has asked you to design a page for its website telling applicants how to apply. Write a paragraph about what kind of information your company requires from job applicants.*

C. *Read at least two classmates' paragraphs. How are they similar to or different from yours?*

EXERCISE 3

Complete the information for a professional networking site. If you have never worked, imagine a job you would like to do and use that information. You may also include part-time jobs and volunteer positions.

Name: _____

Current position: _____

Past position(s): _____

_____

_____

Education: _____

_____

_____

Professional Summary Style and Format

A **professional summary** is a short narrative about your background, skills, and abilities. The way you write it—words you choose to describe yourself, your skills, and your abilities—should also convey your personality.

Example:

Graphic designer with a dual degree in studio art and marketing from Western University seeks freelance design projects. Interned for two summers with top design firm Making Waves in Seattle, WA. Four years of freelance graphic design, including print and online media. Experience with commercial websites and personal blogs. No project is too big—or too small!

Experience with SEO optimization, branding, and both PC and Macintosh operating systems. Eager to listen to clients and help them turn their ideas into workable websites and effective brochures. Client list, references, and website samples available upon request.

Guidelines for Writing a Professional Summary

- Employers will not have much time to read your information, so keep your summary short (one to two paragraphs).

- Often writers leave off the personal pronoun and some auxiliary verbs.
  Example:

  I have experience caring for infants and toddlers. → *Experience caring for infants and toddlers.*

- Use strong verbs.
  Example:

  I was the night shift leader for three years. → *Supervised the night shift for three years.*

You may also choose to divide the summary into easily read parts by using headings or bullets.

Examples:

I am a competent professional with more than five years' experience in retail sales. I bring a love of people and a commitment to customer service, and have led many sales teams to success.

Skills **(Heading)**

Outstanding interpersonal skills and ability to lead and inspire others.

Abilities **(Heading)**

Excellent sense of aesthetics and design. Ability to transform a showroom or retail department into an inviting attractive atmosphere that draws customers.

OR

- *Skills—Outstanding interpersonal skills. Ability to lead and inspire others.* **(Bullet)**
- *Abilities—Excellent sense of aesthetics and design. Ability to transform a showroom or retail department into an inviting, attractive atmosphere that draws customers.* **(Bullet)**

EXERCISE 4

On a separate piece of paper, rewrite these sentences using professional summary style and format. Then compare your new sentences with a partner.

1. I have worked in the insurance industry for two years.
2. I was a coach for a co-ed youth baseball team.
3. I spent some time researching and writing newspaper articles.
4. I took part in an effort to raise money for public health charities.
5. I have some experience in training new employees.
6. When I was a senior, I helped out in the tutoring center in math and physics.
7. It was my job to coordinate communication among five overseas branches.
8. Part of my responsibilities included interviewing and hiring interns.
9. I am committed and energetic, and I enjoy working with people.

A. *Work with another student. Read the summaries below. Then discuss these questions:*

- What essential information does each include? What was missing?
- Is the format effective? Why or why not?
- What words does the writer choose that help to convey his or her personality?
- What do you like or dislike about each one?
- How could you improve them?

Summary 1

> A hardworking and creative young woman interested in working in public relations. Elected by the university to lead two large student organizations while still studying as a full-time student. Recently conducted two successful webinars. Excellent written and oral communication skills, with a passion for working with others.

Summary 2

> Experienced server and cashier looking for a position in restaurant management. Lots of experience, and at some pretty crazy places! Friendly and have a good sense of humor. Too many hobbies and interests to mention. College degree.

Summary 3

> Enthusiastic and dynamic student graduating in June this year with in-depth knowledge of market research. Interested in working at an entry-level position with a small company. Also open to positions in administration. Excellent at working in a team.

B. Begin designing your own professional summary. Follow these steps:

1. On a separate piece of paper, write a short profile (about four lines) about yourself at the top. Include your name.

2. Pass your summary to another classmate. Read the summary you received, and write a comment under it, with your name. Then pass it to another classmate. Continue commenting and passing until your teacher asks you to stop. You don't have to pass to the person right next to you—you can choose any classmate.

3. Find your original summary, and read all of the comments. Write a brief response to two or three of the comments. If you have time, discuss your responses with the people who wrote the original comments.

4. Keep your notes to use when writing your longer summary.

EXERCISE 6

A. Go online and read some of the profiles on LinkedIn®. Browse some member profiles by occupation. Copy and print one summary you like and, if you find one, one that you don't like.

B. Work in a group. Discuss the summaries you found. Did you see other styles of summaries that you liked? If so, describe them to your group.

Note: If you do not have a LinkedIn® account, you will have to create one; however, you can keep your profile and all information private, if you wish. There is no charge to use the basic service.

EXERCISE 7

Write a one to two paragraph personal summary for a professional networking site. Follow these steps:

1. Make some notes on what you would like to include in your summary. Write as many ideas as you can in five minutes.

2. Underline the most important points in your notes.

3. Develop the important points into a summary. Use the summary you wrote in Exercise 5B to help you get started.

4. Make sure that your summary contains the following information:
   • One sentence that gives the reader an overall sense of who you are
   • Clear information about what kind of work you are looking for and why
   • A description of your experience in that type of work
   • A strong statement about what makes you special and why someone should hire you

5. Check your work and correct any spelling mistakes.

LETTERS OF RECOMMENDATION

Professional networking sites such as LinkedIn® can include letters of recommendation written by other people. However, you cannot write a letter about yourself or edit other people's letters.

It is better to have a few letters that add business or professional value rather than a lot of letters of recommendation that say very little about you. Vague letters do not help. For example, "He is an excellent worker" is too vague. Ideally, you want someone to say *how* you are an excellent worker: "He has demonstrated that he is an excellent worker. For example, he has . . . + (examples of actions and results.)" Ask the person who writes your letter of recommendation to be specific and to include both personal and professional comments about you.

It is important to ask people who know you! If they don't know you personally or have not worked with you, their comments will be meaningless.

When you write a letter for someone else, begin by stating how you know the person: *I worked with Samir at . . . ; Carla was my employee for three years at . . . ; I supervised Eun Ji at . . .*

Finally, beware of certain phrases that are overused. LinkedIn® analyzed the profiles of millions of U.S. users and noticed that the same phrases were used repeatedly: *extensive experience, results-oriented, proven track record, team player, fast-paced,* and *problem solver.* You might try some of these instead: *depth of experience, focused on results, outstanding results, accelerated environment,* and *resolve issues.*

EXERCISE 8

A. **Work with a partner. Read these two letters of recommendation. Then answer the questions.**

> I have had the pleasure of working with Ana Mendoza at South Central High School since November 2007. During this time she has shown that she is an excellent teacher. She has extensive knowledge of her subject matter (science) and she is highly efficient—always working above and beyond expectations. Her students respect her enormously, as do her colleagues.
>
> She has a proven track record of remaining calm under pressure and behaving in a gentle but fair manner with our students. Importantly, she is a key contributor to our school, volunteering to take on extra roles such as Parents' Evenings and local community events. I would highly recommend her as an addition to the staff in your school.

(continued)

> *Although I have not worked with Pieter professionally, we have played on the same soccer team for three years, and we often talked about work. He is an exceptionally dedicated man who has worked hard to move up the ranks. In his first role at OPS, he was an office receptionist and was also responsible for office supplies. He managed this so successfully that—one year later—he was asked to take on customer services. Pieter quickly established himself in his new role and soon set up a number of new procedures, which enabled the company to work more efficiently.*
>
> *Pieter is kind, thoughtful, popular, and has a wonderful sense of humor. I would highly recommend him for any position.*

- What do the letters tell you about each person (a) professionally and (b) personally?

- Do the letters contain any overused words or phrases? If so, which ones?

- Which parts of each letter are vague? How are they vague?

- Imagine you are an employer, interested in recruiting one of these two people. Which letter gives you a more specific description of the person? Which one do you find more believable? Why?

B. **Work with another pair. Discuss your comments from Exercise A. Discuss how these letters of recommendation could be improved.**

EXERCISE 9

Browse some member profiles on LinkedIn® by occupation. See if you can find one effective and one ineffective letter of recommendation. Bring them to class to discuss in a group or with the class.

WRITING TASK

Follow these steps to write a letter of recommendation for a classmate:
- Read your classmate's summary from Exercise 7. What examples would you write in a letter to show that those points are true? For this exercise, you may have to invent information.
- Think of some comments about your classmate's personality that you could add.
- Develop your notes into a letter of recommendation of one to two paragraphs.

Check Your Writing

A. *Use this form to check your writing, or exchange letters with another student and check each other's writing.*

Letter Checklist

1. How many paragraphs does the letter have? _____

2. Does the letter talk about these things?

   • education _____

   • skills _____

   • work experience _____

   • personality _____

3. What specific examples were given? _____

   _____

   _____

4. Does the letter finish with a clear recommendation? _____

5. Underline your favorite sentence from the letter.

6. Do you have any other comments or suggestions for the writer? If so, write them here.

   _____

   _____

   _____

   _____

   _____

B. *Make changes to improve your letter. Remember to check your writing for grammar, spelling, and punctuation errors.*

People write opinions for a variety of purposes. For example, you may want to share your opinion of a book or movie by writing an online review; or you may want to write a letter to the editor of a newspaper or magazine about an issue you feel strongly about. A college or university application may require an essay in which you need to explain what makes you a good candidate for acceptance at that school. No matter who is reading your writing, you need to use language appropriate for your audience, clearly state your point of view, and effectively support it. Most opinion writing blends fact and opinion in an attempt to persuade an audience.

In this unit, you will . . .

- consider the importance of audience and purpose.
- practice distinguishing fact, opinion, and informed opinion.
- organize and write an opinion composition or letter.

Warm Up

Work in a group. Discuss these questions:

- Make a quick list of places where you commonly read opinion texts (for example, on the editorial page of a newspaper).

- When was the last time you read a piece of writing that expressed the author's opinion? Describe what you read.

- Have you ever changed your mind about an issue after reading something? If so, what was the issue? What caused you to change your mind?

- When was the last time you wrote something that expressed your opinion? Describe what you wrote and why you wrote it.

PURPOSE AND AUDIENCE

Opinion writing is usually intended to be persuasive. Sometimes it gives a call to action, asking the reader to do something specific, such as vote for a certain political candidate. Sometimes it tries to persuade the reader *not* to do something. For example, a negative book review implies that you—the customer—should not buy that book. When you write an opinion text, you express what you want people to think or do, and then you give several clear reasons to explain why.

In addition, it is important to determine for or to whom you are writing. Is it just your instructor? Your classmates? People in your community? People with similar beliefs to yours or people with different beliefs? You will probably choose to write differently for different audiences.

EXERCISE 1

A. *Write two possible purposes for each topic. Then compare your purposes with another student.*

    Example:

    a letter supporting a political candidate

    a. to persuade people to vote for that candidate

    b. to persuade people to work for that candidate

1. a letter protesting a tuition increase at your college or university

    a. _____

    b. _____

2. an opinion that one computer brand is better than another

    a. _____

    b. _____

3. an explanation of what makes you a unique and talented person

    a. _____

    b. _____

4. an opinion about a politician's plan to raise taxes

    a. _____

    b. _____

5. an opinion that electric cars are not efficient

    a. _____

    b. _____

Work with another student. Discuss at least two possible audiences for each topic in Exercise A.

> **Example:**
>
> an endorsement of a political candidate
>
> *a. businesspeople who might contribute money to a campaign*
>
> *b. voters who might vote for that candidate*

FACTS, OPINIONS, AND INFORMED OPINIONS

A **fact** refers to something that can be proved or disproved. For example, *The sun rises in the east* is a statement of fact; it can be checked and verified, and it happens to be true. *The sun rises in the west* is also a statement of fact, even though it is false.

An **opinion** is a matter of belief; it cannot be proved or disproved. *Ernest Hemingway was a great writer* is an opinion; there is no way that it can be shown to be true or false. People could reasonably disagree about it.

However, most opinions that you read in persuasive writing are not as simplistic as *Ernest Hemingway was a great writer*. Instead, authors give **informed opinions**—that is, opinions that they support with their own arguments or evidence. For example, *Ernest Hemingway was one of the most influential writers of the 20th century* can be supported with a discussion of how many books he sold, which literary prizes he won, and what writers he influenced. It is still possible to argue that he was not "one of the most influential" writers, so it is still not a fact in the same way that *The sun rises in the east* is a fact. However, it is more substantial than just a personal belief.

EXERCISE 2

A. **Read the statements. Write F if they are facts, O if opinions, or IO if informed opinions.**

_____ 1. The United States Postal Service (USPS) was founded in 1841.

_____ 2. It is an independent agency of the U.S. federal government in charge of delivering mail to American homes and businesses.

_____ 3. Home delivery of mail is an essential service in a developed country.

_____ 4. These days, people are sending less and less mail through the postal service because they are using email more often.

_____ 5. Email is cheaper to send, and it is faster, too.

_____ 6. In response to declining revenues, the USPS announced in 2011 that it would close over 50 percent of its mail-processing centers and eliminate 28,000 jobs.

_____ 7. In addition, overnight delivery of first-class mail was abolished.

_____ 8. However, if the postal service becomes less efficient, then people will be even less likely to use it—and so the cycle will continue.

_____ **9.** The postal service is too important to fail.

_____ **10.** The government must increase prices or raise taxes.

_____ **11.** The postal service is the second largest civilian employer in the United States.

_____ **12.** The postal service is, therefore, necessary for a healthy economy.

B. ***Look at the statements in Exercise A again. Underline the information in each sentence that helped you decide whether it was fact, opinion, or informed opinion. Then compare answers with another student.***

Writers sometimes begin opinion writing with phrases such as *I think, In my opinion, I believe that*, and so on. It is not necessary to do this, and doing it too much can make you sound uncertain. Since you are the author of your own writing, it is understood that you are writing from your own point of view.

Do not use phrases such as *It is well-known that, Everybody knows, The fact of the matter is* to present your opinions as if they are facts.

One effective way to introduce an opinion is the use of modals or expressions with similar meanings.

Examples:

Recycling on campus is an excellent solution to the problem.
↓
To solve this problem, we <u>must</u> begin a recycling program now.

Electric cars are better for the environment for two reasons.
↓
In thinking about the environment, there are two important reasons why we <u>should</u> consider electric cars.

Useful Modals and Phrases to Introduce Opinions	
Necessity	**Advice**
had better	ought to
have got to	should
have to	
must	
Other Expressions	
It is critical (that, to)	It is a good idea (to, for)
It is essential (that, to)	I recommend that
It is imperative (that, to)	I suggest that
It is necessary to	

A. *On a separate piece of paper, use the information provided to write two sentences that express an opinion. Use modals and phrases from the chart on page 237 to introduce the opinion.*

1. the USPS/close more processing centers and eliminate jobs

   It is critical that the USPS close more processing centers and eliminate jobs.

2. overnight delivery/be abolished

3. developed countries/have daily mail delivery

4. the government/not increase taxes

5. the Post Office/focus on saving jobs

6. people/use the post office regularly

B. *Compare sentences with another student. How did the way you introduced your opinions affect the meanings of the statements?*

A. *Choose one of these topics and write three facts, three opinions, and three informed opinions on a separate piece of paper.*

- chocolate
- solar energy
- the Olympics
- wood

- Spain
- women
- nutrition

B. *Work in a group. Take turns reading one of your sentences aloud. Do not read your sentences in order. The group decides whether each sentence is a fact, opinion, or informed opinion.*

ORGANIZATION OF OPINION WRITING

Opinion texts should be organized much like academic essays, although the language does not have to be as formal. An opinion text should have a clear thesis or opinion at the beginning, main points to support the opinion, details to support the main points, and then a conclusion that summarizes the main points and adds a final comment or a call to action.

Here are two common ways to order the main points, if you have several:

1. Weakest argument
2. Stronger argument
3. Strongest argument

The reader becomes more convinced with each new point and ends with a strong impression.

OR

1. Strong argument
2. Weaker argument
3. Strongest argument

The reader starts and ends with a strong impression.

Support for opinions includes facts, statistics, examples, anecdotes, quotations from studies or noted experts, informed opinions, and logical reasoning.

You will see opinion pieces that are organized differently, including pieces that are not really organized at all. However, using a clear (and expected) style of organization makes it easier for your readers to understand your arguments and follow your logic. Therefore, you will be more persuasive if your writing is well organized.

EXERCISE 5

A. **Find some examples of opinion writing. Check newspaper editorial pages, the letters to the editor of magazines and newspapers, and online blogs. If possible, find one that is organized well and one that is not. For each one, complete the following:**

1. Thesis or point: _____

2. Purpose: _____

3. Probable audience: _____

4. Number of main ideas: _____

5. Strongest or most convincing main idea: _____

6. Type(s) of support used to support the main idea: _____

7. Conclusion (that is, what does the writer want the readers to do or believe?):

_____

B. **Work with another student or group. Share one of the opinion pieces you read and explain why you did or did not find it convincing. Is there anything the writer could have done to make the piece stronger? If so, what?**

Supporting Your Opinions

After you state your opinion and the main points that support your thesis, you need to provide supporting details to fully develop a strong argument. These supporting details include facts and statistics, examples, anecdotes (a short personal story or experience), quotations from studies or noted experts, and informed opinions. You may already be familiar with some of these types of support and have learned about others in Part 3, Academic Writing.

Choose the types of details that will most effectively support the main points you have selected to develop your thesis. For example, in a movie or book review, you might choose to use examples and anecdotes. In a letter to the editor, you might want to include facts and statistics. The most important thing to remember is that in order to persuade your audience, your writing needs to be organized and logical.

EXERCISE 6

A. *Read this letter to the editor of a university newspaper.*

To the Editor:

I am writing to express my deep disappointment that the Board of Governors is considering a tuition increase for out-of-state students. Our university leaders simply have to find another way to increase revenues. Increasing tuition for non-residents not only will create financial hardship for a large percentage of students, but also may reduce university revenues over time.

The current tuition rates place an incredible strain on students who come from out of state. At the present time, the tuition rate for non-residents is nearly three times that of in-state students. Almost 20 percent of our student body is from out of state. Many of us are not only from neighboring states but also from a substantial number of countries other than the United States. Increases in tuition will make it much more difficult to finance education at this university. Many students come from families who are struggling to support their education now. There are also those students who have little or no support from family and must work, sometimes full-time, while going to school full-time as well. For many of these students, a tuition increase would mean a lost opportunity for education at a school known for its high-quality education. They simply couldn't afford to be here.

Over time, an increase in tuition rates may actually reduce revenue. As fewer out-of-state students apply and attend school here, the number of students paying a lower tuition rate will increase. Eventually that could mean a drastic drop in revenue because more students are paying lower rates. With less revenue, programs would have to be eliminated. With a loss of programs, fewer students, including state residents, might apply because the university cannot offer them the education that they want or need. Ultimately, a decision made to increase revenue actually may decrease it.

It is clear that a tuition increase would immediately increase revenue. What is not as clear is the effect such an increase would have on the students directly affected by it or the university itself over time. It is essential that we make our voices heard and attend the next Board of Governors' meeting on April 28th. One is better than none, but two are better than one. Our strength is in our numbers.

Sincerely,

Letitia Grae

Senior, College of Engineering

B. *Read the letter again. Underline the sentence that states the writer's opinion. Circle the sentences that give reasons to support the opinion. Double underline examples that the writer uses.*

C. *Work with another student. Discuss these questions:*

- What is the purpose of the letter?
- Who is the probable audience?
- What sentence(s) state the opinion?
- What modal or expression does the writer use to introduce her opinion?
- How many main points are there to support the writer's opinion? What are they?
- What details and examples does the writer use to support each main point?
- What sentence(s) summarize the main points of the letter?
- What does the writer want the readers to do or believe?

Further Practice

Research and Write

- Look in the newspaper editorial pages or letters to the editor of magazines, newspapers, or online review sites or blogs. Find a letter (or a posting) that expresses an opinion about a topic that interests you. Bring your letter to class.
- Work with another student. Share your letters and discuss the questions from Exercise 6B.
- Choose one of the letters and work together to write a brief response. Say whether you agree or disagree with the writer's opinion and give one or two reasons. Share your letter with the class.

A. *Read the statements. Decide whether the statements support a "yes" or "no" vote on Proposition 27.*

Proposition 27: The city should widen Vine Drive to include bike lanes and sidewalks.

- Taxes are already too high, and people in this neighborhood can't afford more.
- Children who walk home from school would benefit from sidewalks.
- If bike lanes existed, more people would ride bikes to work, and traffic would lessen.
- There were two serious bicycle accidents on Vine Drive last year, and one pedestrian was hit by a car.
- If the city widens this residential street, people with homes along the street would have to pay for some of the costs, and this isn't fair.
- The city should widen Vine Drive for two reasons. The street is not safe, and it is a good time to restructure the road.
- Putting in bike lanes and sidewalks will cost a lot of money, over half of which will have to come from increased taxes.
- Citizens in a community should help each other, even if their own street isn't part of the project.
- There have been some major problems with Vine Drive over the last few years.
- The city should spend its money on increased bus routes instead.
- Vine Drive is too narrow to be safe for bicyclists and pedestrians.
- Street repairs need to be made this year anyway, so this is the best time to restructure the road.
- The city must not consider widening Vine Drive.
- Vote No on Proposition 27.
- Vote Yes on Proposition 27.

B. *Organize the arguments from Exercise A into an outline that supports either a "yes" or "no" vote on Preposition 27.*

I. Statement of opinion (thesis) _____

II. Main point 1 _____

details and examples _____

_____

_____

III. Main point 2 _____

_____

details and examples _____

_____

_____

IV. Continue main points and details/examples as needed

V. Conclusion _____

_____

C. *Use your outline to write a letter to the editor of the town newspaper on a separate piece of paper. Urge readers to vote either "yes" or "no" on Proposition 27. You may add your own details and examples. Add your own conclusion.*

D. *Exchange letters with another student. On a separate piece of paper, answer these questions about your partner's letter:*

- What is the purpose of the letter?
- Who is the probable audience?
- What sentence(s) state the thesis?
- What modals or expressions does the writer use to introduce his or her opinion?
- How many main points are there to support the opinion? What are they?
- What details and examples does the writer use to support each main point?
- What sentence(s) summarize the main points of the letter?
- What does the writer want the readers to do or believe?
- What changes do you suggest to improve the letter?

E. *Review your answers to the questions with your partner.*

WRITING TASK

Write a composition or letter that expresses and supports an opinion.

A. *Choose a topic, purpose, and audience for an opinion composition or letter of 3–5 paragraphs. Complete this information.*

B. *Think about your purpose for writing and your audience. Then complete the outline.*

Topic: _____

Purpose: _____

_____

Audience: _____

   I.   Statement of opinion (thesis): _____

   II.   Main point 1: _____

            _____

            details and examples: _____

            _____

            _____

   III. Main point 2: _____

            _____

            details and examples: _____

            _____

            _____

   IV. Continue main points and details/examples as needed

   V.   Conclusion: _____

            _____

Check Your Writing

A. *Use this form to check your writing, or exchange compositions or letters with another student and check each other's writing.*

Opinion Composition/Letter Checklist

1. What is the purpose of the composition or letter? _____
_____

2. Who is the intended audience? _____

3. How many major points are there? _____

4. What types of support are used (facts, statistics, examples, anecdotes, and so on)?
_____
_____
_____
_____
_____

5. Was the argument convincing? _____ Why or why not?
_____
_____
_____
_____
_____

6. Underline any parts you had trouble understanding, and write a short note to the writer.

7. Do you have any other comments or suggestions for the writer? If so, write them here:
_____
_____
_____
_____
_____

B. *Make changes to improve your composition or letter. Remember to check your writing for grammar, spelling, and punctuation errors.*

Business correspondence may be an email, a letter mailed through the post office or sent as an attachment to an email, a memo, or even a document such as a business plan. Although there are a number of different types of business correspondence with a variety of formats, they all have one thing in common: written business correspondence must be polite, professional, accurate, and formal in tone.

In this unit, you will . . .

- review the format of a business letter.
- learn how to format a business memo.
- plan and write a business memo.

Warm Up

A. *Work with another student. For five minutes, make a list of types of correspondence people use for business (for example, email messages, reports, and so on). Share your list with another pair or a group. How many different types of correspondence were you able to list?*

B. *Work in a group. Discuss these questions:*

- What are some reasons businesspeople write instead of talking in person or on the phone?

- In what types of business situations is it better *not* to write? Explain.

- What types of business correspondence have you written and received? Have you written or received any business correspondence in English? Describe the circumstances.

BUSINESS LETTER FORMAT

Formal business letters usually follow a set format. This helps writers know how to organize the letter, and it helps readers find the important information.

Here is a standard business letter format:

1616 Blue Ridge Way
Aikenson, NC 28607] **1.** _sender's address_

November 24, 2012] **2.** _date_

Jeff Collins, Human Resources Director
Bloomwood Consulting
1423 Highwood Drive, Suite 12
Ann Abor, MI 48105
] **3.** _recipient's name, title, and address_

Dear Mr. Collins:] **4.** _greeting (or salutation)_

Xxx xxxxxxx xxxxxx xxxxxxxx xxxx x xxxxxxx. xxxxxxx xx
xxxxxxx xxxxx. Xxxxxx xxxx xxxxxxxx xxxxxxxxxx xxx
xxxxx. Xxxxx x xxxxxxxxxxx xxxxx xxxxxx xxx xxxxx
xxxxxxxxxx xxxxx xxxxxxxx.] **5.** _introduction_

Xxx xxxxxxx xxxxx xxxxxxxx xxxx x xxxxxxx xxxxxxx xx
xxxxxxx xxxxx x. Xxxxxx xxxx xxxxxxx xxxxxxxx xxxxxx
xxxxxxxx xxxxxxxxx xxxx. Xxxxx xxxxxxxx xxxxx xxxxxx
xxxxxxx xxx. Xxxxxxxx xxxx xxxxxxx xxxxx xxxx xxxxx.
Xxxxx xxxx xx xxxxxxx xxxx xx xxxxx xxxxxxxx xx xx.
Xxx xxxxxxxxxx xxxxxx xxxxxx.] **6.** _body_

Xxx xxxxxxx xxxxx xxxxxxxx xxxx x xxxxxxx xxxxxxx xx
xxxxxxx xxxxx x. Xxxxxx xxxx xxxx xxxxxxx xxxx. X xxxxx] **7.** _conclusion_
xxxx xxxxxxx xxxx xxxxx.

Sincerely,] **8.** _closing_

Lucia Alvarez] **9.** _signature_

Lucia Alvarez
Senior Marketing Specialist] **10.** _name and job title_

Note: In business communication, the title *Ms.* is the most appropriate for writing to a woman. The titles *Mrs.* and *Miss* are also used to address women.

- *Mrs.* is sometimes used for a married woman who uses her husband's surname (last name). However, some married women prefer *Ms.*

- *Miss* is generally used for a younger, unmarried woman.

Notes:

- In friendly letters, the greeting is most often followed by a comma: *Dear Charles,*

- In business letter greetings, either a comma or a colon is acceptable—*Dear Mr. Dumond,* or *Dear Mrs. Dumond:*—depending on how formal the situation is. The colon is always more formal.

- The closing in American English is always followed by a comma; however, in British English, the greeting and the closing are generally not followed by any punctuation.

EXERCISE 1

Read these common phrases from business letters. Where do they go in a letter? Write the phrases in the chart on page 249. Include the correct punctuation.

Best wishes,

Thank you for your consideration.

Dear Dr. Ibrahim,

I look forward to your reply.

I am writing to inquire about

I appreciate your contacting me about

Dear Sir or Madam:

I would be happy to meet with you to

If you have any questions, please do not hesitate to call.

Dear Ms. Schwartz:

In closing,

I am writing in response to

Kind regards,

Let me know if I can provide you with any further information.

Sincerely,

Thank you for your attention to

This letter is to explain

To whom it may concern:

Yours truly,

greetings	body of the letter	closings
	introduction	
	conclusion	

A. *Choose one of these situations and write a one-page business letter. Invent your own name and address for the recipient of the letter. Use expressions from Exercise 1.*

- You are interested in taking a trip abroad to do volunteer work. Think about where you would like to go and what kind of volunteer work you would like to do. Write to the organization and ask for information.

- You are a college graduate. The advising center of your former college has written to you asking you questions about your career/job. They want to know what qualities and qualifications are important for that career and if you have any advice to someone just starting out. They want to make this information available to graduating seniors interested in the same career.

- You recently returned from vacation. You stayed at a rather expensive hotel, but you experienced many problems. Write a letter to the manager.

- Write a letter to the manager of your apartment building. Suggest some general rules for the residents that would make the apartment building or complex a more pleasant place to live.

B. *Check your own letter with the checklist below. If necessary, make corrections to your letter.*

Business Letter Checklist

1. The letter includes:

- the sender's address ☐
- the date ☐
- the recipient's address ☐
- a greeting ☐
- an introductory paragraph ☐
- body paragraphs ☐
- a concluding paragraph ☐
- a closing ☐
- a signature ☐

2. The letter follows the correct format. ☐

3. The letter uses formal tone and language. ☐

4. The letter does not include slang or abbreviations. ☐

5. The letter uses complete sentences and correct grammar. ☐

6. The letter uses correct punctuation for business letters. ☐

C. *Exchange letters with another student. Answer your partner's letter with another business letter.*

MEMOS

Memo is short for *memorandum*. A **memo** is a type of formal business document, usually sent internally—that is, within the same company or office. Memos are used in situations such as these:

- To announce a change of policy
- To announce important new staff
- To report on a problem that affects a lot of people
- To make a recommendation for change
- To explain a new program

Memos are usually written on a computer and then distributed as email attachments or in hard copy. They are designed to be easy to read. Memos use major headings, minor headings, and bullet points to make it easy for the reader to locate information.

Here is an example of a standard memo format.

Date: April 11, 2012
To: Carl Pikestaff (can be one person or a group of people)
From: Transportation Committee (can be one person or a group of people)
Re: Recommendation on plant relocation (topic of the memo)

The memo begins with a short opening paragraph that states your reason for writing. You do not need a heading for the opening of a 1–2 page memo.

Major Heading

Use major headings to organize your document and make it easy for a reader to skim. Keep your paragraphs short. Avoid block text. In general, paragraphs should have more than one sentence but not more than six lines of text.

If you use bullets or numbered items in your memo, use at least two, but not so many that the list is hard to read. Bullets should be indented one tab space:

- First point
- Second point
- Third point

Left justify your paragraphs and use line breaks between them. Do not indent the first line of a paragraph.

Major Heading

XXX XXXX XXX XXXX XX XXXXXXXX XXXX XXXXXXX XXXXX XXXXXXXXXXX XXXXXX XXXXXXX XXXXXXXXX XXXXXX XXXXXXXXX XXXXXX XXXXXXXX X XXXXXXXXXXXXXX

Minor Heading

Minor Heading

X XXXXXXXXXXX XXXXXXX XXXXXXX XXXXXX XXXXXXX XXXXXXX XXXXXXX XXXXXXX XXXXXX XXX XXXXXXXXXXXXXX XXXXXXXXX XXXXXXXXXX XXXXXXXXX XXXXXXXX

Major Heading

XXXXXXXX X XXXXXXXXXXX XXXXXXX XXXXXXX XXXXX XXXXXX XXXXXXX XXXXXXX XXXXXXX XXXXXX XXXXX XXX XXXXXXXXXXXXXX XXXXXXXX XXXXXXXXXX XXXXXXXXXX

If you use minor, or secondary, headings be sure to use at least two in a section. Use different emphasis than you use for your major heading. For example, use italics instead of bold and keep your formatting consistent. Do not use two forms of emphasis together, such as italics *and* underlining.

End your memo with a brief closing paragraph that includes a call to action. You do not need a heading for the closing of a short memo.

If you have any questions, please email Contact Name at <email@address> or call extension 1234.

A. *Read this memo from an international company with offices in both Japan and the U.S.*

Date: September 24, 2011
To: Employees of XYZ Company
From: Naomi Weston, Director of Human Resources
Re: New email policy

This is to inform you about new company guidelines regarding email communication. Due to different cultural expectations with respect to email correspondence, guidelines have been established to facilitate collaboration between our offices in Japan and the United States. Email is the primary form of communication between offices, so it is important to consider these differences when working in a cross-cultural environment.

AMERICAN EXPECTATIONS
In the United States, email is the dominant form of business communication. Responses are expected within a few hours and are expected to refer to all points in the original message. Americans sometimes send off-topic or humorous emails to establish a friendly relationship with their colleagues.

JAPANESE EXPECTATIONS
In Japan, short texts and fewer focus points are preferred. Replies are sent when the recipient has had sufficient time for a thorough response. Emails are strictly limited to work-related topics. Japanese culture values phone calls as a more personal form of communication.

GUIDELINES
As a consequence of the different expectations, a new email policy has been established. Please be aware of the following guidelines:
- Answer emails within 36 hours. When full response is not possible, confirm receipt.
- Recipients are expected to address all relevant aspects of an email. Copying in the original message can be helpful.
- Keep sentences and paragraphs short; relay only essential information.
- Only Cc people who need copies.
- Email using the company address and servers is limited to work-related subjects. For personal email, please use your personal account outside of your scheduled work hours.
- If an issue would be better resolved over the phone, arrange a mutually agreeable time by email first.

This policy is important for the success of the company. To achieve efficiency, employees need to work according to the same set of rules. As with any type of communication between our offices, respect for our colleagues' cultural background is key. If you have any questions, please don't hesitate to reply by email or call 541-555-6409.

B. *Work in a group. Discuss these questions:*

- Who wrote the memo? To whom is it written?

- Why do you think this memo was written? Briefly summarize the main idea.

- What are the major headings? Minor headings?

- What questions or concerns do you think recipients of this memo might have? How could they express those questions or concerns?

WRITING TASK

Write a memo.

A. *Choose one of these situations, or choose a similar one after asking your teacher.*

- You are a manager at a company, and the company is starting a flextime system. You need to explain the changes in work hours to the employees.

- You are an employee of a company that has a lot of office parties—for birthdays, retirements, marriages, and so on. You want to express your opinions about these parties and some suggestions to your manager.

- You work in the Human Resources office of a large company. Due to construction, the employee parking lot will be closed for four months. You need to explain the situation and recommend several options for your employees who drive to work.

B. *Plan your memo. On a separate piece of paper, make an outline of your ideas. Use the outline below to help you.*

> From:
> To:
> Reason for writing:
> Major heading:
>   minor heading 1 (use bullet points as needed):
>   bullet:
>   bullet:
>   minor heading 2 (use bullet points as needed):
> Major heading 2:
>   minor heading 1 (use bullet points as needed):
>   minor heading 2 (use bullet points as needed):
> Major heading 3:
>   minor heading 1 (use bullet points as needed):
>   minor heading 2 (use bullet points as needed):

C. *Write your memo on a separate piece of paper. Use your own address or a realistic one from your country. Type or email your memo as an attachment to yourself, to a classmate, or to your teacher.*

Check Your Writing

A. *Use this form to check your writing, or exchange memos with another student and check each other's writing.*

Memo Checklist

1. What is the purpose of the memo? _____

   _____

2. How many major headings are there? _____

3. How many minor headings are there? _____

4. How many bullet points are there? _____ What is the purpose of the bullets?

   _____

   _____

5. Was correct memo formatting used? _____

6. Did the writer include contact information? _____

7. Was the memo clear? Underline any parts you had trouble understanding, and write a short note to the writer.

8. Do you have any other comments or suggestions for the writer? If so, write them here:

   _____

   _____

   _____

   _____

   _____

B. *Make changes to improve your composition. Remember to check your writing for grammar, spelling, and punctuation errors.*

UNIT 4 Résumés and Cover Letters

A résumé and cover letter provide a potential employer with a first impression of you as a job applicant and should demonstrate that you are a great fit for the job you are seeking. Your résumé highlights the specific job experience you have that is relevant to the position for which you are applying. Remember that employers often receive hundreds of résumés in response to a job posting, so yours needs to set you apart from other applicants. A well-written cover letter captures an employer's attention and lets that person know that you have taken the time to learn about the company. Your initial goal is to be the applicant who gets the interview.

In this unit you will . . .

- learn about researching a company.
- learn how to organize and write a résumé and cover letter.
- write a basic résumé.
- write a résumé and a cover letter targeted to a specific employer for a specific job.

Warm Up

Work in a group. Discuss these questions:

- Where have you seen books or materials on résumé writing? What information do you think is important to include on a résumé?

- Have you ever applied for a job that required a résumé? If so, what was the job?

- What are some of your work skills? What are some other experiences or qualities that would make you a good employee?

- When do you think you will need a résumé? How confident are you that you could write a good one?

GETTING STARTED

Researching a Company

As an increasing number of job applicants flood the job market, doing your "homework" before you apply for a job is essential. You want your prospective employer to know that you have researched the company and carefully considered why you would be a good candidate for a job there. Once you have done your research, you will be able to create your résumé to show how your skills, abilities, personality traits, and work experience are relevant to the job for which you are applying.

One of the best places to get current information about a company is the Internet. Enter the name of the company as a key word in an Internet search engine, and you will most likely find a number of links that you can follow to learn more about the company. Most companies strive to establish a presence in the virtual world, so it is likely that the company will have a Website that can provide you with a wealth of information.

Here are some things to look for when you are examining a company's Website.

Guidelines for Researching a Company

- Start on the Home page. Then look for a tab or link that says something such as *About* or *About Us*. On this page, you will usually find a brief history of the company, an overview of the services and / or the products it provides, and a vision or mission statement.

- Read the mission statement. Most mission statements are designed to remind employees of what the founder(s) of the company imagined the company would be and why it exists. The mission statement can reveal a lot about the values of the company and what employees are expected to provide to the customers.

- Look for a slogan or tagline—a short memorable phrase that the company uses to identify itself or its goals. Look carefully at the words. Think about the how those specific words communicate what is important to the company.

- Follow the link to the *Employment* page. Look at what it says about working for the company. Think about the qualities you have that would make you a good fit for a job there.

- Follow the links to other pages of the company's website. Make notes about anything you find particularly interesting or significant.

A. Work with another student. Read the statements and slogans from company Websites. Then discuss these questions:

- What kind of service or product do you think the company provides?
- Who would the customers be?
- What makes the company different from others like it?
- What does the company think is important in serving its customers?

Website 1

About Us | Services | Careers | News | Contact

Moneybank's Mission

We're more than money in and money out. We're the neighbor down the street who's always there to help. Low interest on the money out, high interest on your money in—and in you.

Website 2

About Us | Services | Careers | News | Contact

Our Vision

Dress up or dress down—We've got you covered from head to toe.

Our mission is to provide a unique shopping experience for every customer guided by expert fashion consultants in a professional and welcoming environment.

Website 3

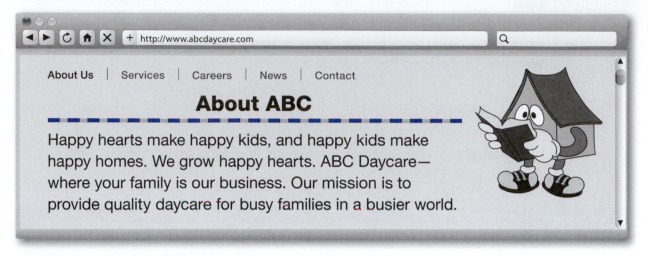

Website 4

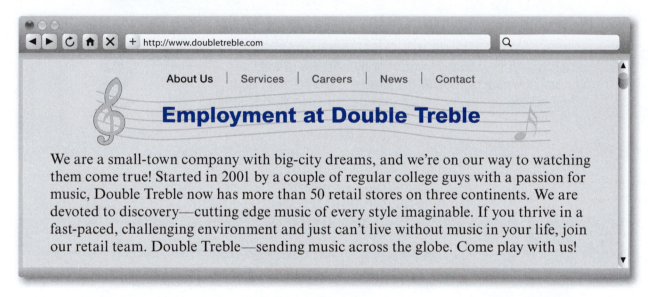

B. *Choose two companies from Exercise A. On a separate piece of paper, make a list of the education, skills, and personality traits that a person would need to be successful at each company. Then share your lists with another student.*

Gathering Information

Another important step in writing a résumé is to brainstorm your outstanding skills, abilities, and personality traits and to gather detailed information about your educational background and work experience. As you learned in Part 3, Unit 5, there are many effective brainstorming techniques from which to choose. What is most important is that you select the technique that will best help you generate ideas. As you brainstorm, remember to write down *any* idea that comes to mind. At this stage of the writing process, it is important to get *all* of your ideas down on paper. Do not consider any thought unimportant. You will review your ideas and select the best ones later in the prewriting stage.

Brainstorm a quick list of your skills, abilities, and personality traits. Remember—every idea counts! You can edit your list later.

EXERCISE 3

A. *Complete the information about your educational background. If there are things you don't know or have forgotten, research the information online or make phone calls. Make notes on a separate piece of paper. Start with your current educational institution. List any others you have attended, starting with the most recent.*

Education

Name of school or institution: _____

Address: _____

Program/Field/Major: _____

(Expected) Diploma, degree or certificate: _____

(Expected) Date of graduation: _____

Scholarships, awards, offices in organizations, etc: _____

Academic advisor or other academic reference: _____

B. *Complete the information about your work history. Make notes on a separate sheet of paper. Start with your current or latest employer, and list any others, starting with the most recent.*

Employer

Date(s): _____

Address and phone: _____

Position(s): _____

Responsibilities: _____

_____

Supervisor(s): _____

A. *Read the résumé. Then discuss the questions with another student.*

Greg Murray

---

298 Hammond Avenue Apt #4   Home phone: (612) 555-2266
Minneapolis, Minnesota 55403   Cell phone: (612) 555-4860
email: gmur93@netmail.net

Position Desired: Seeking full-time entry-level position in health administration

Education: 2011–present   University of Minnesota, Minneapolis, MN
                           School of Public Health

            2011   Southwest High School
                   Minneapolis, MN

Experience: 2011–present   Assistant Activities Coordinator
                            Abergreen Nursing Home, Minneapolis, MN
                            Part-time: plan, schedule, and coordinate evening and
                            weekend art, music, and exercise programs (both on and
                            off site); prepare budgets

             2010–2011   Hays Drugstore
                         Cashier

Skills: 85 words per minute on word processor. Proficient with Microsoft Office
         programs Excel, Word, and Access. Can use QuickBooks and other accounting
         software. Can build and maintain websites. Can navigate all major social
         networking sites. Excellent communication skills.

Interests: Hiking, kayaking, skiing, playing cello, cooking

Honors and awards: Dean's list, departmental scholarship

Volunteer work: Food Pantry; Environmental Advocacy

• Where does Greg live right now?

• Has Greg graduated from the university yet?

• What job does Greg want? What skills do you think this job involves?

- Do you think Greg is qualified for the job? Why?

- When did Greg graduate from high school?

- Does Greg have a job right now? Where in the résumé do you find the answer to this question?

- What are some ways Greg spends his time when he is not busy with school or work?

- Look at the language in the résumé. What are three examples of the use of phrases instead of full sentences? In each example, what part of speech is the first word of the phrase: noun, verb, adjective, or adverb?

- Why do you think Greg includes information about his hobbies?

WRITING A RÉSUMÉ

There are many different formats and styles for a résumé, and examples of them can be found online. Use *résumé* and *sample résumé* as search terms to find them. In general, a résumé should not be more than one page long. You do not have to include information about hobbies or volunteer work, but do include these if your résumé does not fill a page. There should not be any spelling, grammar, punctuation, or formatting mistakes in your résumé. Try writing several drafts. Make small changes to present information in different ways and to get the best fit on a page.

Guidelines for Writing a Résumé

- List your most recent education first. It is not necessary to include high school unless you are a current university student or younger. Never include junior high school or elementary school.

- If you have graduated from a college, name your degree: for example, B.A., Economics. If you are close to graduation, you can indicate this by writing: Expected date of graduation: June 2016.

- If you have work experience, list your most recent employment first. To describe your job responsibilities, use short phrases that begin with verbs rather than complete sentences.

- It is important that the information you include on your résumé be accurate. Keep in mind that many employers check the information in an applicant's résumé. If you misrepresent yourself on your résumé and that is discovered, you will not get the job.

These days, most resumes are sent as attachments to an email. However, some companies still request a paper résumé. In addition, if you go to a job interview, you should have a few hard copies of your résumé with you. Follow these guidelines:

- Use good paper. The paper should be white or off-white. Use a simple, common font in 12-point or 11-point.

- Never fold your résumé. Use a large envelope if you mail it, and use a folder to protect it if you carry it to an interview.

It is a good idea to take your résumé to a career counselor, a friend, or someone else who will proofread your résumé. Even high level managers depend on others to read, format and edit their cover letters and résumés. You might consider hiring a professional writer or editor to help you. If there is a career development center or a writing lab at your school you might also get assistance at these places. Public libraries often offer workshops on writing résumés and cover letters.

You should have a basic résumé and keep it updated as you apply for new positions. That way you can provide specialized versions for specific potential employers more quickly than if you have to write a completely new résumé each time you need one.

Notes: Greg's résumé, on page 260, is a **chronological résumé**. In a chronological resume, information about education and employment history is given in reverse chronological (time) order. List your most recent experience at the top of each section. People without any prior work history might want to try writing a **functional résumé**. You can go to a career or employment agency or to the library for samples, or you can look online. Use the words *example functional résumé* as a search term.

A. *Use your brainstorm from Exercise 2, your information from Exercise 3, and the sample résumé in Exercise 4 to write a draft of your basic résumé on a separate piece of paper. Then check these points and revise as needed.*

- Is your current contact information at the top of the résumé?

- Did you include accurate dates for all education and work history?

- Are the responsibilities at the jobs listed clearly described?

- Is the information arranged clearly in chronological order, starting with the most recent?

- Are columns and tabs even?

- Is there enough space between sections?

- Have you bolded or italicized anything to make it stand out?

- Did you use phrases that begin with verbs instead of complete sentences most of the time?

- Did you mention that you can provide references and transcripts?

B. *Work with another student. Ask your partner the questions in Exercise A about the information on his or her résumé. Make any suggestions you may have for improvement.*

C. *Make a note of any changes you may want to make to your résumé. Save this draft for use later in this unit.*

COVER LETTERS

When you give or send your résumé to a potential employer, you need to include a cover letter with it. Many people apply for a single job. As you learned earlier in this unit, the cover letter should demonstrate that you have some knowledge about the employer and the position. Focus on what the company or the manager wants in an employee. Your cover letter may also repeat basic information from your résumé, such as your main qualifications and relevant work experience.

Be sure to read any job advertisement very carefully. Put yourself in the position of the person who wrote that ad. Your cover letter must convince the employer that you are exactly the right person for the position.

Write a new cover letter each time you apply for a position. It should reflect your knowledge about the company or organization to which you are applying, and it should highlight skills, abilities, personality traits, and work experience that make you a good match for the position you want.

Cover Letter Format

Look at the format for a cover letter.

First and last name
Address
Telephone number
Email address

Month Day, Year

Mr./Ms./Dr. First Name Last Name
Title
Name of Organization
Street or P. O. Box Address
City, State Zip Code

Dear Mr./Ms./Dr. Last Name:

Opening paragraph: State why you are writing, how you learned of the organization or position, and basic information about yourself.

2ⁿᵈ paragraph: Tell why you are interested in the employer or type of work the employer does. Demonstrate that you know enough about the employer or position to relate your background to the employer or position. Mention specific qualifications which make you a good fit for the employer's needs. Focus on what you can do for the employer, not what the employer can do for you, and on how your personality and character are a good fit for the employer and for the job. Mention relevant items from your résumé, and mention that your résumé is enclosed. If an application form or any other items are enclosed, mention them as well.

3ʳᵈ paragraph: Indicate that you would like the opportunity to interview for the position or to talk with the employer. State what you will do to follow up, such as telephone the employer within two weeks. If you will be in the employer's location and could offer to schedule a visit, indicate when. State that you would be glad to provide the employer with any additional information needed. Thank the employer for her/his consideration.

Sincerely,

Your handwritten signature (on hard copy)

Your name typed
(In case of email, your full contact information appears below your printed name instead of at the top, as for hard copy, and, of course, there is no handwritten signature)

Enclosure(s) / attachments (refers to résumé or other relevant attachments)

Note: The contents of your letter might best be arranged into four paragraphs. Consider what you need to say and use good writing style.

Read the example cover letter. Then work with another student and answer the questions.

Cynthia Hazelman
23 56th Avenue, Apt. 12B
New York, NY 10023
CyHaze@myserv.org

March 18, 2013

Mr. John Jamison, Director
Friends of Feathers
PO Box 419
Minneapolis, MN 55403

Dear Mr. Jamison,

I am writing to apply for the Administrative Assistant position advertised in the *Star Tribune* on March 17, 2013.

I am interested in animal welfare, and especially in the protection of birds. I belong to the Audubon Society, and I have volunteered for their bird count every winter. I have also worked in raptor rehabilitation programs, helping to release hawks that had recovered from injury back into the wild. I realize that the work of an administrative assistant is not "field work," and that I would not have direct contact with birds or spend time in their natural environment. However, I am a very thorough and efficient office worker. I have experience with both electronic and paper filing systems.

I can use all Office software applications and all major social media. I have worked as a receptionist, and recently I have been researching and typing documents as an assistant in the biology department at the university. Friends of Feathers has had a positive image in our community for as long as I can remember. It is also ranked very highly on Charity Ratergater. I would be delighted to work for an organization with your reputation. I am honest, hard-working, creative, self-motivated, and I handle stress well. I am supportive of coworkers and supervisors.

I have enclosed my résumé as an MS Word attachment. I would appreciate the opportunity to talk to you about this position. I will contact you in two weeks to check on the status of my application. I would be very happy to provide you with any additional information needed. Thank you very much for your consideration—and for the work you do to maintain the habitats of wild birds in our area.

Sincerely,

Cynthia Hazelman

Cynthia Hazelman

Enclosure: résumé

(continued)

- What job is Cynthia applying for? Where does she state this?
- What is the purpose of her second paragraph?
- What do you think are her strongest qualifications?
- What else is she sending with this letter? Where does she say so?

A. *Read this ad from a Communications and Public Relations department at a hospital.*

Major hospital seeks a motivated individual to work with our outreach team. A qualified candidate for this entry-level position will have a degree or certificate in communications, health administration, or recreation. Experience in a hospital, clinic, or nursing home a plus. The job involves arranging and promoting various health and wellness workshops, classes, and seminars along with follow-up communication and outreach to discharged patients. Must be able to plan, organize, implement, and evaluate programs without much supervision. Must be sensitive to issues of diversity. Must have knowledge of Microsoft Office, QuickBooks, and other accounting software. Excellent oral and written communication skills and ability to work online required. Candidate must be friendly, sensitive, and positive in order to work with individuals and families who are dealing with pain or illness. Send cover and résumé to Claudia Kramer, Unison Health Facilities, Minneapolis, MN 55403.

B. *Reread Greg's résumé on page 260. Highlight anything in the ad that you think would make Greg a good match for this position. Compare ideas with another student.*

C. *On a separate piece of paper, work with your partner to list qualities and personality traits you think Greg should have in order to make this employer happy. List any of Greg's academic or educational experience that might make him a good candidate.*

D. *Take turns role-playing Greg and the interviewer. You may continue to refer to the job posting, but turn your papers over so that you cannot look at your lists. Explain why you would be a great match for this position.*

On a separate piece of paper, write a cover letter for Greg. Then work in a group. Read your cover letters to each other. Based on your group's feedback, write another draft of your cover letter for Greg.

WRITING TASK

Write a cover letter for a job.

A. *Follow these steps to write a cover letter:*

1. Choose one of these job ads.

Now Hiring Sales Associates

Do you need immediate income? Are you enthusiastic and outgoing? Are you motivated and persistent? If you answered "Yes!" we want you on our sales team. Our dynamic group of young men and women are making money (a lot of it) and having fun! Part- or full-time. Flexible schedules. No sales experience needed, but a passion for music a must. Send cover letter and résumé to Human Resources Department, Double Treble, Inc. PO Box 123A, Mescla, CA 11111.

MoneyBank Financial
Financial Services Officer

MoneyBank Financial with headquarters in Charlemagne, NC, has an opening for a Financial Services Officer to work with customers in the Bull City and Smythefield areas. Responsibilities include selling loans and related services to organic farmers and start-up green and eco-friendly businesses. This bank officer will be responsible for analyzing and processing credit applications, managing public relations, and other related activities. Bachelor's degree in agriculture, business, or related field. Lending experience preferred. Excellent salary and benefits package. Send résumé to David Barrington, MoneyBank Financial, PO Box 7777, Bull City, NC. 27777.

Early Child Education Specialist

Premier daycare center in upstate New York seeks a caring, compassionate Education Specialist to work in our new facilities in Livingstone Lodge, NY. Bachelor's degree in Early Childhood Education required. Prefer 2 to 3 years experience in pre-school education, but will consider the right candidate with less experience. Outstanding benefits package, including company paid medical and dental, paid vacation, and flexible spending option. No weekends, and flexible hours available. We are located in the heart of the mountains, less than two hours from New York City. Send cover and résumé to: Celia Fulton-Clarke, ABC Daycare, 173 W. Main Street, Livingstone Lodge, NY. 12333

---

2. Reread the mission statement and/or company slogan from Exercise 1B for one of the ads you have chosen. Think about how you will present yourself as a great match for the job. Highlight or underline sentences or phrases in the ad that make the employer sound like a great fit for you. Then reverse this thinking. Write a cover letter for the job, describing how you would be a great fit for the employer.

Check Your Writing

A. *Use this form to check your writing, or exchange cover letters with another student and check each other's writing.*

Cover Letter Checklist

1. Is the letter formatted correctly? _____ Check for sender's name, date, receiver's name, greeting, closing, and signature.

2. How many main paragraphs are there? _____

3. Do the points in the cover letter refer to language or details in the ad or job posting?

   _____

4. Does the letter indicate that the applicant will follow up? _____

5. Does the letter say that a résumé is enclosed? _____

6. Underline one or two of the most effective sentences in the cover letter.

7. Do you have any other comments or suggestions for the writer? If so, write them here:

   _____

   _____

   _____

   _____

   _____

   _____

B. *Make changes to improve your cover letter. Remember to check your writing for grammar, spelling, and punctuation errors.*

C. *Work in a group. Exchange cover letters. Find out how many in your group would hire you and why.*

Speech and Presentation Writing

Being able to write and deliver a speech or presentation is an important skill, not only in school or academic settings, but also in the work world. A good speech or presentation captures the audience's attention and keeps it. An effective speech, like a good piece of writing, is well organized so that the ideas are easy to follow.

Some speakers write out their speeches and presentations before delivering them. This way, they can plan the content and then time their speeches and practice their presentation skills.

In this unit you will . . .

- learn about how to organize a speech or presentation.
- learn how to write an outline for a speech or presentation.
- learn how to write a strong opening and closing.
- write a speech.
- write notes to use when you speak.
- write a script for a speech.

You will work on both short speeches and longer presentations.

Warm Up

Work in a group. Discuss these questions:

- What occasions do you see in the pictures below? Why is the person giving a speech or presentation?

- What are some other situations in which people give speeches or presentations, and why do they do so?

- What is the last speech or presentation you gave? What was the topic, and how did you feel about your delivery of the speech?

- What is easy for you about giving speeches and presentations? What is challenging?

ORGANIZING YOUR SPEECH OR PRESENTATION

Speeches may be formal or informal, and there are different conventions for each type. For any type of speech, however, you should think carefully about your audience and your purpose.

It is important to organize and present your information clearly. Your listeners cannot go back and check what you said in the same way that a reader can go back and check what was written.

Like an essay, a speech or presentation has an introduction, body, and conclusion. A popular saying about organizing speeches is, "Tell them what you're going to tell them; tell them; and then tell them what you told them." This means that your introduction should clearly outline your speech, the body should present your important points in a logical manner, and your conclusion should clearly summarize your main points.

The Introduction

A typical introduction includes . . .

- a hook to capture the audience's attention, such as an anecdote, saying, quotation, or joke.

- background information about the topic and a statement or two that briefly explains what the speech will be about.

For formal written reports and essays, you have probably been told not to write things such as "This report is going to be about . . ." However, in an oral presentation, you can be more direct. It is completely acceptable to say something such as "Today I'm going to talk about some solutions to the trash problem in our community."

The Body

The body generally includes two to four main points, which are developed and supported with details such as statistics, examples, explanations, or anecdotes. In the body of your speech, it is also important to use clear signal words and phrases such as "First, we can . . .", "The second solution is . . . ," and "Finally, we can . . ."

The Conclusion

The conclusion restates and summarizes the main points of the speech. In the conclusion, it is acceptable to more directly introduce the summary of your main points. For example, you may say something such as, "Today I talked about three solutions to our trash problem and explained how each of them is not only affordable but also will save us money." You might also use a signal word or phrase such as, "In conclusion, . . ." or "To summarize, . . ." The conclusion may also include a call to action or final observation.

Read these sentences from a speech. Write I if they are part of an introduction, B if they are part of a body, and C if they are part of a conclusion.

_____ **1.** Moving on to the second characteristic, . . .

_____ **2.** I'm going to talk first about the history, then describe what it's like in the present, and finally make some predictions about the future.

_____ **3.** That is the main challenge. Now, I have two answers to that challenge. The first one is . . .

_____ **4.** So we looked at how it's made, where it's made, and some of the different things it can do.

_____ **5.** I'd like to tell you a little story that shows just why Jack is such a great friend.

_____ **6.** I hope my photos have convinced you that Alaska is a beautiful, exciting, and educational vacation destination.

_____ **7.** And if those first two reasons weren't enough, here is a third reason to support zoos.

_____ **8.** Whenever I think about the meaning of education, I am reminded of a quote by Aristotle.

OUTLINING THE SPEECH

As you have learned in previous units, an outline will help you to organize your thoughts so that you can present them in a logical order. Notice how this outline is similar to that of an essay.

  I. Introduction
    A. hook
    B. background information
    C. statement of main points

 II. Body
    A. Point 1
      1. detail to support point 1
      2. detail to support point 1
      3. detail to support point 1

    B. Point 2
      1. detail to support point 2
      2. detail to support point 2
      3. detail to support point 2

(continued)

C. Point 3

    1. detail to support point 3

    2. detail to support point 3

    3. detail to support point 3

    (Continue with main points and supporting details as needed)

III. Conclusion

    A. restatement of main points

    B. final comment or call to action

To plan the body of your speech, you may want to begin by sorting information into three or four subtopics. This will help you plan your speech more easily and quickly. You will also find that there are many different ways to organize your ideas about the same main topic.

For example, imagine your topic is "raisins." Here are some different ways to organize your ideas about that topic:

Raisins and agriculture:	**Characteristics of raisins:**
1. How they're made	**1.** Appearance
2. Where they're grown	**2.** Taste
3. What they're used for	**3.** Nutritional value
Cooking with raisins:	**Different food grades of raisins in the U.S.:**
1. Use in salads	**1.** Grade A
2. Use in main dishes	**2.** Grade B
3. Use in desserts	**3.** Grade C

EXERCISE 2

A. *Organize three of these topics into two to four main areas. Try to spend no more than three minutes to write each one. Use the topic organizer above to help you.*

- horses
- trees
- babies
- the sun
- winter
- education
- your childhood
- a recent fad
- socks

B. *Work in a group. Share your ideas. Briefly discuss the kind of information you could use to support each main point.*

Writing Introductions and Conclusions

Anecdotes (short personal stories) or quotations are a popular way to begin an introduction. After you capture your audience's attention with "the hook," you can tell them what main ideas you will discuss. Then in your conclusion, you can summarize your main ideas and—if possible—refer to the hook of your introduction. A conclusion can also recommend an action to the audience or make a prediction. As with other types of writing, do not introduce new ideas in your conclusion.

Look at these examples from the introduction to a speech about friendship. Which one(s) would more likely capture your attention?

Examples:

For me, there are three important qualities of a good friend.

A popular saying about friendship goes like this: "Don't walk behind me; I may not lead. Don't walk in front of me; I may not follow. Just walk beside me and be my friend."

The day I met Margot, it was pouring rain. My car had broken down on an isolated country road, and I had walked for about half a mile. I was soaking wet and my hands were like ice. Of course, my cell phone was sitting on my desk where I had left it after rushing out that morning. I sensed a car approaching from behind. Should I wave my arms and try to stop the driver? Thoughts of my parents' warnings and gruesome stories about what could happen to someone alone on a country road bombarded my brain. The car slowed, and came to a stop beside me. As the driver lowered the window, my heart began to race. But one look at this stranger's face told me it was all going to be OK.

EXERCISE 3

A. **Work with another student. Discuss what kinds of topics could include these quotations or sayings. Try to think of more than one topic for each one.**

   a. In prosperity our friends know us; in adversity we know our friends. –John Churton

   b. A change is as good as a rest. –Proverb

   c. When a man tells you that he got rich through hard work, ask him: "Whose?" –Don Marquis

   d. Laugh, and the world laughs with you; cry, and you cry alone. –Popular saying

   e. A writer is somebody for whom writing is more difficult than it is for other people. –Thomas Mann

   f. Out of sight, out of mind. –Proverb

   g. Even if you're on the right track, you'll get run over if you just sit there. –Will Rogers

   h. Think like a wise man but communicate in the language of the people. –William Butler Yeats

B. *On your own, chose two of the topics that you wrote about in Exercise 2. Go online to find two quotations, proverbs, or sayings that you could use as a hook for each one.*

C. *Now think of a short anecdote you could use to introduce the same topic. Write it on a separate piece of paper.*

D. *Share your hooks with another student.*

A. *Match these concluding sentences to the quotations and sayings in Exercise 3.*

_____ **1.** So now that you've learned some ways to tell if you're on the right track, remember that once you're there, to keep going.

_____ **2.** With these two simple memory tricks, you might find that your most fantastic sights are never out of mind.

_____ **3.** I hope this simple story of a time when plain language was more effective than fancy language will reassure those learning English as a second language.

_____ **4.** As you can see from the examples of these two people, even experts work hard, struggle, and worry about failure just as beginners do.

_____ **5.** Remember, then, no matter how successful you become—you didn't get there alone.

_____ **6.** Those are three positive benefits to change, then: it helps you grow, it helps you learn, and it even helps you rest.

_____ **7.** "A friend in need is a friend indeed" is another saying that sums up this truth about relationships.

_____ **8.** I'm not hoping that you'll have a reason to cry, of course, but if you do, at least now you'll know of some benefits of tears.

B. *Compare answers with another student. Discuss some of the topics you thought of in Exercise 3A.*

WRITING NOTES

Very few people memorize entire speeches. However, it is not interesting for an audience to watch you read a paper word for word. Instead, learn to speak from notes or from the slides of presentation software.

On note cards, write your main points and supporting information. Use one card for each main point, and as many cards for supporting information as necessary. Also use a note card for anything that you might not remember—a long quotation from someone else, for example, or facts and statistics and their source.

Your note cards should remind you of what you want to say—they're prompts, not a script. Practice speaking so that you can glance at your cards to remind you of what to say, and then look up and make eye contact with your audience.

EXERCISE 5

A. **Choose one of the topics you worked on in Exercises 2 and 3. Write out, by hand or on a computer, a brief speech. Then make notecards for your main points and any other information you wish.**

B. **Work in a small group. Take turns giving your speeches. Use your notecards for reference only. When everyone has finished, discuss these questions:**

- What did you write on your notecards?

- Do you wish you had written more notes, fewer notes, or were your notes just right?

- How easy was it to speak from the notecards?

- What is something you think was successful about your speech? Is there anything you wish you had done differently?

WRITING TO BE READ

In general, spoken English is less formal than written English. Speakers use more contractions. They use more idioms and phrasal verbs. They may use more slang and casual expressions. Humor, understatement, and exaggeration are also more common in speaking.

If you wish to draft a speech by writing it out first, remember to include these informal features. However, a speech is still more formal than a conversation; naturally, do not write out words and expressions such as "Um," "I dunno," and "OK, you guys."

A. *Complete the script for a short speech with expressions from the box. Then practice reading it aloud a few times.*

> at all   in fact   practically
> for example   let me tell you something
> imagine   now   this

There are many ways to embarrass yourself when you travel. _____, I remember spending a week in Kyoto, Japan. The food there was delicious, and I went to a restaurant for lunch and dinner every day. _____ I don't speak or read a word of Japanese, so I certainly couldn't handle a menu. But they have _____ great system over there—many restaurants have a window outside the restaurant with plastic models of the food they serve. So I would just take the server outside and point to what I wanted. Well, one day I tried that at a little lunch place. I thought the server was shy or _____, because she didn't want to come with me. But I needed my food! I was hungry! So I took her firmly by the arm and _____ dragged her out to the little window. I pointed to what I wanted—a nice chicken curry—and she finally nodded. Good, I thought! _____ my embarrassment when I realized a little later that she was not, _____, a server at the restaurant _____! I'd dragged another customer outside! I felt terrible, but the customer and the real server just smiled at me. And I got my chicken curry. But _____, I never went back to that restaurant again.

B. *Work with a partner. Read the script in Exercise A again. Which features sound informal? How would you change those if you were writing a formal paper or giving a more formal speech?*

C. *Work with another student. Give the talk in your own words, without reading at all.*

FOCUSING ON DETAILS

Speakers often use a variety of presentation techniques and visual aids to more clearly illustrate their points and keep the audience engaged. As you plan your speech, think about some of the visual aids and techniques that you could use to make your speech more interesting to the audience.

EXERCISE 7

Read the list of visual aids and techniques. Consider whether each technique would appeal to you as a listener, and check the appropriate column. Then compare your answers with a group or the class.

	Like	No Strong Feelings	Don't Like
1. Jokes or humorous stories			
2. Photographs and/or videos			
3. Charts or graphs			
4. Information or research from outside sources			
5. Music			
6. Presentation software (for example, PowerPoint)			
7. Audience asking questions during the presentation			
8. Audience taking notes			
9. Audience participating in some kind of activity			
10. Audience asking questions at the end			
11. Handouts			
12. Speaker asking questions of the audience during the presentation			

WRITING TASK

Write and deliver a speech.

A. **Follow these steps to write a ten-to-fifteen-minute speech.**

1. Choose one of these situations:
   - Give a speech to your classmates to sum up the end of this course.
   - Give a speech about a hobby or interest of yours.
   - Give a speech to congratulate someone on graduating, getting a job, getting married, or retiring.
   - Give a speech about an important value or idea (honesty, hard work, education, success, friendship, etc.).
   - Explain how to do something you can do well.
   - Describe a place you know well.
   - Persuade your classmates to take an action or believe something.

2. Brainstorm a list of ideas that you might include in your speech.

3. Organize your ideas into two to four main areas. Use the idea organizer in Exercise 2 to help you.

4. Select two or three main points you want to include in your speech.

5. Make a simple outline for your speech. Use the format on pages 271–272 to help you. First, fill in the main points. Then select details you want to include.

6. Fill in the introduction section of your outline. What type of hook do you want to use? What background information do you need? Use the main points you wrote in the body of your outline to write a statement of main points for the introduction.

7. Fill in the conclusion section of your outline. How will you summarize your main points? What final observation or call to action do you want to include?

B. **Prepare note cards for your speech. You may also use presentation software instead of notecards.**

Check Your Writing

A. Use this form to check your note cards and your speech.

Presentation/Speech Writing Checklist

1. Who is the (real or imagined) audience? _____

2. What is the purpose of the speech? _____

3. How many main points does the speech have? _____

4. What kind of support is used for each main point? _____
   _____
   _____

5. What is the hook? _____

6. What background information did you include? _____
   _____
   _____

7. Does the conclusion refer to the hook? _____

8. What features of informal speech did you use? _____
   _____
   _____

9. How many notecards will you need? _____

10. Will you use any visual aids or other presentation techniques? _____

B. Make changes to improve your speech and notes. Then practice giving your speech from your notes.

C. Work in a group or with the whole class. Deliver your speeches to each other. After each person speaks, discuss these questions:

- Were the introduction, body, and conclusion clear and easy to follow?

- What hook did the speaker use in the introduction?

- What were the speaker's main points?

- Did the speaker summarize the main points in the conclusion?

- Did the speaker make a final observation or call to action in the conclusion? What was it?

APPENDIX
Frequently Used Words in English

This list was compiled from the Pearson International Corpus of Academic English. It contains the top 3,000 words in the corpus ranked by raw frequency. The Pearson International Corpus of Academic English, Version 1.2010 was developed and is owned by Pearson Language Tests, London, UK, a division of Edexcel Ltd (http://www.pearsonpte.com/).

a	adapt	alien	apparent	assessment	band
abandon	adaptation	alike	apparently	asset	bank
ability	add	alive	appeal	assign	bar
able	addition	all	appear	assignment	barrier
about	additional	allocate	appearance	assist	base
above	address	allow	applicable	assistance	basic
abroad	adequate	ally	applicant	assistant	basically
absence	adequately	almost	application	associate	basis
absent	adjacent	alone	apply	association	battle
absolute	adjust	along	appoint	assume	be
absolutely	adjustment	alongside	appointment	assumption	bear
absorb	administer	already	appreciate	assure	beat
abstract	administration	also	appreciation	at	beautiful
abuse	administrative	alter	approach	atmosphere	beauty
academic	admission	alternative	appropriate	atom	because
accelerate	admit	alternatively	appropriately	attach	become
accept	adopt	although	approval	attachment	bed
acceptable	adoption	altogether	approve	attack	before
acceptance	adult	always	approximately	attain	begin
access	advance	amazing	arbitrary	attempt	beginning
accessible	advanced	ambiguity	architecture	attend	behalf
accident	advantage	ambiguous	area	attention	behave
accommodate	advertising	among	arena	attitude	behavior
accommodation	advice	amongst	argue	attract	behind
accompany	advise	amount	argument	attraction	being
accomplish	advocate	an	arise	attractive	belief
accord	aesthetic	analogy	arm	attribute	believe
accordance	affair	analysis	army	audience	belong
accordingly	affect	analyst	around	author	below
account	afford	analytical	arrange	authority	beneficial
accumulate	afraid	analyze	arrangement	automatic	benefit
accuracy	after	ancient	array	automatically	besides
accurate	afternoon	and	arrest	autonomous	between
accurately	again	anger	arrival	autonomy	beyond
accuse	against	angle	arrive	availability	bias
achieve	age	angry	art	available	big
achievement	agency	animal	article	average	bill
acid	agenda	announce	articulate	avoid	billion
acknowledge	agent	annual	artificial	award	binary
acquire	aggressive	another	artist	aware	bind
acquisition	ago	answer	artistic	awareness	biological
across	agree	anticipate	as	away	biology
act	agreement	anxiety	aside	baby	bird
action	agricultural	any	ask	back	birth
active	ahead	anybody	aspect	background	bit
actively	aid	anyone	aspiration	bad	black
activity	aim	anything	assemble	bag	blame
actor	air	anyway	assert	balance	blind
actual	albeit	anywhere	assertion	ball	block
actually	alcohol	apart	assess	ban	blood

blow	case	closely	completion	consume	credit
blue	cash	closer	complex	consumer	crime
board	cast	clothes	complexity	consumption	criminal
body	catch	clothing	complicate	contact	crisis
bond	category	cloud	complicated	contain	criterion
bone	cause	club	component	contemporary	critic
book	caution	clue	compose	content	critical
border	cease	cluster	composition	contest	critically
borrow	celebrate	coast	compound	context	criticism
both	celebrity	code	comprehensive	continually	criticize
bottom	cell	coffee	comprise	continue	critique
boundary	cent	cognitive	compromise	continued	crop
box	center	coherent	computer	continuity	cross
boy	central	coin	conceive	continuous	crowd
brain	centre	coincide	concentrate	contract	crucial
branch	century	cold	concentration	contradiction	cry
brand	ceremony	collaboration	concept	contrary	cultural
break	certain	collapse	conception	contrast	culture
breakdown	certainly	colleague	conceptual	contribute	curious
bridge	chain	collect	concern	contribution	current
brief	chair	collection	concerned	control	currently
briefly	challenge	collective	conclude	controversial	curriculum
bright	chance	college	conclusion	controversy	curve
brilliant	change	color	concrete	convenient	custom
bring	channel	column	condition	convention	customer
broad	chapter	com	conduct	conventional	cut
broaden	character	combat	conference	conversation	cycle
broadly	characteristic	combination	confidence	conversely	daily
brother	characterize	combine	confident	conversion	damage
budget	charge	combined	configuration	convert	dance
build	chart	come	confine	convey	danger
building	cheap	comfort	confirm	conviction	dangerous
burden	check	comfortable	conflict	convince	dark
burn	chemical	command	conform	cool	data
bus	chemistry	comment	confront	cooperation	database
business	chief	commentary	confuse	coordinate	date
busy	child	commentator	confusion	cope	datum
but	childhood	commercial	conjunction	copy	daughter
buy	choice	commission	connect	core	day
by	choose	commit	connection	corner	dead
calculate	church	commitment	conscious	corporate	deal
calculation	circle	committee	consciousness	corporation	death
call	circuit	commodity	consensus	correct	debate
camera	circumstance	common	consent	correctly	debt
camp	cite	commonly	consequence	correlation	decade
campaign	citizen	communicate	consequently	correspond	decide
campus	city	communication	conservative	correspondence	decision
can	civil	community	consider	corresponding	declare
cancer	claim	company	considerable	cost	decline
candidate	clarify	comparable	considerably	could	decrease
capability	clarity	comparative	consideration	council	dedicate
capable	class	compare	consist	counsel	deem
capacity	classic	comparison	consistency	count	deep
capital	classical	compatible	consistent	counter	deeply
capitalism	classification	compensate	consistently	counterpart	defeat
capitalist	classify	compensation	constant	country	defense
capture	classroom	compete	constantly	couple	defend
car	clean	competence	constituent	course	define
carbon	clear	competition	constitute	court	definitely
card	clearly	competitive	constrain	cover	definition
care	client	complain	constraint	coverage	degree
career	climate	complaint	construct	create	delay
careful	clinical	complement	construction	creation	deliberately
carefully	close	complete	consult	creative	deliver
carry	closed	completely	consultation	creativity	delivery

demand
democracy
democratic
demonstrate
demonstration
denote
density
deny
department
departure
depend
dependence
dependent
depict
deposit
depression
depth
derive
describe
description
deserve
design
designate
desirable
desire
despite
destination
destroy
destruction
detail
detailed
detect
determination
determine
develop
development
device
devise
devote
diagram
dialogue
dictate
die
diet
differ
difference
different
differential
differentiate
differently
difficult
difficulty
digital
dilemma
dimension
diminish
dinner
direct
direction
directly
director
dirt
disability
disadvantage
disagree

disagreement
disappear
disaster
discipline
discourse
discover
discovery
discrete
discrimination
discuss
discussion
disease
dismiss
disorder
displace
display
dispute
dissolve
distance
distant
distinct
distinction
distinctive
distinguish
distribute
distribution
district
diverse
diversity
divide
division
divorce
do
doctor
doctrine
document
dog
dollar
domain
domestic
dominance
dominant
dominate
door
double
doubt
down
dozen
draft
drama
dramatic
dramatically
draw
drawing
dream
dress
drink
drinking
drive
driver
drop
drug
dry
due
duration

during
duty
dynamic
dynamics
each
ear
earlier
early
earn
earth
ease
easily
eastern
easy
eat
echo
economic
economics
economy
edge
edit
edition
editor
educate
education
educational
effect
effective
effectively
effectiveness
efficiency
efficient
effort
eight
either
elaborate
elect
election
electric
electrical
electron
electronic
element
eligible
eliminate
elite
else
elsewhere
email
embed
embody
embrace
emerge
emergence
emergency
emission
emotion
emotional
emphasis
emphasize
empirical
employ
employee
employer
employment

empty
enable
enact
encompass
encounter
encourage
end
endorse
enemy
energy
enforce
engage
engagement
engine
engineer
engineering
enhance
enjoy
enormous
enough
ensure
entail
enter
enterprise
entertainment
enthusiasm
entire
entirely
entitle
entity
entry
environment
environmental
episode
equal
equality
equally
equation
equilibrium
equip
equipment
equivalent
era
error
escape
especially
essay
essence
essential
essentially
establish
established
establishment
estate
estimate
ethic
ethical
ethnic
evaluate
evaluation
even
evening
event
eventually
ever

every
everybody
everyday
everyone
everything
everywhere
evidence
evident
evil
evolution
evolve
exact
exactly
exam
examination
examine
example
exceed
excellent
except
exception
exceptional
excess
excessive
exchange
excite
exciting
exclude
exclusion
exclusive
exclusively
excuse
executive
exemplify
exercise
exert
exhibit
exhibition
exist
existence
existing
expand
expansion
expect
expectation
expenditure
expense
expensive
experience
experienced
experiment
experimental
expert
expertise
explain
explanation
explicit
explicitly
exploit
exploitation
exploration
explore
export
expose
exposure

express
expression
extend
extended
extension
extensive
extent
external
extra
extract
extraordinary
extreme
extremely
eye
face
facilitate
facility
fact
factor
factory
faculty
fail
failure
fair
fairly
faith
fall
familiar
family
famous
fan
fantastic
fantasy
far
farm
farmer
fascinating
fashion
fast
faster
fat
fate
father
fault
favor
fear
feature
federal
fee
feed
feedback
feel
feeling
fellow
female
feminist
few
fiction
field
fifth
fifty
fight
figure
file
fill

film	freely	grasp	hit	impulse	integrated
filter	frequency	great	hold	in	integration
final	frequent	greatly	hole	inability	integrity
finally	frequently	green	holiday	inadequate	intellectual
finance	fresh	gross	home	inappropriate	intelligence
financial	friend	ground	honest	incentive	intend
find	friendly	group	hope	incident	intense
finding	friendship	grow	hopefully	include	intensity
fine	from	growth	horse	inclusion	intensive
finger	front	guarantee	hospital	income	intent
finish	fruit	guard	host	incorporate	intention
fire	fuel	guess	hot	increase	interact
firm	fulfill	guest	hour	increasingly	interaction
firmly	full	guidance	house	indeed	interactive
first	fully	guide	household	independence	interest
firstly	fun	guideline	housing	independent	interested
fish	function	guilty	how	independently	interesting
fit	functional	guy	however	index	interfere
five	fund	habit	huge	indicate	intermediate
fix	fundamental	hair	human	indication	internal
flat	fundamentally	half	humanity	indicator	international
flexibility	funding	hall	hundred	indigenous	interpret
flexible	funny	hand	hurt	indirect	interpretation
flight	further	handle	husband	individual	interrupt
flood	furthermore	hang	hybrid	individually	interval
floor	future	happen	hypothesis	induce	intervene
flow	gain	happy	ice	industrial	intervention
fluid	game	hard	idea	industry	interview
fly	gap	hardly	ideal	inequality	intimate
focus	garden	harm	identical	inevitable	into
folk	gas	hate	identification	inevitably	introduce
follow	gather	have	identify	infant	introduction
following	gay	he	identity	influence	invent
food	gender	head	ideological	influential	invest
foot	general	health	ideology	inform	investigate
football	generally	healthy	if	informal	investigation
for	generate	hear	ignore	information	investment
force	generation	hearing	ill	infrastructure	invite
foreign	generic	heart	illegal	inherent	invoke
forest	genetic	heat	illness	inherit	involve
forget	genre	heavily	illustrate	initial	involvement
form	genuine	heavy	illustration	initially	ion
formal	geographical	height	image	initiate	iron
formally	geography	help	imagination	initiative	irrelevant
format	gesture	helpful	imagine	injury	island
formation	get	hence	immediate	inner	isolate
former	giant	her	immediately	innovation	isolated
formula	gift	here	impact	innovative	isolation
formulate	girl	hero	imperative	input	issue
formulation	give	herself	implement	inquiry	it
forth	glass	hidden	implementation	insert	item
forum	global	hide	implication	inside	its
forward	go	hierarchy	implicit	insight	itself
foster	goal	high	imply	insist	job
found	god	highlight	import	inspiration	join
foundation	gold	highly	importance	inspire	joint
founder	good	him	important	instance	joke
four	govern	himself	importantly	instead	journal
fourth	government	hint	impose	institution	journalist
fraction	grade	hire	impossible	institutional	journey
fragment	gradually	his	impress	instruction	judge
frame	graduate	historian	impression	instrument	judgment
framework	grand	historical	impressive	insurance	jump
free	grant	historically	improve	integral	just
freedom	graph	history	improvement	integrate	justice

justification	likelihood	map	mission	need	ocean
justify	likely	margin	mistake	negative	odd
keen	likewise	mark	mix	neglect	of
keep	limit	market	mixed	negotiate	off
key	limitation	marketing	mixture	negotiation	offer
kick	limited	marriage	mobile	neither	office
kid	line	marry	mobility	nervous	officer
kill	linear	mass	mode	net	official
kind	linguistic	massive	model	network	often
know	link	master	moderate	neutral	oil
knowledge	liquid	match	modern	never	okay
label	list	material	modest	nevertheless	old
labor	listen	mathematical	modification	new	on
laboratory	literally	matrix	modify	newly	once
lack	literary	matter	molecular	news	one
lady	literature	mature	molecule	newspaper	ongoing
land	little	maximum	moment	next	online
landscape	live	may	money	nice	only
language	living	maybe	monitor	night	onto
large	load	me	month	nine	open
largely	loan	meal	mood	nineteenth	opening
last	local	mean	moral	no	operate
late	locate	meaning	more	nobody	operation
later	location	meaningful	moreover	noise	operator
latter	lock	means	morning	none	opinion
laugh	log	measure	most	nonetheless	opponent
launch	logic	measurement	mostly	nor	opportunity
law	logical	mechanical	mother	norm	oppose
lawyer	long	mechanism	motion	normal	opposite
lay	longer	medical	motivate	normally	opposition
layer	look	medicine	motivation	north	optical
lead	loose	medium	motive	northern	option
leader	lose	meet	motor	not	or
leadership	loss	meeting	mount	notable	oral
learn	lot	member	mountain	notably	order
learning	love	membership	mouth	note	ordinary
least	low	memory	move	nothing	organ
leave	lower	mental	movement	notice	organic
lecture	machine	mention	movie	notion	organization
lecturer	magazine	mere	much	novel	organize
left	magnitude	merely	multiple	now	orient
leg	main	merge	multiply	nowhere	orientation
legacy	mainly	merit	murder	nuclear	origin
legal	mainstream	message	music	number	original
legislation	maintain	metal	musical	numerous	originally
legitimate	maintenance	metaphor	must	nurse	originate
leisure	major	method	mutual	object	other
lend	majority	methodology	my	objection	otherwise
length	make	middle	myself	objective	ought
less	maker	might	myth	obligation	our
lesser	making	migration	name	obscure	ourselves
lesson	male	mile	namely	observation	out
let	man	military	narrative	observe	outcome
letter	manage	million	narrow	observer	outline
level	management	mind	nation	obstacle	output
liberal	manager	mine	national	obtain	outside
liberty	manifest	minimal	native	obvious	outstanding
library	manifestation	minimum	natural	obviously	over
lie	manipulate	minister	naturally	occasion	overall
life	manipulation	minor	nature	occasional	overcome
lifestyle	manner	minority	near	occasionally	overlap
lifetime	manual	minute	nearly	occupation	overlook
lift	manufacture	mirror	necessarily	occupy	overseas
light	manufacturing	mislead	necessary	occur	overview
like	many	miss	necessity	occurrence	overwhelming

owe	personal	possibility	produce	question	reflect
own	personality	possible	producer	quick	reflection
owner	personally	possibly	product	quickly	reform
ownership	personnel	post	production	quiet	refuse
pace	perspective	potential	productive	quite	regard
pack	persuade	potentially	productivity	quote	regardless
package	phase	pound	profession	race	regime
page	phenomenon	poverty	professional	racial	region
pain	philosopher	power	professor	racism	regional
paint	philosophical	powerful	profile	radical	register
painting	philosophy	practical	profit	radically	regular
pair	phone	practice	profound	radio	regularly
panel	photo	practitioner	program	rain	regulate
paper	photograph	praise	progress	raise	regulation
paradigm	phrase	precede	progressive	random	reinforce
paragraph	physical	precise	prohibit	range	reject
parallel	physically	precisely	project	rank	relate
parameter	pick	predict	prominent	rapid	related
parent	picture	prediction	promise	rapidly	relation
park	piece	predominantly	promote	rare	relationship
part	pioneer	prefer	promotion	rarely	relative
partial	place	preference	prompt	rate	relatively
partially	placement	preferred	proof	rather	relax
participant	plain	prejudice	proper	rating	release
participate	plan	preliminary	properly	ratio	relevance
participation	plane	premise	property	rational	relevant
particle	planet	preparation	proportion	raw	reliable
particular	planning	prepare	proposal	reach	relief
particularly	plant	presence	propose	react	religion
partly	plastic	present	proposition	reaction	religious
partner	plate	presentation	prospect	read	rely
partnership	platform	preserve	protect	reader	remain
party	play	president	protection	readily	remainder
pass	player	press	protest	reading	remark
passage	please	pressure	proud	ready	remarkable
passion	pleasure	presumably	prove	real	remember
passive	plenty	pretend	provide	realistic	remind
past	plot	pretty	provider	reality	remote
path	plus	prevail	provision	realize	removal
pathway	poem	prevent	provoke	really	remove
patient	poet	previous	psychological	realm	render
pattern	poetry	previously	psychologist	reason	rent
pay	point	price	psychology	reasonable	repair
payment	police	pride	public	reasonably	repeat
peace	policy	primarily	publication	reasoning	repeated
peak	political	primary	publicly	recall	repeatedly
peer	politically	prime	publish	receive	replace
penalty	politician	principal	publishing	recent	replacement
people	politics	principle	pull	recently	reply
per	pollution	print	punishment	reception	report
perceive	pool	prior	purchase	recipient	represent
percent	poor	priority	pure	recognition	representation
percentage	poorly	prison	purely	recognize	representative
perception	pop	private	purpose	recommend	reproduce
perfect	popular	privilege	pursue	recommendation	reputation
perfectly	popularity	prize	pursuit	record	request
perform	population	probability	push	recording	require
performance	portion	probably	put	recover	requirement
perhaps	portray	problem	qualification	recovery	research
period	pose	problematic	qualify	recruit	researcher
permanent	position	procedure	qualitative	red	resemble
permission	positive	proceed	quality	reduce	reserve
permit	positively	proceeding	quantitative	reduction	reside
persist	possess	process	quantity	refer	residence
person	possession	processing	quarter	reference	resident

resist	sanction	setting	small	spring	style
resistance	satellite	settle	smile	square	subject
resolution	satisfaction	settlement	smoke	stability	subjective
resolve	satisfactory	seven	smooth	stable	submit
resort	satisfy	several	so	staff	subordinate
resource	save	severe	social	stage	subsequent
respect	say	sex	socially	stake	subsequently
respective	scale	sexual	society	stance	substance
respectively	scenario	sexuality	sociology	stand	substantial
respond	scene	shake	soft	standard	substantially
response	schedule	shall	software	standing	substitute
responsibility	scheme	shape	soil	star	subtle
responsible	scholar	share	soldier	start	succeed
rest	scholarship	sharp	sole	state	success
restore	school	she	solely	statement	successful
restrict	science	sheet	solid	static	successfully
restriction	scientific	shift	solution	station	successive
result	scientist	ship	solve	statistic	such
retain	scope	shock	some	statistical	sudden
return	score	shoot	somebody	status	suddenly
reveal	screen	shop	somehow	stay	suffer
revenue	script	short	someone	steady	sufficient
reverse	sea	shortly	something	steal	sufficiently
review	search	shot	sometimes	stem	suggest
revise	season	should	somewhat	step	suggestion
revision	seat	show	somewhere	stereotype	suit
revolution	second	shut	son	stick	suitable
revolutionary	secondary	sick	song	still	sum
reward	secondly	side	soon	stimulate	summarize
rhetoric	secret	sight	sophisticated	stimulus	summary
rich	section	sign	sorry	stock	summer
ride	sector	signal	sort	stone	sun
right	secure	significance	soul	stop	superior
ring	security	significant	sound	storage	supplement
rise	see	significantly	source	store	supply
risk	seed	signify	south	storm	support
ritual	seek	silence	southern	story	supporter
rival	seem	similar	space	straight	supportive
river	seemingly	similarity	span	straightforward	suppose
road	segment	similarly	spatial	strain	suppress
rock	select	simple	speak	strand	sure
role	selected	simplify	speaker	strange	surely
roll	selection	simply	special	strategic	surface
romantic	selective	simultaneously	specialist	strategy	surprise
room	self	since	specie	stream	surprising
root	sell	sing	species	street	surprisingly
rough	semester	single	specific	strength	surround
roughly	seminar	sister	specifically	strengthen	survey
round	send	sit	specify	stress	survival
route	senior	site	spectrum	stretch	survive
routine	sense	situate	speech	strict	suspect
row	sensitive	situation	speed	strictly	suspend
rule	sensitivity	six	spell	strike	sweet
run	sentence	size	spend	striking	switch
rural	separate	sketch	spending	string	symbol
rush	separately	skill	sphere	strip	symbolic
sacrifice	separation	skilled	spin	strive	symptom
sad	sequence	skin	spirit	strong	synthesis
safe	series	sleep	spiritual	strongly	system
safety	serious	slide	spite	structural	systematic
sake	seriously	slight	split	structure	table
sale	serve	slightly	sponsor	struggle	tackle
salt	service	slip	sport	student	take
same	session	slow	spot	study	tale
sample	set	slowly	spread	stuff	talent

talk
tape
target
task
taste
tax
teach
teacher
teaching
team
tear
technical
technique
technological
technology
telephone
television
tell
temperature
temporary
ten
tend
tendency
tension
term
terminology
territory
test
testing
text
textbook
than
thank
that
the
theater
their
them
theme
themselves
then
theoretical
theorist
theory
therapy
there
thereby
therefore
these
thesis
they
thick
thin
thing
think
thinking
third
thirty

this
thoroughly
those
though
thought
thousand
threat
threaten
three
threshold
through
throughout
throw
thus
ticket
tie
tight
time
timing
tiny
tip
title
to
today
together
tomorrow
tone
tonight
too
tool
top
topic
total
totally
touch
tough
tour
toward
towards
town
trace
track
trade
tradition
traditional
traditionally
traffic
train
training
trait
transfer
transform
transformation
transition
translate
translation
transmission
transmit

transport
trap
travel
treat
treatment
tree
trend
trial
trigger
trip
trouble
truly
trust
truth
try
tune
turn
tutor
twelve
twentieth
twenty
twice
two
type
typical
typically
ultimate
ultimately
unable
uncertain
uncertainty
under
undergo
undergraduate
underlie
undermine
understand
understanding
undertake
undoubtedly
unexpected
unfortunately
uniform
union
unique
unit
unite
unity
universal
universe
university
unknown
unless
unlike
unlikely
unnecessary
until
unusual

up
update
upon
upper
upset
urban
urge
us
usage
use
useful
user
usual
usually
utility
valid
validity
valuable
value
van
variable
variation
varied
variety
various
vary
vast
vehicle
venture
verbal
version
versus
vertical
very
via
vice
victim
victory
video
view
viewer
viewpoint
village
violate
violence
violent
virtual
virtually
virtue
visible
vision
visit
visitor
visual
vital
vocabulary
voice
volume

voluntary
volunteer
vote
vulnerable
wage
wait
wake
walk
wall
want
war
warm
warn
warning
wash
waste
watch
water
wave
way
we
weak
weakness
wealth
weapon
wear
weather
web
website
week
weekend
weekly
weigh
weight
welcome
welfare
well
west
western
what
whatever
when
whenever
where
whereas
whereby
wherever
whether
which
while
whilst
white
who
whole
whom
whose
why
wide

widely
widespread
wife
wild
will
willing
win
wind
window
winner
winter
wire
wisdom
wish
with
withdraw
within
without
witness
woman
wonder
wonderful
wood
word
work
worker
working
workplace
workshop
world
worldwide
worry
worth
worthy
would
write
writer
writing
written
wrong
year
yes
yet
yield
you
young
your
yourself
youth
zero
zone